GW00357147

Leaving Certificate
Higher Level Paper 1

Mathematics

John Scannell

The Educational Company of Ireland

Published 2015

The Educational Company of Ireland
Ballymount Road
Walkinstown
Dublin 12

www.edco.ie

A member of the Smurfit Kappa Group plc

© John Scannell, 2015

All rights reserved. No part of this publication may be reproduced, stored in a retrieval system, or transmitted in any form or by any means, electronic, mechanical, photocopying, recording or otherwise, without either the prior permission of the Publisher or a licence permitting restricted copying in Ireland issued by the Irish Copyright Licensing Agency, 25 Denzille Lane, Dublin 2.

ISBN: 978-1-84536-645-2

Book design: Liz White Designs

Cover design: Identikit

Layout: Compuscript

Editor: Sam Hartburn

Illustrations: Compuscript

Proofreaders: Sam Hartburn, Anne Trevillion, Lyn Imeson

The paper used in this book comes from Managed Forests in Northern Europe For every tree felled, at least one new tree is planted

While every care has been taken to trace and acknowledge copyright, the publishers tender their apologies for any accidental infringement where copyright has proved untraceable. They would be pleased to come to a suitable arrangement with the rightful owner in each case.

Web references in this book are intended as a guide for teachers. At the time of going to press, all web addresses were active and contained information relevant to the topics in this book. However, The Educational Company of Ireland and the authors do not accept responsibility for the views or information contained on these websites. Content and addresses may change beyond our control and students should be supervised when investigating websites.

CONTENTS

Introduction	ix

1 Number Systems — 1

Natural numbers ($\mathbb{N}$)	1
Integers ($\mathbb{Z}$)	3
Rational numbers ($\mathbb{Q}$)	3
Irrational numbers	4
Constructions	7
Proof by contradiction	8
Order of operations	9
Checklist	10

2 Indices and Logarithms — 11

Indices and logs	11
Laws of indices	12
Solving index equations	14
Exponential functions and graphs	15
Natural exponential function (e^x)	18
Rules of logarithms	19
Solving log equations	20
Problem solving – exponential and logarithmic functions	23
Checklist	25

3 Algebra 1 — 26

Expression vs equation	26
Terms, variables, coefficients and constants	27
Polynomials	27

Algebraic expressions	28
Expanding brackets	29
Factorising expressions	32
Simplifying algebraic fractions	35
Adding and subtracting algebraic fractions	36
Multiplying and dividing algebraic fractions	37
Rearranging formulae	38
Checklist	40

4 Algebra 2 — 41

Surds	41
Solving quadratic equations	43
Linear and non-linear simultaneous equations	47
Simultaneous linear equations with two unknowns	48
Simultaneous equations with three unknowns	49
Factor theorem for polynomials	52
Checklist	56

5 Algebra 3 — 57

Inequalities	57
Modulus (absolute value)	65
Abstract inequalities	70
Checklist	71

6 Functions and Graphing Functions — 72

Relations	72
Functions	73

Types of function 83

Composition of functions 85

Inverse of functions 87

Limit of a function 90

Continuous functions 91

Graphing of functions 94

Quadratic functions in completed square form 95

Summary of graph transformations 97

Checklist 102

7 Patterns 103

Number patterns 103

Linear patterns 104

Quadratic patterns 105

Cubic patterns 110

Exponential sequences 113

Checklist 116

8 Arithmetic and Geometric Sequences and Series 117

Notation for sequences 117

Arithmetic sequences 118

Limit of a sequence 120

Arithmetic series 121

Geometric sequences 124

Sigma notation 127

Infinite geometric series 128

Checklist 130

9 Financial Maths and Arithmetic 131

Relative and percentage error	131
Tolerance interval	131
Percentage profit and loss	132
Income tax	133
Present value and future value	134
Compound interest	137
Depreciation	138
Interest periods and rates	140
Savings and investments	142
Loans and mortgages	144
Amortisation formula	145
Checklist	150

10 Nets, Length, Area and Volume 151

Glossary of terms	151
Nets of prisms, cylinders and cones	156
Properties of 3D shapes	157
Length and area formulae	157
Surface area and volume	158
Checklist	166

11 Differentiation 1 167

Introduction	167
Evaluating derivatives	173
Differentiation by rule	173
Checklist	182

12 Differentiation 2 — 183

Increasing and decreasing functions — 183

Stationary points — 186

Point of inflection — 189

Second derivative test for turning points — 191

Curve sketching — 193

Matching derivatives — 196

Checklist — 200

13 Differentiation 3 — 201

Differentiating with respect to other variables — 201

Maximum and minimum problems — 202

Rates of change — 210

Implicit differentiation — 212

Related rates of change — 213

Checklist — 217

14 Integration — 218

Introduction — 218

Working out the indefinite integral — 220

Numerical methods for finding area under a curve — 223

Applications of integration — 234

Average velocity and average value of a function — 238

Checklist — 241

15 Complex Numbers   242

    Introduction   242

    Operations with complex numbers   247

    Geometrical transformations of complex numbers   251

    Equality of complex numbers   255

    Complex equations   255

    Conjugate root theorem   256

    Polar form of a complex number   259

    De Moivre's theorem   267

    Checklist   276

16 Proof by Induction   277

    Introduction   277

    Series   278

    Divisibility   279

    Inequalities   280

    Proof of De Moivre's theorem by induction   282

    Checklist   282

17 Binomial Theorem   283

    $\binom{n}{r}$ notation   283

    Binomial coefficients and Pascal's triangle   284

    Binomial theorem   285

    General term of binomial expansion   287

    Binomial distribution   288

    Checklist   289

Appendix: Questions to Practise   290

Introduction

This book covers the material needed for Paper 1 of the Leaving Certificate Higher Level mathematics examination. The examination consists of two written papers, each carrying 300 marks.

Paper 1 generally tests the material in strands 3, 4 and 5 of the syllabus (number, algebra and functions). The paper is split into two sections:

- Section A: Concepts and Skills, worth 150 marks
- Section B: Contexts and Applications, worth 150 marks.

The book contains numerous questions of the type that you will see in the exam, with worked solutions. Attempt each question yourself before looking at the solution. Make a note of any that you can't do by yourself and try again in your next revision session. That way, you will make the most of your revision time by focusing on the areas you find hardest.

Make sure to practise your basic skills in algebra, arithmetic, indices and logarithms, and so on. These skills will be needed in many different contexts. You should know them well.

When you get into the exam, take five minutes at the start to read through the paper. Allow 70 minutes for Section A, and 70 for Section B, with five minutes at the end to check that you haven't missed anything.

Be prepared for the unfamiliar. Section B in particular involves problem solving skills, and will be challenging. Don't give up if a problem is not working out.

Read each question carefully before starting. The first step might involve stating a correct formula, drawing a graph or completing a table. Make sure that the axes and points on graphs are clearly labelled. Use a pencil for graphs, diagrams and constructions, so that you can easily rub them out if necessary.

Double check what the question has asked for. Give your answer to the correct number of decimal places or in the correct form, and in the simplest form if relevant.

Show all your work clearly, and make your final answer clear. You will lose marks if you haven't shown all the necessary work, or if the examiner cannot read or make sense of what you have written. Minus signs can sometimes be hard to read on squared paper, so take extra care to make them obvious. Don't forget units of measurement if applicable – you will lose marks if you leave them out.

Don't leave any question blank. If you don't write anything you can't get any marks. Write down any formulae that you think are relevant, even if you don't know how to use them. You will get partial credit for any work of merit. Avoid crossing out work if you can – anything you have written might be worth marks.

If you are struggling with a particular question, leave it and move on to the next one. You can always come back to it at the end if you have time.

The *Formulae and Tables* booklet is your friend! Study it carefully before the exam and make sure you know how to find the information you need. Practise using your calculator. Read the manual and ensure that you know how to calculate indices and logarithms, trigonometric functions and functions such as *nCr*.

There are many websites that are useful for revision. Here are just a few.

- **www.projectmaths.ie** has a wealth of activities in the Student Area, including tips for getting the most out of your calculator.

- **www.examinations.ie** contains lots of information about the examinations. The most relevant part for students is the examination material archive, where you can find past papers and marking schemes.

- **www.betterexaminations.ie** also makes past papers available.

- **www.ncca.ie** gives information about the Leaving Certificate Mathematics Syllabus.

- **www.mathopenref.com** is an easy to use maths reference site with animations and interactive tools that illustrate key concepts.

Number Systems

Learning objectives

In this chapter you will learn how to:

- Recognise number sets and properties of $\mathbb{N}$, $\mathbb{Z}$, $\mathbb{Q}$ and the set of irrational numbers $\mathbb{R}\backslash\mathbb{Q}$
- Understand factors, multiples and prime numbers in $\mathbb{N}$
- Express numbers in terms of their prime factors
- Geometrically construct $\sqrt{2}$ and $\sqrt{3}$
- Prove by contradiction that $\sqrt{2}$ is an irrational number
- Appreciate the order of operations including brackets.

Natural numbers ($\mathbb{N}$)

The set of **natural numbers** is the set of all positive whole numbers excluding zero. It is denoted by $\mathbb{N}$.

$\mathbb{N} = \{1, 2, 3, 4, 5, \ldots\}$

A **factor**, or **divisor**, of a natural number is any number that divides exactly into it. The **highest common factor (HCF)** of two or more natural numbers is the highest number that divides exactly into both given numbers.

The **multiples** of a natural number are the numbers into which it divides exactly. The **lowest common multiple (LCM)** of two or more numbers is the smallest multiple that the given numbers have in common.

Prime numbers are natural numbers bigger than 1 that have only two factors: the number itself and 1. There are infinitely many prime numbers

> **Point to note**
>
> 0 and 1 are not prime numbers. 2 is the only even prime number.
>
> Natural numbers greater than 1 which are not prime are called **composite numbers**.

Examples

Find the HCF and LCM of **(a)** 12, 48 and 144   **(b)** n, $4n$ and $12n$, where n is a natural number.

Solutions

(a) To find the HCF, list the factors of each number in the question.

Factors of 12 = {1, 2, 3, 4, 6, 12}

Factors of 48 = {1, 2, 3, 4, 6, 8, 12, 16, 24, 48}

Factors of 144 = {1, 2, 3, 4, 6, 9, 12, 16, 24, 36, 48, 72, 144}

HCF = 12

To find the LCM, list the first few multiples of each number in the question.

Multiples of 12 = {12, 24, 36, 48, 60, 72, 84, 96, 108, 120, 132, 144, ...}

Multiples of 48 = {48, 96, 144, ...}

Multiples of 144 = {144, ...}

LCM = 144

(b) The highest factor of n is n, and n is also a factor of $4n$ and of $12n$. Therefore, HCF = n.

The lowest multiple of $12n$ is $12n$, and $12n$ is also a multiple of n and $4n$. Therefore, LCM = $12n$.

Note that this is an algebraic generalisation of the example in part (a).

Point to note

Any composite number can be written as a product of prime numbers. This can be useful for finding the HCF and LCM.

Examples

(a) Express 290 and 120 as a product of prime numbers.

(b) Find the HCF and LCM of 290 and 120.

Solutions

(a) To express a number as a product of prime numbers, start by finding its lowest prime factor. Divide the number by this factor, then find the lowest prime factor of the answer. Continue in the same manner until you get to a prime answer.

2	120
2	60
2	30
3	15
5	5

2	290
5	145
29	29

290 = 2 × 5 × 29

120 = 2 × 2 × 2 × 3 × 5

= 2^3 × 3 × 5

The common factors are 2 and 5.

(b) To find the HCF, multiply the common prime factors. HCF = $2 \times 5 = 10$.

To find the LCM, multiply the highest power of each prime factor.

LCM = $2^3 \times 3 \times 5 \times 29 = 3480$.

Integers ($\mathbb{Z}$)

The set of **integers** is the set of all whole numbers, positive, negative and zero. It is denoted by $\mathbb{Z}$.

$\mathbb{Z} = \{\ldots -3, -2, -1, 0, 1, 2, 3, \ldots\}$

Properties of integers

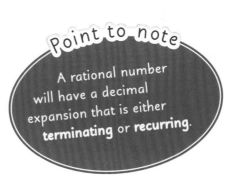

Remember

Make sure you know how to find the HCF and LCM of a pair of numbers. Practise the techniques until you can do them easily.

1 **Commutative** property (applies to addition and multiplication)

$x + y = y + x$ and $xy = yx$

Note that $x - y \ne y - x$ (i.e. subtraction is not commutative).

2 **Associative** property (applies to addition and multiplication)

$(x + y) + z = x + (y + z)$ and $(xy)z = x(yz)$

Note that $(x - y) - z \ne x - (y - z)$ (i.e. subtraction is not associative).

3 **Distributive** property

$x(y + c) = xy + xc$

Rational numbers ($\mathbb{Q}$)

The set of **rational numbers** is the set of numbers that can be written as a ratio of two integers $\frac{p}{q}$, where $p, q \in \mathbb{Z}$, $q \ne 0$. It is denoted by $\mathbb{Q}$.

Point to note

A rational number will have a decimal expansion that is either **terminating** or **recurring**.

Examples

Express the following as rational numbers:

(a) $1 \cdot \dot{3}$ **(b)** $2 \cdot 45$ **(c)** $0 \cdot 125$ **(d)** $\frac{1}{0 \cdot 3}$.

Solutions

(a) $\frac{4}{3}$ **(b)** $\frac{49}{20}$ **(c)** $\frac{1}{8}$ **(d)** $\frac{10}{3}$

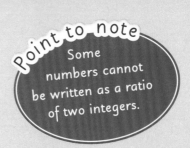

Point to note

Some numbers cannot be written as a ratio of two integers.

Irrational numbers

An **irrational number** is any number that cannot be expressed as a ratio of two integers $\frac{p}{q}$, where $p, q \in \mathbb{Z}$ and $q \neq 0$.

The set of **real numbers** is the set of all rational and irrational numbers. It is denoted by $\mathbb{R}$. The **set of irrational numbers** contains all the real numbers that are not rational, i.e. all numbers that are in $\mathbb{R}$ but not in $\mathbb{Q}$. It is denoted by $\mathbb{R}\backslash\mathbb{Q}$.

> **Point to note**
>
> $\mathbb{R}\backslash\mathbb{Q}$ means $\mathbb{R}$ less $\mathbb{Q}$. It is another way of writing 'all numbers that are in $\mathbb{R}$ but not in $\mathbb{Q}$'.

> **Point to note**
>
> Irrational numbers cannot be expressed as fractions. They are non-terminating, non-recurring decimals.

A **surd** is an irrational number containing a root term. For example, $\sqrt{2} = 1 \cdot 414213562....$ This is a number that will continue indefinitely and has no pattern. Other important irrational numbers are π and e.

The set of rational and irrational numbers together make up the real number system ($\mathbb{R}$).

The set of real numbers is a subset of the set of complex numbers, $\mathbb{C}$.

$\mathbb{C} = \{a + bi,\ a \in \mathbb{R},\ b \in \mathbb{R},\ i^2 = -1\}$

Complex numbers are dealt with in more detail in Chapter 15.

Note that $\mathbb{N} \subset \mathbb{Z} \subset \mathbb{Q} \subset \mathbb{R} \subset \mathbb{C}$.

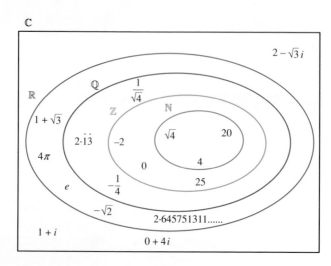

Remember

The symbol $\subset$ means 'contained in' or 'is a subset of'. So $\mathbb{N} \subset \mathbb{Z}$ means that every element of $\mathbb{N}$ is also an element of $\mathbb{Z}$.

Example

Fill in the table below, indicating which number sets contain each number.
List all that apply in each case.

	$\mathbb{N}$ (Natural)	$\mathbb{Z}$ (Integer)	$\mathbb{Q}$ (Rational)	$\mathbb{R}\backslash\mathbb{Q}$ (Irrational)	$\mathbb{R}$ (Real)	$\mathbb{C}$ (Complex)
2						
$1 + \sqrt{7}$						
$\dfrac{2}{3}$						
π						
$2 + 3i$						
$1 \cdot \dot{3}$						
$\sqrt[3]{64}$						

Solution

	$\mathbb{N}$ (Natural)	$\mathbb{Z}$ (Integer)	$\mathbb{Q}$ (Rational)	$\mathbb{R}\backslash\mathbb{Q}$ (Irrational)	$\mathbb{R}$ (Real)	$\mathbb{C}$ (Complex)
2	✓	✓	✓		✓	✓
$1 + \sqrt{7}$				✓	✓	✓
$\dfrac{2}{3}$			✓		✓	✓
π				✓	✓	✓
$2 + 3i$						✓
$1 \cdot \dot{3}$			✓		✓	✓
$\sqrt[3]{64}$	✓	✓	✓		✓	✓

Let G be the set $\{x + yi \mid x, y \in \mathbb{Z}, i^2 = -1\}$.

Consider the Venn diagram below.

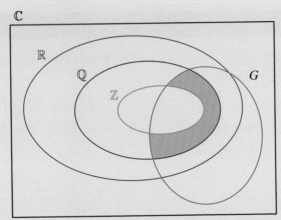

(a) There are three regions in the diagram that represent empty sets. One of these is shaded. Shade in the other two.

(b) Insert each of the following numbers in its correct region on the diagram.

$$\sqrt{2} \qquad 7 \qquad \sqrt{3} - i \qquad 4 + 3i \qquad \frac{1}{2} \qquad \frac{1}{2} + 2i$$

(c) Consider the product ab, where $a \in G$ and $b \in \mathbb{Q}$. There is a non-empty region in the diagram where ab cannot be. Write the word 'here' in this region.

(SEC 2012)

Solutions

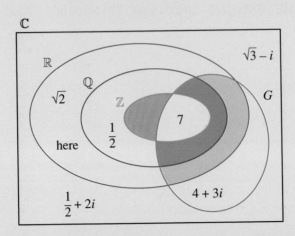

(a) Every integer can be written in the form $x + yi$, with $y = 0$. Therefore every element of $\mathbb{Z}$ is also in G, so the area representing $\mathbb{Z} \backslash G$ is empty.

Because x and y are integers, $x + yi$ cannot be irrational. Therefore the intersection of $\mathbb{R} \backslash \mathbb{Q}$ and G is also empty.

(b) See the diagram.

(c) The real and imaginary parts of ab must both be rational, because they are composed of a rational multiplied by an integer. So ab cannot be in $\mathbb{R}\backslash\mathbb{Q}$.

 Top-Tip

Make sure you know how to classify numbers into the correct number sets.

Constructions

Examples

(a) Given a line segment of one unit, show clearly how to construct a line segment of **(i)** $\sqrt{2}$ and **(ii)** $\sqrt{3}$ units, using only a compass and straight edge.

(b) Explain what it means to say that $\sqrt{2}$ is not a rational number.

Solutions

(a) (i) 1 Label each end of the line segment A and B.

    2 Draw a line perpendicular to AB at B (refer to Construction 4 from the Junior Certificate part of the Student Area on the Project Maths website if you are not sure how to do this).

    3 Draw a circle of radius length 1 and centre B.

    4 Find where the circle and line meet; mark this point C.

    5 Draw the line segments $[AC]$ and $[BC]$.

    6 Draw a circle of centre A and radius $|AC|$. Draw a straight line joining A, B and the circle. This line segment has length $\sqrt{2}$.

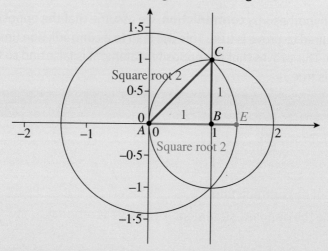

(ii) **1** Draw a line AC of length equal to $\sqrt{2}$.

2 Draw a line perpendicular to AC at C.

3 Draw a circle of radius 1 with centre C.

4 Find where the circle and line meet; mark this point D.

5 Draw the line segments $[AD]$ and $[CD]$.

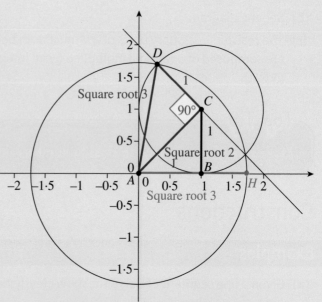

6 Draw a circle of centre A and radius $|AD|$. Draw a straight line joining A, B and the circle. This line segment has length $\sqrt{3}$.

(b) It cannot be written as a fraction of integers in the form $\dfrac{p}{q}$, where p, $q \in \mathbb{Z}$ and $q \neq 0$.

Top Tip

Practise constructions for $\sqrt{2}$ and $\sqrt{3}$. Study the GeoGebra constructions and try the student activity in the Number section of the Student Area on the Project Maths website.

Proof by contradiction

To prove a hypothesis by **contradiction**, we assume that the opposite of what we are required to prove is true. This will lead to a contradiction (impossible statement). This proves that the opposite statement is false and so the original statement is true.

Example

Prove that $\sqrt{2}$ is irrational.

Solution

We will use proof by contradiction.

Step 1: Assume the opposite statement is true: $\sqrt{2}$ is rational.

Then $\sqrt{2} = \dfrac{p}{q}$, where p and q have no common factors (the fraction is in its simplest form).

Squaring both sides gives $\dfrac{p^2}{q^2} = 2 \Rightarrow p^2 = 2q^2$. This means that 2 is a factor of p^2, so 2 must also be a factor of p.

Step 2: Let $p = 2k$ for some $k \in \mathbb{Z}$. Then:

$$(2k)^2 = 2q^2$$
$$4k^2 = 2q^2$$
$$q^2 = 2k^2$$

Therefore 2 is a factor of q^2 and so 2 is also a factor of q.

Step 3: Therefore 2 is a common factor of p and q. This contradicts the original assumption. Thus $\sqrt{2}$ is an irrational number.

Top Tip

Learn the above proof well. You can use the basic idea as a framework for other proofs.

Order of operations

The order of operations is BIRDMAS: Brackets, Indices and Roots, Division and Multiplication, Addition and Subtraction.

Examples

Evaluate:

(a) $\dfrac{3(1{\cdot}2 - 0{\cdot}3)^2 + (1{\cdot}3 + 0{\cdot}4)}{\sqrt{0{\cdot}09}}$

(b) $2\left(1 + \dfrac{1}{3} + \dfrac{1 \times 2}{3 \times 5} + \dfrac{1 \times 2 \times 3}{3 \times 5 \times 7}\right)$.

Solutions

(a) $\dfrac{3(0{\cdot}9)^2 + (1{\cdot}7)}{0{\cdot}3} = \dfrac{2{\cdot}43 + 1{\cdot}7}{0{\cdot}3} = \dfrac{4{\cdot}13}{0{\cdot}3} = 13{\cdot}7\dot{6}$

(b) $2\left(1 + \dfrac{1}{3} + \dfrac{2}{15} + \dfrac{6}{105}\right) = 2\left(\dfrac{32}{21}\right) = \dfrac{64}{21} = 3{\cdot}05$ (correct to 2 decimal places)

Note that if the pattern in (b) was continued it would give an approximation for π.

Remember

Practise using the order of operations until it is second nature. Remember to always show your working in the exam.

Checklist

✓ Practise constructions for $\sqrt{2}$ and $\sqrt{3}$. Study the GeoGebra constructions and try the student activity in the Number section of the Student Area on the Project Maths website.

✓ Know how to use proof by contradiction to show that $\sqrt{2}$ is an irrational number.

✓ Know how to classify numbers into number sets.

✓ Know how to use the order of operations and understand the importance of showing all your working in the exam.

✓ Know how to calculate the HCF and LCM of numbers.

Indices and Logarithms   **2**

Learning objectives

In this chapter you will learn how to:

- Understand the connection between indices and logarithms
- Solve problems using the rules for indices
- Solve problems using the rules of logarithms
- Solve problems based on the graphs of exponential and logarithmic functions.

Indices and logs

Logarithms and **indices** are closely linked. Raising a base to a power and finding the logarithm to the base are **inverse operations**.

$$2^3 = 8 \iff \log_2 8 = 3$$

In the above equation:

- 2 is the **base**

- 3 is the **exponent**, also called the **power** or **index**

- 8 is the value or number.

> **Point to note**
>
> $$y = a^n \iff \log_a y = n$$
>
> (This is on page 21 of the *Formulae and Tables* booklet.)

Consider the functions $f(x) = 2^x$ and $g(x) = \log_2 x$.

x (input values)	$f(x)$ (output values)	x (input values)	$g(x)$ (output values)
−1	$2^{-1} = \dfrac{1}{2}$	$\dfrac{1}{2}$	$\log_2 \dfrac{1}{2} = -1$
0	$2^0 = 1$	1	$\log_2 1 = 0$
1	$2^1 = 2$	2	$\log_2 2 = 1$
2	$2^2 = 4$	4	$\log_2 4 = 2$
3	$2^3 = 8$	8	$\log_2 8 = 3$

Notice that if we reverse the co-ordinates of $f(x) = 2^x$ we get $g(x) = \log_2 x$.
So $f^{-1}(x) = g(x)$ and $g^{-1}(x) = f(x)$, i.e. they are inverse functions.

We can see this on this graph below. If we reflect either graph through the line $y = x$ it will give the other function.

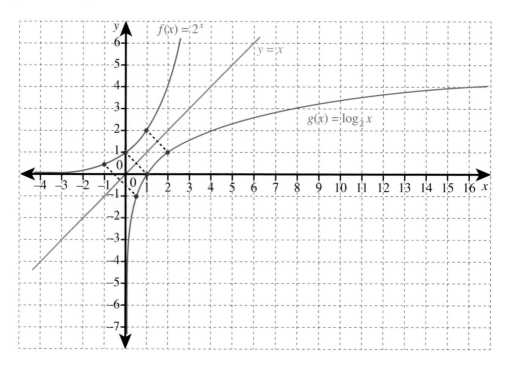

Laws of indices

The nine laws of indices are on page 21 of the *Formulae and Tables* booklet.

$$a^p a^q = a^{p+q}$$

$$\frac{a^p}{a^q} = a^{p-q}$$

$$(a^p)^q = a^{pq}$$

$$a^0 = 1$$

$$a^{-p} = \frac{1}{a^p}$$

$$a^{\frac{1}{q}} = \sqrt[q]{a}$$

$$a^{\frac{p}{q}} = \sqrt[q]{a^p} = \left(\sqrt[q]{a}\right)^p$$

$$(ab)^p = a^p b^p$$

$$\left(\frac{a}{b}\right)^p = \frac{a^p}{b^p}$$

Some examples of the laws are shown in the table below.

Law 1 (product rule)	$3^2 \times 3^4 = 3^{2+4} = 3^6$
Law 2 (quotient rule)	$\dfrac{7^6}{7^3} = 7^{6-3} = 7^3$
Law 3 (power to a power)	$\left(4^2\right)^3 = 4^{2\times 3} = 4^6$
Law 4 (zero exponent)	$6^0 = 1$
Law 5 (n^{th} root)	$27^{\frac{1}{3}} = \sqrt[3]{27} = 3$
Law 6 (fractional exponent)	$4^{\frac{3}{2}} = \left(\sqrt[2]{4}\right)^3 = 8$
Law 7 (negative exponent)	$3^{-2} = \dfrac{1}{3^2} = \dfrac{1}{9}$
Law 8	$(2 \times 3)^6 = 2^6 \times 3^6$
Law 9	$\left(\dfrac{4}{3}\right)^5 = \dfrac{4^5}{3^5}$

These rules also apply when the index is a variable or if the base is a variable.

Examples

Simplify the following expressions:

(a) $3^x \times 3^{2x}$

(b) $(5^x)^2$

(c) $\dfrac{2^x}{2}$

(d) x^{-2}

(e) $x^{\frac{5}{2}}$

(f) $\left(\dfrac{a}{b}\right)^6$.

Solutions

(a) $3^x \times 3^{2x} = 3^{x+2x} = 3^{3x}$ (Law 1)

(b) $(5^x)^2 = 5^{2x}$ (Law 3)

(c) $\dfrac{2^x}{2} = 2^{x-1}$ (Law 2)

(d) $x^{-2} = \dfrac{1}{x^2}$ (Law 7)

(e) $x^{\frac{5}{2}} = \left(\sqrt{x}\right)^5$ (Law 6)

(f) $\left(\dfrac{a}{b}\right)^6 = \dfrac{a^6}{b^6}$ (Law 9)

Solving index equations

Point to note

$a^x = a^y \Rightarrow x = y$, where $a > 0$, $a \neq 1$

As long as we have the *same base* on both sides we can equate indices, use laws of indices and solve index equations.

Solving an index equation can lead to a linear (one solution) or quadratic (two possible solutions) equation. Check the solutions if required.

Examples

Solve the following index equations.

(a) $4^{2x+1} = 64$

(b) $3^{3x-1} = \left(\dfrac{9}{\sqrt{3}}\right)^2$

Solutions

(a) We need to express 64 as a power of 4, to give the same base on both sides of the equation.

$4^{2x+1} = 64$

$4^{2x+1} = 4^3$

$2x + 1 = 3$ Equate exponents.

$x = 1$ Solve for x.

(b) Write each side as a power of 3.

$3^{3x-1} = \left(\dfrac{9}{\sqrt{3}}\right)^2$

$3^{3x-1} = \left(\dfrac{3^2}{3^{0.5}}\right)^2$

$3^{3x-1} = (3^{1.5})^2 = 3^3$ Use laws of indices.

$3x - 1 = 3$ Equate exponents.

$x = \dfrac{4}{3}$ Solve for x.

Example

Solve the equation $5^{2x+1} - 20(5^x) - 25 = 0$.

Solution

In this type of question, find a common base with x as the exponent.

Here, let $y = 5^x$ and express the index equation as a quadratic in terms of y.

So $5^{2x+1} = 5^{2x} \times 5^1 = (5^x)^2 \times 5 = y^2 \times 5 = 5y^2$ (This is the most difficult part of the question.)

The index equation now becomes a quadratic in terms of y:

$5y^2 - 20y - 25 = 0$

$(5y + 5)(y - 5) = 0$ Solve the quadratic by factorising.

y values are $y = -1$ or $y = 5$.

We're not finished yet! Now we need to solve the equation for x.

If $y = 5^x$ then $5^x = -1$ or $5^x = 5 = 5^1$.

There is no possible value for x that would satisfy $5^x = -1$, therefore $x = 1$.

Exponential functions and graphs

Exponential functions have their independent variable in the exponent.

$f(x) = ab^x$

In the above expression:

- x is the **independent variable**, or input value ($x \in \mathbb{R}$)

- b is the **base**, a constant ($b > 0$, $b \in \mathbb{R}$ (i.e. it is a positive real number) and $b \neq 1$)

- a is a real number and $a \neq 0$.

Examples of exponential functions are 2^x, $3 \cdot 4^x$, $\left(\dfrac{1}{2}\right)^x$, $12\,000(2)^t$, 3^{-x}, e^{2x}.

There are two main types of exponential functions: exponential growth and exponential decay. What are the similarities and differences between the two types? We will look at the graphs and properties of two basic exponential functions to find out.

$f(x) = 2^x$ and $g(x) = \left(\frac{1}{2}\right)^x$ (equivalent to $g(x) = 2^{-x}$).

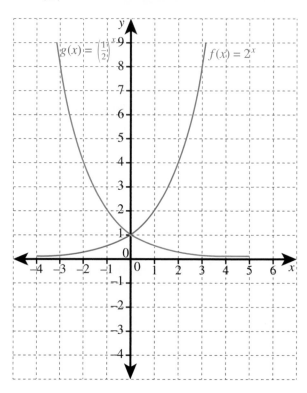

For both functions:

- domain = $\mathbb{R}$
- range = $\mathbb{R}^+$
- there is no x intercept
- y intercept = $(0, 1)$
- the x-axis is a horizontal asymptote
- the y values can form a geometric progression
  (1, 2, 4, 8, ... for $f(x)$, 8, 4, 2, 1, ... for $g(x)$)
- the graph is continuous.

Differences are listed in the table below.

$f(x)$	$g(x)$
Base: $b = 2 > 1$	Base: $0 < b = \frac{1}{2} < 1$
Graph is increasing for all values of x	Graph is decreasing for all values of x
Exponential growth (doubling)	Exponential decay (halving)

Note that $g(x)$ is a reflection of $f(x)$ in the y-axis.

Examples

(a) Graph the function $f(x) = 3^x$ in the domain $-3 \leq x \leq 2$.

(b) Use your graph to estimate **(i)** $3^{1\cdot5}$ **(ii)** $\sqrt{3}$.

(c) Solve $f(x) = 8$ using the graph (correct to 1 decimal place). Check your answer by solving using logs.

(d) Complete the table for the function $g(x) = 3^{-x}$.

x	-3	-2	-1	0	1	2
$g(x)$						

Hence draw $g(x)$ on the same scale and axes.

(e) Find from your graph the values of x for which **(i)** $f(x) = g(x)$ **(ii)** $f(x) < g(x)$.

Solutions

(a)

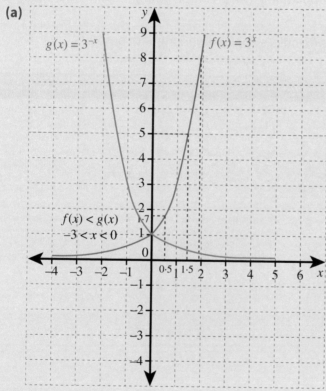

(b) (i) 5 **(ii)** 1·7

(c) From the graph, $x \approx 1\cdot9$.

To solve using logs, use the formula on page 21 of the *Formulae and Tables* booklet: $a^x = y \Leftrightarrow \log_a y = x$.

So $3^x = 8 \Leftrightarrow \log_3 8 = x \Rightarrow x \approx 1\cdot89$.

(d)

x	−3	−2	−1	0	1	2
g(x)	27	9	3	1	$\frac{1}{3}$ = 0·33	$\frac{1}{9}$

(e) (i) $f(x) = g(x)$ at $x = 0$.

(ii) $f(x) < g(x)$ when $-3 < x < 0$ for the given domain of values for $f(x)$ and $g(x)$.

Natural exponential function (e^x)

We often use base e for exponential functions. $f(x) = e^x$ is called the **natural exponential function**.

Like π, e is an irrational number; $e \approx 2 \cdot 7128....$ This might seem an awkward base to work with, but it has a unique property: there is a direct, natural link between the rate of change and the value of the function which reflects real-world problems such as population growth, carbon dating, exponential decay and finance.

Note that the normal rules of indices apply to working with base e.

Examples

Simplify the following:

(a) e^{-1}

(b) $\dfrac{e^2}{e^4}$

(c) $\left(e^3\right)^2$

(d) $e^x \times e^{2x}$

(e) e^0

(f) $e^{\frac{1}{2}}$.

Solutions

(a) $e^{-1} = \dfrac{1}{e}$

(b) $\dfrac{e^2}{e^4} = e^{2-4} = e^{-2} = \dfrac{1}{e^2}$

(c) $\left(e^3\right)^2 = e^{2 \times 3} = e^6$

(d) $e^x \times e^{2x} = e^{x+2x} = e^{3x}$

(e) $e^0 = 1$

(f) $e^{\frac{1}{2}} = \sqrt{e}$

As $e^x = (2 \cdot 7128....)^x$, the graph $y = e^x$ is between $y = 2^x$ and $y = 3^x$.

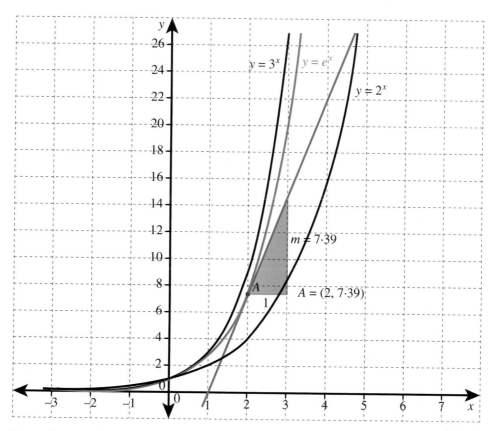

From the graph, we can see that at the point $A = (2, 7 \cdot 39)$
the rate of change = slope of tangent = y value = $7 \cdot 39$.

Rules of logarithms

The rules of logarithms are on page 21 of the *Formulae and Tables* booklet.

$\log_a (xy) = \log_a x + \log_a y$

$\log_a \left(\dfrac{x}{y} \right) = \log_a x - \log_a y$

$\log_a (x^q) = q \log_a x$

$\log_a 1 = 0$

$\log_a \left(\dfrac{1}{x} \right) = -\log_a x$

$a^x = y \iff \log_a y = x$

$\log_a (a^x) = x$

$a^{\log_a x} = x$

$\log_b x = \dfrac{\log_a x}{\log_a b}$

Examples

Given that $\log_2 3 = x$ and $\log_2 5 = y$, express the following in terms of x and y:

(a) $\log_2 15$ (b) $\log_2 \dfrac{5}{3}$ (c) $\log_2 125$ (d) $\log_2 \left(\dfrac{1}{3}\right)$ (e) $\log_2 \sqrt{3}$ (f) $\log_2 2 + \log_2 3$.

Solutions

(a) $\log_2 15 = \log_2 (3 \times 5) = \log_2 3 + \log_2 5 = x + y$

(b) $\log_2 \dfrac{5}{3} = \log_2 5 - \log_2 3 = y - x$

(c) $\log_2 125 = \log_2 5^3 = 3 \log_2 5 = 3y$

(d) $\log_2 \left(\dfrac{1}{3}\right) = -\log_2 3 = -x$

(e) $\log_2 \sqrt{3} = \log_2 3^{\frac{1}{2}} = \dfrac{1}{2}\log_2 3 = \dfrac{x}{2}$

(f) $\log_2 2 + \log_2 3 = 1 + x$

Example

Given that $p = \log_c x$, express $\log_c \sqrt{x} + \log_c (cx)$ in terms of p.   (SEC 2011)

Solution

Express each term separately in terms of p, then combine the terms.

$\log_c \sqrt{x} = \log_c x^{\frac{1}{2}} = \dfrac{1}{2}\log_c x$

$\log_c (cx) = \log_c c + \log_c x = 1 + \log_c x$

$\dfrac{1}{2}\log_c x + 1 + \log_c x = \dfrac{3}{2}\log_c x + 1 = \dfrac{3}{2}p + 1$

Solving log equations

The most common log bases used are:

- base 10 (common logarithm) used for decibel scale for sound intensity, pH scale for acidity and Richter scale for comparing earthquake sizes

- base 2 used for computer science

- base e (**natural logarithm**) used for economics, statistics, physics and chemistry.

Top Tip!

The log button on your calculator uses base 10.

When solving log equations always check that you have the same base on both sides of the equation. Use rules of logs to simplify the equation.

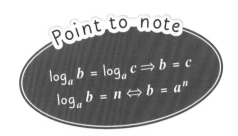

Point to note

$$\log_a b = \log_a c \Rightarrow b = c$$
$$\log_a b = n \Leftrightarrow b = a^n$$

Top Tip

The log of any negative number is not defined. The base of any log cannot be negative either. Always check your solutions for negative numbers!

Examples

(a) Solve $\log_x 8 = 3$.

(b) Solve $3^x = 12$.

Solutions

(a) $\log_x 8 = 3 \Rightarrow x^3 = 8 \Rightarrow x = 2$

(b) $3^x = 12 \Rightarrow x = \log_3 12 = 2 \cdot 26$ (2 decimal places)

Example

Solve the equation $\log_3 (x + 1) + \log_3 (x - 1) = 1$.

Solution

$\log_3 (x + 1) + \log_3 (x - 1) = \log_3 (x + 1)(x - 1)$ Simplify LHS using rules of logs.
$\qquad\qquad\qquad\qquad\qquad\quad = \log_3 (x^2 - 1)$

$\log_3 (x^2 - 1) = 1 \Rightarrow x^2 - 1 = 3^1$

$x^2 = 4 \Rightarrow x = \pm 2$

Answer: $x = 2$, as the log of a negative number is undefined.

Examples

(a) Graph the function $f(x) = \log_3 x$ where $x \in \mathbb{R}$, $x > 0$.

(b) From your graph evaluate **(i)** $f(2)$ **(ii)** $\log_3 5$ **(iii)** $3^{1.5}$, correct to 1 decimal place.

(c) Using your graph **(i)** solve $f(x) = 0$ **(ii)** given $g(x) = 2.5$, solve $g(x)$ for x at the point where $f(x) = g(x)$. Give your answers correct to 1 decimal place, and check them using rules of logs.

Solutions

(a)

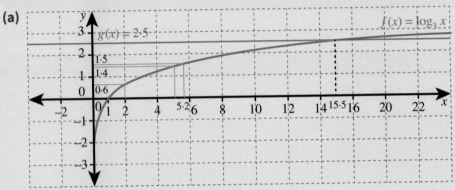

(b) **(i)** $f(2) = 0.6$ **(ii)** $\log_3 5 = 1.4$ **(iii)** $3^{1.5} = 5.2$

(c) **(i)** From the graph, $x = 1$.

Using rules of logs, $\log_3 x = 0 \Rightarrow x = 3^0 = 1$.

(ii) From the graph, $x = 15.5$.

Using rules of logs, $\log_3 x = 2.5 \Rightarrow x = 3^{2.5} \approx 15.6$.

Example

The points $(1, 0)$, $(5, 1)$ and $(125, 3)$ are on the graph of $f(x) = \log_b x$.

Find the value of b where $b > 0$.

Solution

Choose the second point: $x = 5$ and $y = 1$.

$f(x) = \log_b x \Rightarrow 1 = \log_b 5 \Rightarrow b = 5$

The natural logarithm is usually denoted by $\ln(x)$ or $\log_e x$. The natural log function and the exponential function are inverse functions, so $\ln(e^x) = x$ and $e^{\log_e x} = x$.

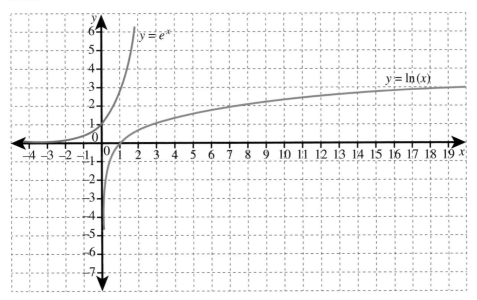

Problem solving – exponential and logarithmic functions

Examples

The exponential growth of a colony of bacteria can be modelled by the function

$$A(t) = 50e^{0.02t}$$

where A is the number of bacteria and t is the time in hours from the time at which the colony is first examined ($t \geq 0$).

(a) Find the initial population of the bacteria.

(b) Estimate the number of bacteria after 5 hours (nearest whole number).

(c) At what time will the colony size reach 1000 (correct to 2 decimal places)?

Solutions

(a) The initial population is the population at time $t = 0$.

$t = 0 \implies A(0) = 50e^{0.02(0)} = 50(1) = 50$

(b) $A(5) = 50e^{0.02(5)} = 50e^{0.1} \approx 55$

(c) $1000 = 50e^{0.02(t)} \implies 20 = e^{0.02(t)} \implies \ln(20) = \ln(e^{0.02(t)})$

$\implies \ln(20) = 0.02t$ (since $\ln(e^x) = x$)

$\therefore t = \dfrac{\ln(20)}{0.02} = 149.79$ hours

Examples

A liquid is cooling so that its temperature θ °C after t seconds can be predicted from the formula $\theta = A e^{-ct}$. A and c are constants.

(a) If the initial temperature of the heated liquid was 70 °C, find the value of A.

(b) After the first minute, the liquid had cooled by 10 °C. Find the value of c (correct to 3 decimal places).

(c) Predict the temperature of the liquid after 4 minutes.

(d) How long will it take for the liquid to cool to 20 °C?

(e) Using suitable values, draw a sketch of the exponential graph for $0 \le t \le 500$.

Solutions

(a) Substitute the initial temperature into the equation and rearrange to find A.

$t = 0 \Rightarrow 70 = A e^{-ct} = A e^{-c(0)} = A e^0 = A$

$\therefore A = 70$

(b) Temperature (θ) has cooled by 10 °C, so temperature is 60 °C after 60 seconds (t).

$60 = 70 e^{-c(60)}$

$\dfrac{6}{7} = e^{-60c}$

$\ln\left(\dfrac{6}{7}\right) = \ln e^{-60c}$

$\ln\left(\dfrac{6}{7}\right) = -60c$

$\therefore c = \dfrac{\ln\left(\dfrac{6}{7}\right)}{-60} = 0.003$

(c) $t = 240$, $A = 70$, $c = 0.003$

$\theta = 70 e^{-0.003(240)} = 70 e^{\frac{-18}{25}} \approx 34.07$ °C

(d) $\theta = 20 = 70 e^{-0.003t}$

$\dfrac{2}{7} = e^{-0.003t}$

$\ln\left(\dfrac{2}{7}\right) = \ln\left(e^{-0.003t}\right)$

$-0.003t = \ln\left(\dfrac{2}{7}\right)$

$t = \dfrac{\ln\left(\dfrac{2}{7}\right)}{-0.003} = 417.6$ seconds

(e) Use the points from parts (a) to (d): (0, 70), (60, 60), (240, 34) and (418, 20). Draw a smooth curve to join them.

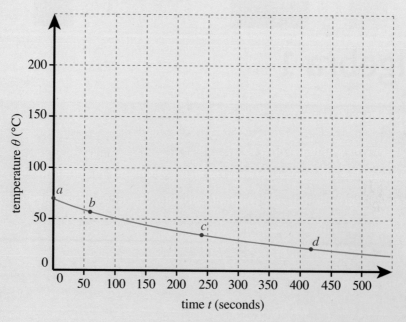

Checklist

✓   Practise drawing graphs of exponential and log graphs.

✓   Use GeoGebra to check your work when drawing graphs.

✓   Label axes carefully, making sure your scales are correct.

✓   Practise working with your calculator to evaluate exponential and log values.

3 Algebra 1

Learning objectives

In this chapter you will learn how to:

- Understand the difference between an expression and an equation
- Understand terminology: polynomial, variable, term, coefficient and constant
- Expand and simplify expressions
- Factorise expressions of order 2
- Add expressions such as

$$\frac{ax + b}{c} \pm \cdots \pm \frac{dx + e}{f} \text{ where } a, b, c, d, e, f \in \mathbb{Z}$$

$$\frac{a}{bx + c} \pm \frac{q}{px + r} \text{ where } a, b, c, p, q, r \in \mathbb{Z}$$

- Perform the arithmetic operations of addition, subtraction, multiplication and division on polynomials and rational algebraic expressions, paying attention to the use of brackets and surds
- Rearrange formulae.

Expression vs equation

What is the difference between an **equation** and an **expression**? Look at the following examples.

Expression	Equation
$x - 2$	$x - 2 = 0$
$x^2 - 3x + 4$	$x^2 - 3x + 4 = 5x - 2$
$x^3 - 3x^2 + 5x + 2$	$x^3 - 3x^2 + 5x + 2 = -7$

It is obvious that with an equation we have a left-hand side (LHS), a right-hand side (RHS) and an = sign. The above examples all have a single **variable**, x. In the first example we can solve the equation for one value of x ($x = 2$).

We can substitute any value of x into the expression $x - 2$.

Other examples of expressions are $4abc - 3, 6xy^2 - 8y, \sqrt{x} - 2$. Some of these have more than one variable.

Terms, variables, coefficients and constants

Consider the expression $1x^3 - 3x^2 + 5x + 2$. This expression has four **terms**. x is the **variable** (its value can vary) and 2 is a constant (its value doesn't change). Each term containing x has a coefficient, as shown in the table.

Term	Coefficient
$1x^3$	1
$-3x^2$	-3
$5x$	5
2	No coefficient

Examples

Consider the expression $x^4 - 4x^3 + 3x^2 - 4x$.

(a) How many terms are in the expression?

(b) What is the coefficient of x^2?

(c) What is the constant term in the expression?

(d) Evaluate the expression when the value of x is 3.

Solutions

(a) There are four terms in the expression.

(b) 3

(c) There is no constant term in the expression, so the constant term = 0.

(d) $x = 3 \Rightarrow (3)^4 - 4(3)^3 + 3(3)^2 - 4(3) = 81 - 108 + 27 - 12 = -12$

Top Tip

When you substitute a value into an expression, rewrite the expression replacing the variable with the value in brackets. This will help you to avoid making mistakes when you evaluate the expression.

Polynomials

'Poly' means many and 'nomial' refers to terms, so a **polynomial** is an expression with many terms, each consisting of a variable raised to a positive whole number power.

The degree of the polynomial is the highest power of the variable (usually x) in the polynomial, so a polynomial of degree 6 will have x to the power of 6 as the highest power. Notice that sometimes not all powers will be in the expression.

Degree	Type	Example
0	Constant	$5 = 5x^0$
1	Linear	$2x^1 - 1 = 2x - 1$
2	Quadratic	$x^2 - 3x + 1$
3	Cubic	$4x^3 - 9x + 1$
4	Quartic	$x^4 - 3x^2 - x - 1$
5	Quintic	$5x^5 - 4x^4 + 3x - 2$

Note that $\sqrt{x} + 3$, $x^{-3} + 2x$, $x^2 + y^2$, $x^2 y - 1$, etc. are not polynomials, either because the powers are not positive whole numbers or because there is a second variable, y.

Algebraic expressions

Top Tip

It is very important to be able to expand brackets and to know the rules for simplifying expressions. These skills are important for both papers.

Commutative law

The commutative law states that the order of terms does not matter. Reversing the order does not change the result.

$a + b = b + a \qquad a \times b = b \times a$

$2x - 3 = -3 + 2x \qquad (2x)(4y) = (4y)(2x) = 8xy$

Point to note

The commutative law works only for addition and multiplication. For subtraction or division, changing the order of the numbers or terms will affect the outcome.

Subtraction: $a - b \neq b - a$, $3x - 3 \neq -3 - 3x$

Division: $\dfrac{12}{4} \neq \dfrac{4}{12}$

Associative law

The associative law states that it does not matter how we group terms.

$(a + b) + c = a + (b + c)$ $(2x - 8) + 5 = 2x + (-8 + 5) = 2x - 3$

$(a \times b) \times c = a \times (b \times c)$ $(3a \times 4) \times 8 = 3a \times (4 \times 8) = 96a$

> **Point to note**
>
> The associative law works only for addition and multiplication. The grouping of terms is important for subtraction and division.
>
> Subtraction: $9 - (4 - 3) = 9 - 1 = 8$ is not equal to $(9 - 4) - 3 = 5 - 3 = 2$.
>
> Division: $15 \div (10 \div 2) = 15 \div 5 = 3$ is not equal to $(15 \div 10) \div 2 = 1.5 \div 2 = 0.75$.

Distributive law

The distributive law states that multiplying by the sum of two terms is the same as multiplying by each term separately.

$a \times (b + c) = a \times b + a \times c$ $8a(4b + 3) = 8a \times 4b + 8a \times 3 = 32ab + 24a$

> **Point to note**
>
> The distributive law doesn't apply to subtraction or division.

Expanding brackets

Single brackets

Examples

(a) Expand $x(x^2 - xy + 8)$.

(b) Expand $-3(x^2 - 2x + 4)$.

Solutions

(a) $x(x^2 - xy + 8)$

$= x(x^2) - x(xy) + x(8)$ Multiply each term in the brackets by x^2.

$= x^3 - x^2y + 8x$ Simplify the terms.

(b) $-3(x^2 - 2x + 4)$

$= (-3)(x^2) - (-3)(2x) + (-3)(4)$ Multiply each term in the brackets by -3.

$= -3x^2 + 6x - 12$ Simplify the terms.

Double brackets

Examples

(a) Expand $(a + b)(x + y)$.

(b) Expand $(2x - 3)(x - 4)$.

Solutions

(a) $(a + b)(x + y)$

$\quad = a(x + y) + b(x + y)$ — Multiply each term in the first bracket by each term in the second bracket.

$\quad = ax + ay + bx + by$ — Multiply out the single brackets as before.

(b) $(2x - 3)(x - 4)$

$\quad = 2x(x - 4) - 3(x - 4)$ — Multiply each term in the first bracket by each term in the second bracket.

$\quad = 2x^2 - 8x - 3x + 12$ — Multiply out the single brackets and simplify.

$\quad = 2x^2 - 11x + 12$

Squaring brackets

Squaring brackets is a special case of multiplying out double brackets.

$(x + y)^2 = (x + y)(x + y) = x^2 + 2xy + y^2$

$(x - y)^2 = (x - y)(x - y) = x^2 - 2xy + y^2$

> **Top Tip**
>
> $(\text{first} \pm \text{second})^2 = \text{first}^2 \pm (2 \times \text{first} \times \text{second}) + \text{second}^2$

In each case the resulting expression has three terms. This is a binomial expansion, which is covered in more detail in Chapter 17.

Examples

(a) Expand $(4x + 2b)^2$.

(b) Expand $(\sqrt{x} - 3)^2$.

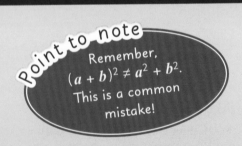

Point to note

Remember,
$(a + b)^2 \neq a^2 + b^2$.
This is a common mistake!

Solutions

(a) $(4x + 2b)^2 = (4x)^2 + 2(4x)(2b) + (2b)^2$

$\quad\quad\quad\quad\quad = 16x^2 + 16xb + 4b^2$

(b) $(\sqrt{x} - 3)^2 = (\sqrt{x})^2 - 2(\sqrt{x})(3) + 3^2$

$\quad\quad\quad\quad\quad = x - 6\sqrt{x} + 9$

Long brackets

Example

Given that $(2x - 3)^2(x^2 - 3x) = ax^4 + bx^3 + cx^2 + dx$, where $a, b, c, d \in \mathbb{Z}$, find the values of a, b, c and d.

Solution

$(2x - 3)^2(x^2 - 3x) = 4x^2 - 12x + 9\,(x^2 - 3x)$ Expand the square bracket first.

$\qquad = x^2(4x^2 - 12x + 9) - 3x(4x^2 - 12x + 9)$ Multiply this expression by the second bracket.

$\qquad = 4x^4 - 12x^3 + 9x^2 - 12x^3 + 36x^2 - 27x$

$\qquad = 4x^4 - 24x^3 + 45x^2 - 27x$ Collect like terms to simplify the expression.

Now the expression is in the right format to equate coefficients:

$ax^4 + bx^3 + cx^2 + dx = 4x^4 - 24x^3 + 45x^2 - 27x \implies a = 4, b = -24, c = 45, d = -27$

> **Point to note**
>
> The example above is known as undetermined or unknown coefficients.
> There are more examples in Chapter 4.

Many brackets

Example

Expand $(x - 3)(x + 4)(x - 5)$.

Solution

Multiply any two sets of brackets, then multiply the result by the third bracket.

$(x - 3)(x + 4)(x - 5) = (x^2 + x - 12)(x - 5)$ Multiply the first two pairs of brackets.

$\qquad = x(x^2 + x - 12) - 5(x^2 + x - 12)$ Multiply the result by the third bracket.

$\qquad = x^3 + x^2 - 12x - 5x^2 - 5x + 60$

$\qquad = x^3 - 4x^2 - 17x + 60$

This is a polynomial of degree 3 (a cubic expression).

> **Point to note**
>
> $(x + y)^3 = x^3 + 3x^2y + 3xy^2 + y^3$
> $(x - y)^3 = x^3 - 3x^2y + 3xy^2 - y^3$

Factorising expressions

Common factor

Example

Factorise fully $2x^2z + 6x^2yz + 10x^2y^2z$.

Solution

$2x^2z$ is a common factor of all the terms, so take this outside the bracket.

$2x^2z + 6x^2yz + 10x^2y^2z = 2x^2z(1 + 3y + 5y^2)$

> **Remember**
>
> Check your factorisation by multiplying out the factors. If the result is the same as the original expression then you've done it right!

Grouping

Example

Factorise fully $6xy - 3y^2 + 4by - 8bx$.

Solution

$6xy - 3y^2 + 4by - 8bx = 3y(2x - y) - 4b(2x - y)$ Group first pair of terms and second pair of terms.

$\qquad\qquad\qquad\qquad = (3y - 4b)(2x - y)$ Now $(2x - y)$ is a common factor.

Difference of two squares

The difference of two squares is a special form of expression which is easy to factorise:

$x^2 - y^2 = (x + y)(x - y)$

Examples

(a) Factorise fully $4x^2 - 100y^2$.

(b) Factorise fully $2a^2b^2 - 8c^2d^2$.

Solutions

(a) $4x^2 - 100y^2 = 4(x^2 - 25y^2)$ Take out the common factor first.

$\qquad\qquad\quad = 4(x + 5y)(x - 5y)$ Use the difference of two squares to factorise the remaining terms.

(b) This example looks more complicated, but it is still the difference of two square terms.

$2a^2b^2 - 8c^2d^2 = 2(a^2b^2 - 4c^2d^2)$ Take out the common factor first.

$\qquad\qquad\quad = 2(ab - 2cd)(ab + 2cd)$ Use the difference of two squares to factorise the remaining terms.

Trinomials

A trinomial is an expression with three terms, such as $5x^2 + 9x - 2$.

Examples

(a) Factorise $2x^2 + 5x + 3$.

(b) Factorise $2a^2 - 11a + 12$.

(c) Factorise $16x^2 + 38x - 5$.

(d) Factorise $8p^2 - 2pq - q^2$.

Solutions

(a) The x^2 term has a coefficient of 2, so the x terms in the factors must be x and $2x$.

$2x^2 + 5x + 3 = (2x + a)(x + b)$

Now we try to find a and b. We know that $ab = 3$ and $2b + a = 5$.
Therefore, $a = 3$ and $b = 1$.

$2x^2 + 5x + 3 = (2x + 3)(x + 1)$

> **Top Tip**
>
> Always check factors of trinomials by testing for the middle term.
>
> $(2x + 3)(x + 1)$: $3x + 2x = 5x$

(b) The a^2 term has a coefficient of 2, so the a terms in the factors must be a and $2a$.

$2a^2 - 11a + 12 = (2a + x)(a + y)$

Look for numbers x and y that satisfy $xy = 12$ and $2y + x = -11$.

$(-3) \times (-4) = 12$ and $2(-4) + (-3) = 11$.

$2a^2 - 11a + 12 = (2a - 3)(a - 4)$

(c) The x^2 term has a coefficient of 16, so the x terms in the factors could be x and $16x$ or $2x$ and $8x$ or $4x$ and $4x$. Try $2x$ and $8x$.

$16x^2 + 38x - 5 = (2x + a)(8x + b)$

Look for numbers a and b that satisfy $ab = -5$ and $2b + 8a = 38$.
The numbers must be either -1 and 5 or -5 and 1.

$2(-5) + 8(1) = -2$ ✗
$2(-1) + 8(5) = 38$ ✓

So $a = -1$ and $b = 5$, and $16x^2 + 38x - 5 = (8x - 1)(2x + 5)$.

(d) Here we know that the q^2 factors must be q and $-q$.

$8p^2 - 2pq - q^2 = (ap + q)(bp - q)$

Look for numbers a and b that satisfy $ab = 8$ and $b - a = -2$.
The factors of 8 that we can try are (8 and 1), (-8 and -1), (4 and 2), (-4 and -2).
The only pair that satisfies $b - a = -2$ is (4 and 2)

$8p^2 - 2pq - q^2 = (4p + q)(2p - q)$

Sum and difference of two cubes

A sum of two cubes factorises as

$x^3 + y^3 = (x + y)(x^2 - xy + y^2).$

Point to note

$(first)^3 + (second)^3 = (first + second)(first^2 - (first \times second) + second^2)$

Example

Factorise fully $27p^3 + 1000q^3$.

Solution

$27p^3 + 1000q^3 = (3p)^3 + (10q)^3$ This is a sum of two cubes.

$= (3p + 10q)(9p^2 - 30pq + 100q^2)$

A difference of two cubes factorises as:

$x^3 - y^3 = (x - y)(x^2 + xy + y^2).$

Point to note

$(first)^3 - (second)^3 = (first - second)(first^2 + (first \times second) + second^2)$

Example

Factorise fully $64 - 216x^3$.

Solution

$64 - 216x^3 = 8(8 - 27x^3)$ Take out the common factor first.

$\qquad\qquad\quad = 8(2^3 - (3x)^3)$ The expression in brackets is a difference of two cubes.

$\qquad\qquad\quad = 8(2 - 3x)(4 + 6x + 9x^2)$

Top Tip

You could do the example above without taking out the common factor first, but taking out the common factor makes the numbers much easier to deal with.

Remember

Learn the formulae for the difference of two squares and the sum and difference of two cubes.

Simplifying algebraic fractions

When simplifying algebraic fractions:

- factorise the numerator and denominator
- look for common factors
- simplify where possible.

Examples

Put the following expressions in their simplest form:

(a) $\dfrac{x - 1}{x^2 - 1}$ (b) $\dfrac{x^3 - 8}{x - 2}$

(c) $\dfrac{4 + \frac{1}{x}}{2 - \frac{1}{x}}$ (d) $\dfrac{x^4 - 16}{4 - x^2}$.

Solutions

(a) $\dfrac{x - 1}{x^2 - 1} = \dfrac{(x - 1)}{(x - 1)(x + 1)}$ Factorise the denominator.

$\qquad = \dfrac{\cancel{(x - 1)}}{\cancel{(x - 1)}(x + 1)} = \dfrac{1}{x + 1}$ Remove the common factor.

(b) $\dfrac{x^3-8}{x-2} = \dfrac{(x-2)(x^2+2x+4)}{(x-2)}$ Factorise the numerator.

$\qquad = \dfrac{\cancel{(x-2)}(x^2+2x+4)}{\cancel{(x-2)}} = x^2+2x+4$ Remove the common factor.

(c) $\dfrac{4+\frac{1}{x}}{2-\frac{1}{x}} = \dfrac{4+\frac{1}{x}}{2-\frac{1}{x}} \times \dfrac{x}{x}$ Multiply by $\dfrac{x}{x}$ to remove the fractions within a fraction.

$\qquad = \dfrac{4x+1}{2x-1}$

> ## Top Tip
> When you have fractions within a fraction, multiply above and below by the lowest common multiple of the denominators of the smaller fractions.

(d) $\dfrac{x^4-16}{4-x^2} = \dfrac{(x^2-4)(x^2+4)}{(4-x^2)}$ Factorise the numerator and denominator.

$\qquad = \dfrac{(x^2-4)(x^2+4)}{-1(x^2-4)}$ Notice that $4-x^2 = -1(x^2-4)$.

$\qquad = \dfrac{(x^2+4)}{-1}$ Remove the common factor.

$\qquad = -x^2-4$

Adding and subtracting algebraic fractions

Example

Express $\dfrac{1}{x-1} - \dfrac{1}{x+1}$ as a single fraction.

Solution

$\dfrac{1}{x-1} - \dfrac{1}{x+1} = \dfrac{1(x+1)}{(x-1)(x+1)} - \dfrac{1(x-1)}{(x-1)(x+1)}$ Write both fractions with the same denominator.

$\qquad = \dfrac{1(x+1)-1(x-1)}{(x-1)(x+1)}$ Combine the fractions by adding the numerators.

> ## Top Tip
> Always use brackets at this step, so that you don't forget to multiply by the minus.

$\qquad = \dfrac{x+1-x+1}{x^2-1} = \dfrac{2}{x^2-1}$

Example

Simplify $\dfrac{3}{x+1} + \dfrac{6}{2x^2+x-1}$.

Solution

$$\dfrac{3}{x+1} + \dfrac{6}{2x^2+x-1} = \dfrac{3}{x+1} + \dfrac{6}{(2x-1)(x+1)}$$ Factorise the denominator.

$$= \dfrac{3(2x-1)+6(1)}{(2x-1)(x+1)} = \dfrac{6x-3+6}{(2x-1)(x+1)}$$ Write both fractions with the same denominator and add the numerators.

$$= \dfrac{6x+3}{(2x-1)(x+1)} = \dfrac{3(2x+1)}{(2x-1)(x+1)}$$ Simplify and factorise the numerator.

Multiplying and dividing algebraic fractions

Example

Simplify $\dfrac{x^2-4}{6x-3} \times \dfrac{2x^2+5x-3}{x^2+2x}$.

Solution

$$\dfrac{x^2-4}{6x-3} \times \dfrac{2x^2+5x-3}{x^2+2x} = \dfrac{(x-2)(x+2)}{3(2x-1)} \times \dfrac{(2x-1)(x+3)}{x(x+2)}$$ Factorise numerators and denominators.

$$= \dfrac{(x-2)\cancel{(x+2)}}{3\cancel{(2x-1)}} \times \dfrac{\cancel{(2x-1)}(x+3)}{x\cancel{(x+2)}} = \dfrac{(x-2)(x+3)}{3x}$$ Remove common factors.

Examples

Given that $f(x) = \dfrac{6}{x-1}$, $g(x) = \dfrac{3}{x^2-1}$.

(a) Express $\dfrac{f(x)}{g(x)}$ in its simplest form.

(b) Hence, or otherwise, evaluate $\dfrac{f(2)}{g(2)}$.

(c) For what values of x are $f(x)$ and $g(x)$ not possible or undefined?

Solutions

(a) $\dfrac{f(x)}{g(x)} = \dfrac{\dfrac{6}{x-1}}{\dfrac{3}{x^2-1}} = \dfrac{6}{x-1} \times \dfrac{x^2-1}{3}$ Invert the second fraction and multiply.

$$= \dfrac{6}{(x-1)} \times \dfrac{(x-1)(x+1)}{3}$$ Factorise where possible.

$$= \dfrac{6(x+1)}{3} = 2(x+1)$$ Cancel common factors and simplify.

(b) $2(2+1) = 6$

Substitute $x = 2$ into the simplest form calculated in part (a).

or

$f(2) = \dfrac{6}{(2)-1} = 6$, $g(2) = \dfrac{3}{(2)^2-1} = 1$ Substitute $x = 2$ into $f(x)$ and $g(x)$.

$\dfrac{f(2)}{g(2)} = \dfrac{6}{1} = 6$

Use the answers to calculate $\dfrac{f(2)}{g(2)}$.

Top Tip

Evaluating the expression is a good way to check your answer is in simplest form.

(c) For $f(x)$, x cannot have a value of 1 and for $g(x)$, x cannot have a value of ± 1. If we substitute these values into the functions we have division by zero, which is undefined.

Rearranging formulae

Rearranging a formula involves expressing it in terms of one variable. The skill for rearranging formulae well is required in many sections of the course, so practise it as much as you can.

Notice that every formula has a LHS and a RHS. When you rearrange a formula, you must always carry out the same action on both the LHS and the RHS.

Example

Express $ax + by + c = 0$ in terms of y.

Solution

$by = -ax - c$ Subtract ax and c from both sides.

$\dfrac{by}{b} = \dfrac{-ax - c}{b} \Rightarrow y = \dfrac{-ax - c}{b}$ Divide both sides by b.

Example

The formula for the volume of a cone is $V = \dfrac{1}{3}\pi r^2 h$. Express r in terms of the other variables.

Solution

$V = \dfrac{1}{3}\pi r^2 h \Rightarrow 3V = \pi r^2 h$ Multiply both sides by 3.

$\Rightarrow \dfrac{3V}{\pi h} = r^2$ Divide both sides by πh.

$r = \sqrt{\dfrac{3V}{\pi h}}$ Take square roots of both sides.

Point to note

Note that if $x^2 = 4$ this implies that $x = \pm\sqrt{4} = \pm 2$. We must include both signs. In the above example we know that r cannot have a negative value because it is the radius of a cone.

Example

If $\dfrac{1}{a} = \dfrac{1}{b} + \dfrac{1}{c}$, then express a in terms of b and c and hence evaluate a if $b = 4$ and $c = 0.5$.

Top Tip

$\dfrac{1}{a} = \dfrac{1}{b} + \dfrac{1}{c}$ does *not* imply that $a = b + c$.

We can only invert on a one-to-one basis, i.e. $\dfrac{1}{a} = \dfrac{1}{b} \Rightarrow a = b$.

Solution

We have one fraction on the LHS and two fractions on the RHS.

$\dfrac{1}{a} = \dfrac{1}{b} + \dfrac{1}{c} \Rightarrow \dfrac{1}{a} = \dfrac{c+b}{bc}$ Add the fractions on the RHS.

$\Rightarrow a = \dfrac{bc}{c+b}$ Invert both sides.

If $b = 4$ and $c = 0.5$ then $a = \dfrac{(4) \times (0.5)}{(0.5) + (4)} = \dfrac{2}{4.5} = \dfrac{4}{9}$.

Example

Make q the subject of the formula $s = \sqrt{\dfrac{p-r}{q}}$.

Solution

$s = \sqrt{\dfrac{p-r}{q}} \Rightarrow s^2 = \dfrac{p-r}{q}$ Square both sides to remove the square root sign.

$\Rightarrow qs^2 = p - r$ Multiply both sides by q.

$\Rightarrow q = \dfrac{p-r}{s^2}$ Divide both sides by s^2.

Example

Given $x = \dfrac{4t-1}{t+3}$, express t in terms of x.

Solution

$x = \dfrac{4t-1}{t+3} \implies x(t+3) = 4t-1$ Multiply both sides by $(t+3)$.

$\implies tx + 3x = 4t - 1$ Multiply out the brackets on the LHS.

$\implies tx - 4t = -1 - 3x$ Isolate the required variable on one side.

$\implies t(x-4) = -1 - 3x$ Factorise.

$t = \dfrac{-1-3x}{x-4}$

Remember

Manipulation of formulae comes up in lots of different types of question. Practise plenty of examples.

Checklist

✓ An expression is not the same as an equation.

✓ Be careful with signs and powers when expanding brackets.

✓ Learn the formulae for factors of difference of two squares and sum and difference of two cubes.

✓ Practise factorising different types of expressions.

✓ Practise simplifying algebraic equations.

✓ Practise plenty of examples involving manipulation of formulae.

Algebra 2

In this chapter you will learn how to:

- Select and use suitable strategies (graphic, numerical, algebraic and mental) for finding solutions to equations of the form:
  - $f(x) = g(x)$ with $f(x) = \dfrac{a}{bx+c} \pm \dfrac{p}{qx+r}$, $g(x) = \dfrac{e}{f}$ where $a, b, c, e, f, p, q, r \in \mathbb{Z}$
  - $f(x) = g(x)$ with $f(x) = \dfrac{ax+b}{ex+f} \pm \dfrac{cx+d}{qx+r}$, $g(x) = k$ where $a, b, c, d, e, f, q, r \in \mathbb{Z}$
  - $f(x) = k$ with $f(x) = ax^2 + bx + c$ (not necessarily factorisable) where $a, b, c \in \mathbb{Q}$

  and interpret the results

- Form polynomial equations given the roots

- Solve one linear equation and one equation of order 2 with two unknowns and interpret the results

- Solve simultaneous linear equations with two unknowns and interpret the results

- Solve simultaneous linear equations with three unknowns and interpret the results

- Use the factor theorem for polynomials

- Select and use strategies (graphic, numerical, algebraic and mental) for finding solutions to cubic equations with at least one integer root and interpret the results.

Surds

An irrational number is a number that cannot be expressed as a fraction.
A **surd** is a root (e.g. square root or cube root) that cannot be expressed as a rational number.

$\sqrt{4} = 2$, which is rational (the square root of a perfect square is rational).

$\sqrt{2}$ and $\sqrt{3}$ are irrational. You have already seen their geometrical constructions in Chapter 1.

Rules for surds

- Addition and subtraction

$$\sqrt{a} \pm \sqrt{b} \neq \sqrt{a \pm b} \quad \sqrt{2} + \sqrt{3} \neq \sqrt{5} \text{ (you can check this with a calculator)}.$$

We can only add or subtract like surds: $\sqrt{2} + \sqrt{2} = 2\sqrt{2}, \quad 2\sqrt{3} - 4\sqrt{3} = -2\sqrt{3}$.

- Multiplication and division

$$\sqrt{a} \times \sqrt{b} = \sqrt{ab} \quad \sqrt{2} \times \sqrt{3} = \sqrt{6}$$

(Note that $\sqrt{a} \times \sqrt{a} = a$, $\sqrt{6} \times \sqrt{6} = \sqrt{36} = 6$)

$$\sqrt{\frac{a}{b}} = \frac{\sqrt{a}}{\sqrt{b}} \quad \sqrt{\frac{4}{9}} = \frac{\sqrt{4}}{\sqrt{9}} = \frac{2}{3}$$

Simplifying and reducing surds

Examples

Simplify the following surds:

(a) $\sqrt{12}$

(b) $\sqrt{48}$.

Solutions

(a) $\sqrt{12} = \sqrt{4 \times 3} = \sqrt{4} \times \sqrt{3} = 2\sqrt{3}$

(b) $\sqrt{48} = \sqrt{16 \times 3} = \sqrt{16} \times \sqrt{3} = 4\sqrt{3}$

A surd in the form $4\sqrt{3}$ is called a **simple surd**. A surd in the form $2 + \sqrt{3}$ is called a **compound surd**. If $a + \sqrt{b}$ is a compound surd then its **conjugate surd** is $a - \sqrt{b}$.

It is important to know that when you multiply a surd by its conjugate the result is a rational number. This is very useful for rationalising a denominator.

$(a + \sqrt{b})(a - \sqrt{b})$ = factors of a difference of two squares = $a^2 - b$.

For example, $(2 - \sqrt{3})(2 + \sqrt{3}) = 4 - 3 = 1$ and

$(\sqrt{2} + \sqrt{3})(\sqrt{2} - \sqrt{3}) = 2 - 3 = -1$.

To **rationalise a denominator** means to remove the surds from the denominator of a fraction. It is important to know the steps involved in this.

Examples

Simplify:

(a) $\dfrac{3}{\sqrt{5}}$ **(b)** $\dfrac{1}{2 + \sqrt{2}}$.

Solutions

(a) $\dfrac{3}{\sqrt{5}} = \dfrac{3}{\sqrt{5}} \times \dfrac{\sqrt{5}}{\sqrt{5}} = \dfrac{3\sqrt{5}}{5}$ Multiply above and below by the denominator.

(b) $\dfrac{1}{2 + \sqrt{2}} = \dfrac{1}{2 + \sqrt{2}} \times \dfrac{2 - \sqrt{2}}{2 - \sqrt{2}}$ Multiply above and below by the conjugate of the denominator.

$= \dfrac{2 - \sqrt{2}}{4 - 2} = \dfrac{2 - \sqrt{2}}{2}$

Solving quadratic equations

The quickest way to solve a quadratic equation is to factorise it – *if* this is possible! Not all quadratic equations can be factorised. If you can't factorise the equation use the **quadratic formula**, which is on page 20 of the *Formulae and Tables* booklet.

Example

Solve $x^2 + x - 12 = 0$.

Solution

$x^2 + x - 12 = 0 \Rightarrow (x + 4)(x - 3) = 0$ Factorise the quadratic.

$\Rightarrow x + 4 = 0$ or $x - 3 = 0$ One of the factors must be equal to 0.

$\Rightarrow x = -4$ or $x = 3$.

Remember

These are the **solutions**, or **roots**, of the equation. If you draw a graph of $x^2 + x - 12$, it will intercept the x-axis at $x = -4$ and $x = 3$. These are called the x intercepts.

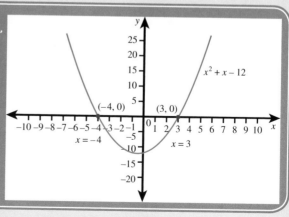

Solve $x^2 + 4x - 14 = 0$. Give your answers in surd form.

Top Tip

If you are asked to give your answers in surd form, it means that the quadratic won't factorise and you should use the quadratic formula.

Solution

The coefficients of the quadratic are $a = 1$, $b = 4$, $c = -14$.

$$x = \frac{-b \pm \sqrt{b^2 - 4ac}}{2a}$$ Write out the quadratic formula.

$$x = \frac{-(4) \pm \sqrt{(4)^2 - 4(1)(-14)}}{2(1)}$$ Substitute in the values of the coefficients.

$$= \frac{-4 \pm \sqrt{72}}{2} = \frac{-4 \pm 6\sqrt{2}}{2}$$ Simplify.

$$= -2 \pm 3\sqrt{2}$$

The solutions are in surd form (a conjugate pair) and are irrational numbers.

Top Tip

When you use the quadratic formula, start by writing it out in full. Then substitute in the coefficients, using brackets around each one. This minimises the chance of making a mistake with minus signs.

Given the two roots of a quadratic, how can we form the quadratic equation?

Roots	Factors	Equation
1, 2	$(x - 1)(x - 2)$	$x^2 - 3x + 2 = 0$
-2, 3	$(x + 2)(x - 3)$	$x^2 - x - 6 = 0$
4, 4	$(x - 4)(x - 4)$	$x^2 - 8x + 16 = 0$
6, 0	$(x - 6)(x - 0)$	$x^2 - 6x = 0$
a, b	$(x - a)(x - b)$	$x^2 - (a + b)x + ab = 0$

We can use the formula from the final row to form a quadratic given its roots:

$x^2 - $ (*sum of roots*) $x + $ *product of roots* $ = 0$.

Example

Form a quadratic equation given the pair of roots $1 \pm \sqrt{3}$. Give your answer in the form $ax^2 + bx + c = 0$, where $a, b, c \in \mathbb{Z}$.

Solution

Sum of roots $= 1 + \sqrt{3} + 1 - \sqrt{3} = 2$

Product of roots: $\left(1 + \sqrt{3}\right)\left(1 - \sqrt{3}\right) = 1 - 3 = -2$

Using the formula, the equation is $x^2 - 2x - 2 = 0$.

Solving rational equations

A **rational equation** is an equation with rational expressions (i.e. one or more of the terms is in rational or fraction form).

Example

A positive integer is 2 less than another positive integer. The sum of the reciprocals of the two integers is equal to $\dfrac{7}{24}$. Find the values of the integers.

Solution

Let x be the first integer and $x - 2$ be the second integer.

> **Top Tip**
>
> Always state clearly any variables that you set up for your calculations.

The sum of the reciprocals $= \dfrac{1}{x} + \dfrac{1}{x - 2}$.

$\dfrac{1}{x} + \dfrac{1}{x - 2} = \dfrac{7}{24}$

Form a rational equation.

$\dfrac{1}{\cancel{x}}(\cancel{x})(x - 2)(24) + \dfrac{1}{\cancel{x - 2}}(x)(\cancel{x - 2})(24) = \dfrac{7}{\cancel{24}}(x)(x - 2)(\cancel{24})$

Multiply each term by the LCM of the denominators, $(x)(x - 2)(24)$.

$(x - 2)(24) + 24x = 7x(x - 2)$

Simplify and rearrange.

$24x - 48 + 24x = 7x^2 - 14x$

$7x^2 - 62x + 48 = 0$

$(7x - 6)(x - 8) = 0 \Rightarrow x = \dfrac{6}{7}$ or $x = 8$.

Factorise to solve for x.

When solving rational equations there might be invalid or erroneous solutions. Check that your answers make sense in the context of the question.

In this example we know that x is a positive integer, so we ignore the fraction $x = \frac{6}{7}$.

Answer: The positive integers are $x = 8$ and $x - 2 = 6$.

Solving surd and irrational equations

To solve an equation involving surds, isolate the surd part on one side of equation. Then square both sides to remove the surd and solve the resulting quadratic equation.

Remember

Always check both solutions in the original equation.

Example

Solve $\sqrt{x + 4} - 2 = x$.

Solution

$\sqrt{x + 4} = x + 2$	Isolate the surd on the LHS.
$\left(\sqrt{x + 4}\right)^2 = (x + 2)^2$	Square both sides.
$x + 4 = x^2 + 4x + 4 \Rightarrow x^2 + 3x = 0$	Solve the resulting quadratic equation.

$x(x + 3) = 0 \Rightarrow x = -3$ or $x = 0$

Test the solutions in the original equation:

$x = 0 \Rightarrow \sqrt{0 + 4} - 2 = 0 \Rightarrow 2 - 2 = 0 ✓$

$x = -3 \Rightarrow \sqrt{-3 + 4} - 2 = -3 \Rightarrow 1 - 2 = -3 \Rightarrow -1 = -3 ✗$

So $x = -3$ is a not a solution, and the answer is $x = 0$.

Point to note

You might be wondering why we end up with a solution that is not really a solution. When we squared both sides in the second step, we changed the equation into a quadratic – and quadratics have two solutions. This means that we have a solution that is not a solution to the original equation. That's why you must *always* check both solutions!

Linear and non-linear simultaneous equations

Example

Solve the simultaneous equations: $x + 2y = 4$ and $x^2 + y^2 = 16$.

Solution

This is the equation of a line and a circle.

Always start with the linear equation and express the equation in terms of one variable.

Here it is much easier to work with x: $x = 4 - 2y$. (This avoids a fraction, i.e. $y = \dfrac{4 - x}{2}$, which would be more difficult to work with.)

$(4 - 2y)^2 + y^2 = 16$ Substitute $x = 4 - 2y$ into the non-linear equation.

$16 - 16y + 4y^2 + y^2 = 16$ Rearrange and solve the quadratic as normal.

$$5y^2 - 16y = 0$$

$$y(5y - 16) = 0$$

$y = 0$ or $y = 3\cdot2$

Top Tip

Don't forget to calculate the corresponding x values by substituting the y values into the linear equation.

$y = 0 \Rightarrow x = 4 - 2(0) = 4$

$y = 3\cdot2 \Rightarrow x = 4 - 2(3\cdot2) = -2\cdot4$

In this example there are two points of intersection between the line and circle: $(4, 0)$ and $(-2\cdot4, 3\cdot2)$.

Examples

A golfer hits a golf ball on the first tee as shown in the diagram. The path of the ball is modelled by the parabola $h(t) = -0\cdot5t^2 + 4t + 10$, where h is the height in metres and t is the time in seconds.

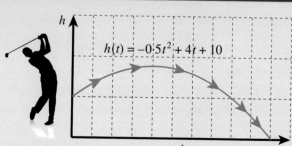

$h(t) = -0\cdot5t^2 + 4t + 10$

(a) Find the time it takes the golf ball to strike the ground.

(b) After how many seconds does the golf ball reach a height of 10 metres?

Solutions

(a) When the ball hits the ground, $h(t) = 0$. This is the point at which the graph cuts the x-axis.

Solve the equation $-0\cdot5t^2 + 4t + 10 = 0$.

This factorises to $(-0\cdot5t + 5)(t + 2) = 0$, giving the solutions $t = -2$ or $t = 10$.

The answer must be positive, so the ball will hit the ground when $t = 10$ seconds.

(b) To find where the ball reaches a height of 10 metres we must solve $h(t) = 10$.

$$-0\cdot5t^2 + 4t + 10 = 10$$

$$-0\cdot5t^2 + 4t = 0 \qquad \text{Rearrange so that the RHS is 0.}$$

$$t(-0\cdot5t + 4) = 0 \qquad \text{Factorise.}$$

$$t = 0 \text{ or } -0\cdot5t = -4 \Rightarrow t = 8$$

We can see from the diagram that the golfer is on a platform above the ground when hitting the ball at $t = 0$, so the ball reaches a height of 10 metres at $t = 8$ seconds.

Simultaneous linear equations with two unknowns

Example

Solve the simultaneous equations:

$$y + \frac{2}{3}x = 7$$

$$y - \frac{1}{2}x = \frac{21}{2}.$$

Solution

We can solve these equations by using elimination or by graphing these lines and finding the point of intersection.

Using elimination gives the exact answers. Graphing sometimes gives only approximate answers.

Elimination method

(A) $y + \dfrac{2}{3}x = 7 \Rightarrow 3y + 2x = 21$ Give each equation a label. Eliminate the fractions by multiplying each equation by the

(B) $y - \dfrac{1}{2}x = \dfrac{21}{2} \Rightarrow 2y - x = 21$ LCM of its denominators.

Eliminate one variable. In this example, equation *(A)* has a $2x$ term and equation *(B)* has an x term.

(2B) $4y - 2x = 42$ Multiply equation *(B)* by 2 to give it a $-2x$ term.

(A + 2B) $7y = 63 \Rightarrow y = 9$ Add *(A)* and *(2B)* to eliminate x.

$y = 9 \Rightarrow 2(9) - x = 21 \Rightarrow x = -3$ Substitute $y = 9$ into *(B)* to find x.

On a graph, these lines intersect at the point $(-3, 9)$.

Top Tip

Always label the equations in a simultaneous equation problem so that you can refer back to them in your working.

Simultaneous equations with three unknowns

Example

Solve the simultaneous equations:

$x + y + z = 16$

$\dfrac{5}{2}x + y + 10z = 40$

$2x + \dfrac{1}{2}y + 4z = 21.$

(SEC 2013)

Solution

(A) $x + y + z = 16$

(B) $5x + 2y + 20z = 80$ Multiply the second and third equation by 2 to eliminate the fractions.

(C) $4x + y + 8z = 42$

Choose one variable to eliminate in two pairs of equations. Look at the coefficients to determine the easier variable.

In this example y is the easiest option.

(B) $5x + 2y + 20z = 80$ (A) $x + y + z = 16$

(2A) $-2x - 2y - 2z = -32$ (−1C) $-4x - y - 8z = -42$

Adding each pair gives us two equations with two unknowns. We can solve these using elimination.

(B + 2A) $3x + 18z = 48$

(A − C) $-3x - 7z = -26$

Adding these equations gives $11z = 22$ so $z = 2$.

$3x + 18z = 48 \Rightarrow 3x = 48 - 36 = 12 \Rightarrow x = 4$ Substitute $z = 2$ into (B + 2A) to find x.

$x + y + z = 16 \Rightarrow 4 + y + 2 = 16 \Rightarrow y = 10$ Substitute into (A) to find y.

Answer: $x = 4$, $y = 10$ and $z = 2$. If you have time, check your answers by substituting them into the original equations.

Examples

The diagram below shows the path of a missile: a parabola of the form $f(x) = ax^2 + bx + c$.

(a) Find the values of a, b and c where $a, b, c \in \mathbb{R}$.

(b) Hence solve $f(x) = 0$ correct to 2 decimal places.

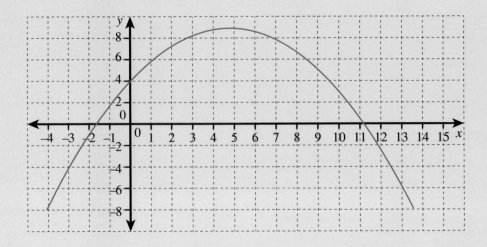

Solutions

(a) Choose three points on the curve and determine their x and y values.

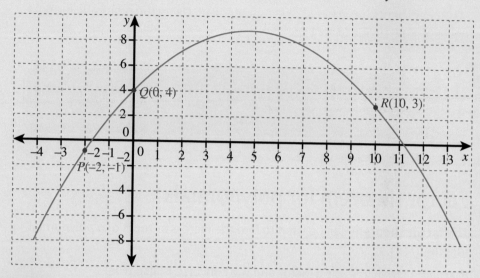

Point	x	$ax^2 + bx + c$	y
P	-2	$4a - 2b + c$	-1
Q	0	$0a + 0b + c$	4
R	10	$100a + 10b + c$	3

This gives three equations:

$4a - 2b + c = -1$

$c = 4$

$100a + 10b + c = 3$

Substitute $c = 4$ into the other two equations.

$4a - 2b + (4) = -1 \Rightarrow 4a - 2b = -5$

$100a + 10b + (4) = 3 \Rightarrow 100a + 10b = -1$

Solving these two equations in two variables gives $a = \dfrac{-13}{60}$ and $b = \dfrac{31}{15}$.

So $f(x) = ax^2 + bx + c = \dfrac{-13}{60}x^2 + \dfrac{31}{15}x + 4$.

(b) Solve $f(x) = \dfrac{-13}{60}x^2 + \dfrac{31}{15}x + 4 = 0$

$-13x^2 + 124x + 240 = 0$ Multiply each term by 60 to eliminate the fractions.

The coefficients are $a = -13$, $b = 124$, $c = 240$. Using the quadratic formula gives $x = 11·19$ and $x = -1·65$.

Top Tip

Practise using the quadratic formula by checking this answer for yourself.

Factor theorem for polynomials

The **factor theorem** can be used to find the factors or roots of a polynomial function $f(x)$.

If $f(a) = 0$, then $x - a$ is a factor and the converse is also true.

If $f(2) = 0$, then $x - 2$ is a factor and if $x - 2$ is a factor then $f(2) = 0$ ($x = 2$ is a root).

If $f(3) = 0$, then $x - 3$ is a factor and if $x - 3$ is a factor then $f(3) = 0$ ($x = 3$ is a root).

If $f(-1) = 0$, then $x + 1$ is a factor and if $x + 1$ is a factor then $f(-1) = 0$ ($x = -1$ is a root).

If $f\left(\dfrac{b}{a}\right) = 0$ then $ax - b$ is a factor. If $f\left(\dfrac{2}{3}\right) = 0$ then $3x - 2$ is a factor and $x = \dfrac{2}{3}$ is a root.

The table below gives some examples.

Roots	Factors	Polynomial in factor form
$x = 2, x = -3$	$(x - 2)(x + 3)$	$f(x) = (x - 2)(x + 3)$ Quadratic
$x = -3, x = 2,$ $x = -4$	$(x + 3)(x - 2)(x + 4)$	$f(x) = (x + 3)(x - 2)(x + 4)$ Cubic
$x = \dfrac{1}{2}, x = \dfrac{2}{3}$	$(2x - 1)(3x - 2)$	$f(x) = (2x - 1)(3x - 2)$ Quadratic
$x = -2, x = -2,$ $x = 3, x = \dfrac{1}{3}$	$(x + 2)(x + 2)(x - 3)(3x - 1)$	$f(x) = (x + 2)^2 (x - 3)(3x - 1)$ Quartic

Example

Show that $x + 3$ is a factor of $x^2 + x - 6$ and find the other factor.

Solution

Using the factor theorem, if $x + 3$ is a factor then $f(-3) = 0$.

$f(-3) = (-3)^2 + (-3) - 6 = 9 - 9 = 0$ ✓

Therefore $x + 3$ is a factor.

We can use long division **or** undetermined coefficients to find the second factor.

Long division

$$
\begin{array}{r}
x - 2 \\
x + 3 \overline{)\,x^2 + x - 6} \\
\underline{x^2 \mp 3x} \\
-2x - 6 \\
\underline{\pm 2x \pm 6}
\end{array}
$$

Remainder = 0, so the other factor is $x - 2$.

Undetermined coefficients

Let $(x + k)$ be the other factor.

$(x + 3)(x + k) = x^2 + x - 6$

$x^2 + 3x + kx + 3k = x^2 + x - 6$

$x^2 + (3 + k)x + 3k = x^2 + x - 6$

Equating coefficients: $3 + k = 1 \Rightarrow k = -2$. So the other factor is $x + k = x - 2$.

Example

Solve the cubic equation $2x^3 - 9x^2 + 7x + 6$.

Solution

We can assume that this equation has at least one integer root as the coefficients are real values.

To find a root we use trial and error and substitute an x value (input value) into the cubic equation which will give an output value of 0. (This is the factor theorem in use again.)

The root will be a factor of the constant term 6, so there are many factors to try.

Try factors of $\dfrac{6}{2} = 3$. Factors can be ± 1 or ± 3.

$x = 1 \Rightarrow f(1) = 2(1)^3 - 9(1)^2 + 7(1) + 6 = 2 - 9 + 7 + 6 = 6$

So $x = 1$ is not a root.

$x = 3 \Rightarrow f(3) = 2(3)^3 - 9(3)^2 + 7(3) + 6 = 54 - 81 + 21 + 6 = -27 + 27 = 0$

So $x = 3$ is a root and $x - 3$ is a factor.

To find the other factors we use long division. We divide the linear factor into the cubic expression and this gives a quadratic expression. This quadratic expression contains the other two factors.

$$
\begin{array}{r}
2x^2 - 3x - 2 \\
x - 3 \overline{\smash{\big)}\, 2x^3 - 9x^2 + 7x + 6} \\
\underline{\mp 2x^3 \pm 6x^2} \\
-3x^2 + 7x \\
\underline{\pm 3x^2 \mp 9x} \\
-2x + 6 \\
\underline{\pm 2x \mp 6}
\end{array}
$$

Remainder = 0

So $(x - 3)(2x^2 - 3x - 2) = 2x^3 - 9x^2 + 7x + 6$

$(x - 3)(x - 2)(2x + 1) = 2x^3 - 9x^2 + 7x + 6$

Solving gives 3 roots: $x = 2$, $x = 3$ and $x = \dfrac{-1}{2}$.

Example

A cubic function $f(x)$ cuts the x-axis at $x = -2$, $x = 0$ and $x = 3$.
If $f(x) = ax^3 + bx^2 + cx + d$, where $a, b, c, d \in \mathbb{R}$, find the values of a, b, c and d.

Solution

The roots are $x = -2$, $x = 0$ and $x = 3$. Using the factor theorem, the factors of $f(x)$ are $(x + 2)$, $(x - 0)$ and $(x - 3)$.

If $x = 0$ is a root then the factor could be x or $-x$ so another possible solution is $(x + 2)(x - 3)(-x)$.

Multiply the factors to find the cubic equation.

$(x + 2)(x)(x - 3) = (x^2 + 2x)(x - 3) = x^3 - x^2 - 6x = 0$

or

$(x + 2)(x - 3)(-x) = (x^2 - x - 6)(-x) = -x^3 + x^2 + 6x = 0$

Answer: $a = 1, b = -1, c = -6, d = 0$ or $a = 1, b = -1, c = -1, d = 0$

Example

Find the equation of the function $f(x) = ax^3 + bx^2 + cx + d$ in the diagram below.

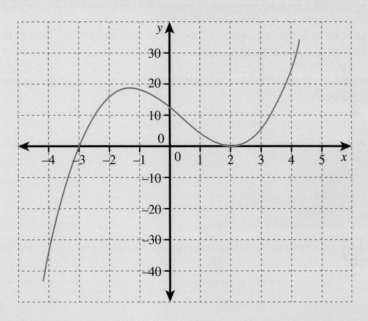

Solution

The graph intersects the x-axis at $x = -3$ and $x = 2$. We know that a cubic function has three roots.

Notice that the graph touches the x-axis at $x = 2$ (the x-axis is a tangent) so this means that we have two equal roots.

Roots: $x = -3$, $x = 2$, $x = 2$

Factors: $(x + 3)(x - 2)(x - 2)$

Multiply factors: $(x + 3)(x - 2)^2 = (x + 3)(x^2 - 4x + 4)$

Cubic equation: $f(x) = x^3 - x^2 - 8x + 12$

✓ Practise solving quadratic and cubic equations algebraically and graphically.

✓ Learn the formula for forming a quadratic equation given the roots.

✓ Always check answers when solving surd/irrational equations.

✓ Practise solving linear and non-linear equations. Don't forget to find the second variable!

✓ Know how to work with quadratic graphs.

✓ Practise solving linear equations (two and three variables). Select the variable that is easiest to eliminate.

✓ Practise using long division and undetermined coefficients to factorise and solve polynomials.

Algebra 3   5

Learning objectives

In this chapter you will learn how to:

- Select and use suitable strategies (graphic, numeric, algebraic, mental) for finding solutions to inequalities of the form

  $g(x) \le k, g(x) \ge k, g(x) < k, g(x) > k$

  where

  $g(x) = ax + b$ or $g(x) = ax^2 + bx + c$ or $g(x) = \dfrac{ax + b}{cx + d}$, $a, b, c, d, k \in \mathbb{Q}, x \in \mathbb{R}$

- Use the notation $|x|$

- Select and use suitable strategies (graphic, numeric, algebraic, mental) for finding solutions to inequalities of the form $|x - a| < b$, $|x - a| > b$ and combinations of these, where $a, b \in \mathbb{Q}, x \in \mathbb{R}$.

Inequalities

There are four **inequality** symbols:

Symbol	Meaning
>	Greater than
≥	Greater than or equal to
<	Less than
≤	Less than or equal to

We can show inequalities on a number line. The way they are shown depends on which number set the solutions are in. The table on page 58 shows how to display $x \le 3$ for three different number sets.

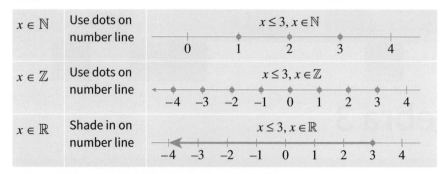

$x \in \mathbb{N}$	Use dots on number line	$x \leq 3, x \in \mathbb{N}$
$x \in \mathbb{Z}$	Use dots on number line	$x \leq 3, x \in \mathbb{Z}$
$x \in \mathbb{R}$	Shade in on number line	$x \leq 3, x \in \mathbb{R}$

Point to note

$a > b \Leftrightarrow b < a$. So if $3 > 2$ then $2 < 3$.

We try to have a positive x on the LHS of the inequality sign where possible. To solve $8 < 3x$, first rearrange to $3x > 8$ (note that the sign has changed direction). Then divide both sides by 3 to get $x > \dfrac{8}{3}$ (x is greater than $\dfrac{8}{3}$).

Rules for solving inequalities

We solve inequalities in the same way as equations, but there's one important difference to remember. If you multiply or divide both sides by a negative number, you *must* reverse the inequality sign. For example, $8 > -3$ but $-8 < 3$.

Example

Solve the inequality $\dfrac{x+2}{4} > \dfrac{x+1}{3} + \dfrac{1}{3}$, where $x \in \mathbb{R}$, and show the solution set on a number line.

Solution

$\dfrac{x+2}{4}(12) > \dfrac{x+1}{3}(12) + \dfrac{1}{3}(12)$ Remove the fractions by multiplying both sides by 12.

$\Rightarrow 3(x + 2) > 4(x + 1) + 4$

$\Rightarrow 3x + 6 > 4x + 4 + 4$ Simplify.

$\Rightarrow 3x - 4x > 8 - 6 \Rightarrow -x > -2$

$\Rightarrow x < 2$ Multiply both sides by -1. Remember to reverse the inequality sign!

$x < 2, x \in \mathbb{R}$

Remember

Don't forget to reverse the sign when you multiply or divide through by -1. It makes a big difference!

Combined inequalities

A **combined inequality** is the combination of two or more inequalities.

For example, $x < 2$ or $x > 5$, where $x \in \mathbb{R}$. Graphing this combined inequality, we see that the solution set is in opposite directions on the number line. The word **or** indicates the **union** of the inequalities.

$$x < 2 \text{ or } x > 5, x \in \mathbb{R}$$

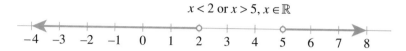

Consider $-1 \le x < 7$, where $x \in \mathbb{Z}$. Graphing this combined inequality we see that the solution set satisfies $-1 \le x$ and $x < 7$. The word **and** indicates the **intersection** of the inequalities

$$-1 \le x < 7, x \in \mathbb{Z}$$

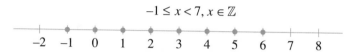

Examples

(a) Graph the solution set A of $-2 < \dfrac{3x+1}{4}$, $x \in \mathbb{R}$.

(b) Graph the solution set B of $8 \ge \dfrac{4x-4}{2}$, $x \in \mathbb{R}$.

(c) Find the solution set of $A \cap B$ and show the solution set on a number line.

Solutions

(a) $-2 < \dfrac{3x+1}{4} \Rightarrow -8 < 3x + 1 \Rightarrow -9 < 3x$ Rearrange to get x on the right.

$\Rightarrow -3 < x \Rightarrow x > -3$ Multiply through by -1. Remember to reverse the sign!

$$x > -3, x \in \mathbb{R}$$

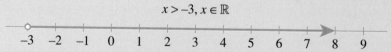

(b) $16 \ge 4x - 4 \Rightarrow 20 \ge 4x \Rightarrow 5 \ge x \Rightarrow x \le 5$

$$x \le 5, x \in \mathbb{R}$$

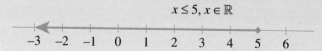

(c) Combining the two inequalities $x > -3$ and $x \le 5$ can be written as $-3 < x \le 5$. This is the intersection of the two sets.

$$-3 < x \le 5, x \in \mathbb{R}$$

Quadratic inequalities

When we work with a quadratic inequality, we always make **the coefficient of the x^2 term positive**. To solve a quadratic inequality we need to find the **roots**, or **critical values**, of the quadratic.

The solution set will be either between the roots or outside the roots. This is determined by the inequality sign.

Quadratic inequality	Solution set
$ax^2 + bx + c > 0$	Outside roots
$ax^2 + bx + c \geq 0$	Outside and including roots
$ax^2 + bx + c < 0$	Between roots
$ax^2 + bx + c \leq 0$	Between and including roots

Note that since the coefficient of the x^2 term is positive, $a > 0$.

Example

Find the set of all real values of x for which $2x^2 + x - 15 \geq 0$.

(SEC 2013)

Solution

First, find the roots of the quadratic using the equation $2x^2 + x - 15 = 0$.

$2x^2 + x - 15 = 0 \Rightarrow (2x - 5)(x + 3) = 0$ Factorise.

$\Rightarrow 2x - 5 = 0$ or $x + 3 = 0$

$\Rightarrow x = \dfrac{5}{2}$ or $x = -3$

Since $ax^2 + bx + c \geq 0$, the solution set is outside and including the roots.

$$\{x \mid x \leq -3\} \cup \{x \mid x \geq 2\cdot 5\}, x \in \mathbb{R}$$

$x \leq -3$ or $x \geq \dfrac{5}{2}$. This means that any value less than or equal to 3 or greater than or equal to 2·5 will satisfy the quadratic inequality.

Top-Tip

It is important to write the word 'or' in the solution.

Example

Find the solution set of the inequality $-3 < x(-2x - 5)$, where $x \in \mathbb{R}$.

Solution

$-3 < x(-2x - 5) \Rightarrow -3 < -2x^2 - 5x$	Multiply out RHS.
$\Rightarrow 2x^2 + 5x - 3 < 0$	Rearrange terms.
$2x^2 + 5x - 3 = 0 \Rightarrow (2x - 1)(x + 3) = 0$	Write as an equation and factorise to find roots.

$\Rightarrow 2x - 1 = 0$ or $x + 3 = 0$

$\Rightarrow x = \dfrac{1}{2}$ or $x = -3$

$ax^2 + bx + c < 0$, so the solution set is between the roots.

$$-3 < x < \frac{1}{2}, x \in \mathbb{R}$$

```
 +----o----+----+----+----o----+----+----+
   -4   -3   -2   -1   0 0·5 1    2
```

The answer is $-3 < x < \dfrac{1}{2}$.

Examples

The path of a table tennis ball that bounces over the net can be modelled by the parabola $h(t) = -5t^2 + 2t$, as shown in the diagram, where h is the height in metres and t is the time in seconds.

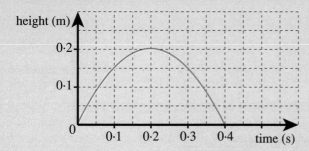

(a) Estimate from the graph the maximum height of the ball and the time taken to reach its maximum height.

(b) Estimate from the graph the time at which the ball hits the table. Check your answer by solving algebraically.

(c) If the height of the net is approximately 16 cm, for what time interval is the ball above the net?

Solutions

(a)

From the graph, the maximum height is 0·2 metres, and the time taken to reach this height is 0·2 seconds.

(b) From the graph, the ball hits the table at 0·4 seconds.

The ball is at table height when $h = 0$. Set the equation equal to zero and solve for t.

$-5t^2 + 2t = 0$

$t(-5t + 2) = 0$

$t = 0$ or $t = \dfrac{2}{5} = 0\cdot4$

$t = 0$ is the time at the start, so the answer is $t = 0\cdot4$ seconds. This agrees with the answer from the graph.

> ## Top Tip
> Always remember to include the units in your final answer.

(c) 16 cm = 0·16 metres.

Using the graph

Draw a horizontal line at $y = 0\cdot16$. (This is shown in the answer to part (a).)

Draw lines down to the x-axis at the points where this line meets the parabola. Estimate the x values at these points: 0·1 seconds and 0·3 seconds. The ball was above the net between these two times.

Algebraically

$-5t^2 + 2t > 0\cdot16$	The ball is above the net when $h(t) > 0\cdot16$. Write this as an inequality.
$\Rightarrow -5t^2 + 2t - 0\cdot16 > 0$	Rearrange to get 0 on the RHS.
$\Rightarrow 5t^2 - 2t + 0\cdot16 < 0$	Multiply through by -1 to get a positive t^2 coefficient.

The inequality sign is 'less than', so the interval we want is between the roots.

Find the roots using the quadratic formula. This gives $t = 0.11$ and $t = 0.29$ correct to 2 decimal places. The range of values will be between these values: 0.11 seconds $< t < 0.29$ seconds. This agrees with the approximate solution from the graph.

Discriminants

We know that the solution of any quadratic equation can be found using the formula $x = \dfrac{-b \pm \sqrt{b^2 - 4ac}}{2a}$.

The nature of the roots (solutions) of a quadratic equation depends on the value of the **discriminant**: $b^2 - 4ac$.

Discriminant value	Nature of roots
$b^2 - 4ac = 0$	Repeated real roots (two equal roots)
$b^2 - 4ac > 0$	Two distinct real roots
$b^2 - 4ac < 0$	No real roots (two complex roots)
$b^2 - 4ac \geq 0$	Use this to prove that the roots are real

Examples

Without solving, determine the nature of the roots of the quadratic in each case:

(a) $x^2 - 6x + 4 = 0$

(b) $x^2 - 6x + 9 = 0$

(c) $4x^2 + 8x + 20 = 0$.

Solutions

(a) $a = 1$, $b = -6$, $c = 4$

Discriminant $= b^2 - 4ac = (6)^2 - 4(1)(4) = 36 - 16 = 20 > 0$, therefore there are two distinct real roots.

(b) $a = 1$, $b = -6$, $c = 9$

$b^2 - 4ac = (-6^2) - 4(1)(9) = 0$, therefore there are repeated real roots (two equal roots).

(c) $a = 4$, $b = 8$, $c = 20$

$b^2 - 4ac = (8)^2 - 4(4)(20) = -256 < 0$, therefore there are no real roots.

Rational inequalities

Rational inequalities are in rational or fraction form. We don't know if the denominator is positive or negative. We must multiply both sides of the inequality by a positive quantity (a squared term) to be certain so that we don't have to reverse the inequality symbol.

> **Top Tip**
>
> For rational inequalities multiply both sides of the inequality by (denominator)^2 and then solve the quadratic inequality.

Example

Solve $\dfrac{2x + 1}{x - 3} < 1$, $x \neq 3$ where $x \in \mathbb{R}$.

Solution

$\dfrac{2x + 1}{x - 3} < 1 \Rightarrow \dfrac{2x + 1}{x - 3}(x - 3)^2 < 1(x - 3)^2$ Multiply both sides by $(x - 3)^2$.

This is positive, so there will be no change in the inequality sign.

$\Rightarrow (2x + 1)(x - 3) < x^2 - 6x + 9$ Multiply out the brackets and simplify.

$\Rightarrow 2x^2 - 5x - 3 < x^2 - 6x + 9$

$\Rightarrow x^2 - 5x + 6x - 3 - 9 < 0$

$\Rightarrow x^2 + x - 12 < 0$

$x^2 + x - 12 = 0 \Rightarrow (x + 4)(x - 3) = 0$ Write as an equation and solve for x.

$\Rightarrow x = -4$ or $x = 3$

Since the quadratic inequality is 'less than zero', the solution is between these roots.

Answer: $-4 < x < 3$

$$-4 < x < 3, x \in \mathbb{R}$$

Examples

The concentration, c, of a chemical in a liquid at t hours is given by $c(t) = \dfrac{2t}{1 + t}$, where c is measured in milligrams per litre.

(a) What is the concentration of the chemical after 5 hours correct to 2 decimal places?

(b) If the maximum allowed concentration was 1·5 mg/litre, after how many hours would the concentration exceed the maximum?

Solutions

(a) $c(5) = \dfrac{2(5)}{1 + (5)} = \dfrac{10}{6} = 1.67$ mg/litre   Substitute $t = 5$ into the formula and evaluate.

(b) We need to work out at what times the concentration is above 1.5 mg/litre.

We can write this as the inequality $\dfrac{2t}{1 + t} > 1.5$ and solve for t.

$\dfrac{2t}{1 + t} > 1.5 \Rightarrow \dfrac{2t}{1 + t}(1 + t)^2 > 1.5(1 + t)^2$ Multiply both sides by $(1 + t)^2$.

$\Rightarrow 2t(1 + t) > 1.5(1 + 2t + t^2)$ Multiply out the brackets and simplify.

$\Rightarrow 2t + 2t^2 > 1.5 + 3t + 1.5t^2$

$\Rightarrow 0.5t^2 - t - 1.5 > 0$

$0.5t^2 - t - 1.5 = 0 \Rightarrow t^2 - 2t - 3 = 0$ Write as an equation, multiply by 2 and factorise.

$\Rightarrow (t - 3)(t + 1) = 0$

The roots are $t = 3$ and $t = -1$. We know that $t > 0$ (time must be positive) so we can disregard $t = -1$.

The quadratic inequality is 'greater than zero' so the solution is outside the roots.

Answer: $t > 3$, so after 3 hours the concentration will exceed the maximum allowed concentration.

Note: Since $t > 0$, we can multiply by $(1 + t)$.

$2t > 1.5(1 + t) \Rightarrow 2t - 1.5t > 1.5 \Rightarrow 0.5t > 1.5 \Rightarrow t > 3$

Modulus (absolute value)

The **absolute value** or **modulus** of a real number is the positive value of that number. The absolute value of x is written as $|x|$.

$|-6| = 6$ and $|6| = 6$

If $|x| = 6$ then $x = \pm 6$. So if $|x| = a$ then $x = \pm a$.

Modulus graphs

A **modulus graph** is a graph of the form $f(x) = |x - a|$. Modulus graphs are V shaped, made up of two half lines. The point of the V is on the x-axis at $x - a = 0$.

Because the modulus is always positive, the graph for $f(x) = |x - a|$ does not go below the x-axis.

It's helpful to construct a table of values before drawing a graph.

Examples

Solve the following equations by sketching a graph:

Point to note

The apex is the point of the V.

(a) $|x - 2| = 3$

(b) $|2x + 1| = 4$.

Solutions

(a) We need to sketch a graph of $y = |x - 2|$. Find the apex of the graph first. This occurs when $x - 2 = 0$, so $x = 2$.

Construct a table of values less than $x = 2$ and greater than $x = 2$.

x	-2	-1	0	1	2	3	4	-5
$x - 2$	-4	-3	-2	-1	0	1	2	3
$y = \|x - 2\|$	4	3	2	1	0	1	2	3
Co-ordinates	$(-2, 4)$	$(-1, 3)$	$(0, 2)$	$(1, 1)$	$(2, 0)$	$(3, 1)$	$(4, 2)$	$(5, 3)$

Notice that all the y values are positive. Use the co-ordinates to sketch a graph.

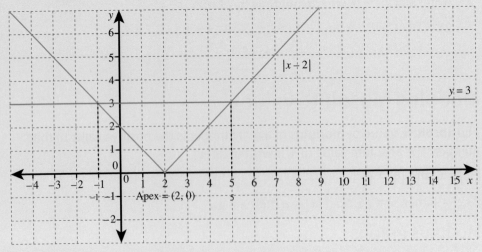

We can see from the graph that $y = |x - 2| = 3$ when $x = -1$ and $x = 5$.

(b) We need to sketch a graph of $y = |2x + 1|$. Find the apex of the graph first. This occurs when $2x + 1 = 0 \Rightarrow 2x = -1 \Rightarrow x = \dfrac{-1}{2}$.

So construct a table of values less than $x = \dfrac{-1}{2}$ and greater than $x = \dfrac{-1}{2}$. Then draw the graph.

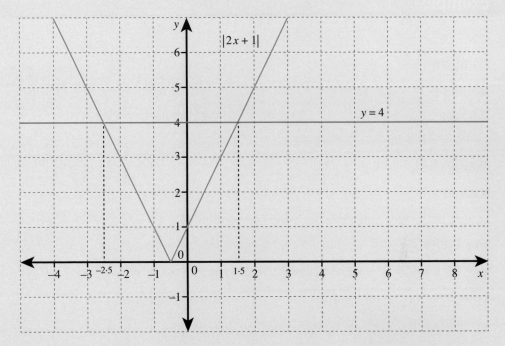

Answer: $x = -2{\cdot}5$ or $x = 1{\cdot}5$.

Modulus equations

Example

Solve $\left| x + 2 \right| = 6$.

Solution

$\left| x + 2 \right| = 6 \Rightarrow x + 2 = 6$ or $x + 2 = -6$

$\Rightarrow x = 4$ or $x = -8$

Test the values in the modulus equation to check your answers.

$\left| (4) + 2 \right| = \left| 6 \right| = 6 ✓$

$\left| (-8) + 2 \right| = \left| -6 \right| = 6 ✓$

You could also solve this by squaring both sides and solving the resulting quadratic equation, or by using a graph.

Example

Solve $2|x + 1| = |x - 2|$ for x, $x \in \mathbb{R}$.

Solution

Method 1

$2(x + 1) = \pm(x - 2)$ Take positive/negative case on RHS.

$2x + 2 = x - 2$ or $2x + 2 = -x + 2$

Solving gives $x = -4$ or $x = 0$.

Method 2

Square both sides and solve the quadratic inequality.

$2^2(x + 1)^2 = (x - 2)^2$

$4(x^2 + 2x + 1) = x^2 - 4x + 4$

$4x^2 + 8x + 4 = x^2 - 4x + 4$

$3x^2 + 12x = 0$

$x^2 + 4x = 0$

$x(x + 4) = 0$

$x = 0$ or $x = -4$

You can test these values in the original modulus equation if required.

Modulus inequalities

$|x| = 3 \Rightarrow x = -3$ or $x = 3$ ($\pm$ values)

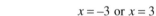

$x = -3$ or $x = 3$

$|x| > 3 \Rightarrow x > 3$ or $x < -3$ (outside values)

$x < -3$ or $x > 3$, $x \in \mathbb{R}$

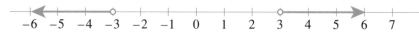

$|x| < 3 \Rightarrow -3 < x < 3$ (between values)

$$-3 < x < 3, x \in \mathbb{R}$$

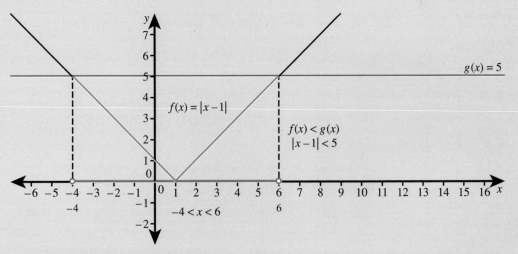

Example

Solve $|x - 1| < 5$ where $x \in \mathbb{R}$. Check your answer by using a graph.

Solution

Solving algebraically

$-5 < x - 1 < 5$ (between values)

Add 1 to each part to get x in the middle.

$-5 + 1 < x - 1 + 1 < 5 + 1 \Rightarrow -4 < x < 6.$

It is also possible to square both sides and solve the quadratic inequality.

Using a graph

We have two functions in this modulus inequality:

$f(x) = |x - 1|$ and $g(x) = 5.$

Plot these functions on a graph and find the points of intersection to solve $f(x) < g(x).$

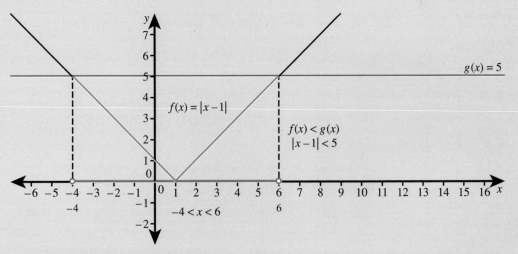

We can see from the graph the points of intersection and the x values on the x-axis (red) where $f(x)$ is below $g(x)$ (green).

Abstract inequalities

The following table shows examples of **abstract inequalities**.

$a, b \in \mathbb{R}$	Example
$a^2 \geq 0$	$(-5)^2 = 25 \geq 0$
$b^2 \geq 0$	$\left(\sqrt{2}\right)^2 = 2 \geq 0$
$(a + b)^2 \geq 0$	$\left(-5 + \sqrt{2}\right)^2 = 27 - 10\sqrt{2} \geq 0$
$(a - b)^2 \geq 0$	$(5 - 5)^2 = 0 \geq 0$
$-(a + b)^2 \leq 0$	$-(2 - 3)^2 = -1 \leq 0$
$-(a - b)^2 \leq 0$	$-(0{\cdot}5 - 1{\cdot}3)^2 = -0{\cdot}64 \leq 0$

Note that $(a - 1)^2$ and $(x - 2)^2$ etc. are perfect squares.

When proving abstract inequalities we must prove the inequality for all values or for certain conditions. It is not enough to substitute random values as above to prove an inequality.

Example

Prove that $a + \dfrac{1}{a} \geq 2$ for $a > 0$.

Solution

$a + \dfrac{1}{a} \geq 2$

$\Leftrightarrow a^2 + 1 \geq 2a$ Clear the fraction by multiplying both sides by a. We know that a is positive so the inequality sign remains the same.

$\Leftrightarrow a^2 - 2a + 1 \geq 0$

$\Leftrightarrow (a - 1)^2 \geq 0$ We know that this is true, because $(a - 1)^2$ is a perfect square, so must be ≥ 0.

$\Rightarrow a + \dfrac{1}{a} \geq 2$ This allows us to deduce that the original inequality is true.

Examples

Given the equation $x^2 + (k - 2)x + (k - 3) = 0$:

(a) Show that the roots are real for all values of $k \in \mathbb{R}$.

(b) Find the roots of the equation in terms of k.

Solutions

(a) We know that for a quadratic to have real roots, its discriminant must be greater than or equal to zero: $b^2 - 4ac \geq 0$.

Find the coefficients and substitute them into this inequality.

$a = 1$, $b = k - 2$, $c = k - 3$

$b^2 - 4ac = (k - 2)^2 - 4(1)(k - 3) = k^2 - 4k + 4 - 4k + 12 = k^2 - 8k + 16 = (k - 4)^2$

This gives us a perfect square, $(k - 4)^2$, which we know is ≥ 0. Therefore, the roots are real for all values of $k \in \mathbb{R}$.

(b) We use the formula $x = \dfrac{-b \pm \sqrt{b^2 - 4ac}}{2a}$ to solve the quadratic.

$x = \dfrac{-(k - 2) \pm \sqrt{(k - 4)^2}}{2(1)}$ Use the value for $b^2 - 4ac$ from part (a).

$x = \dfrac{-k + 2 \pm (k - 4)}{2}$

$x = \dfrac{-k + 2 + k - 4}{2} = \dfrac{-2}{2} = -1$

$x = \dfrac{-k + 2 - k + 4}{2} = \dfrac{-2k + 6}{2} = -k + 3$

The roots are $x = -1$ and $x = 3 - k$.

Checklist

✓ Know the rules for inequalities.

✓ Practise solving combined inequalities and showing the answers on a number line.

✓ Practise solving quadratic and rational inequalities and solving real-life problems.

✓ Know how the type of quadratic inequality determines the location of the solution set.

✓ Know how to use the value of the discriminant to determine the nature of quadratic roots.

✓ Practise solving modulus equations and inequalities using different methods: algebraic and graphical.

✓ Practise steps for solving abstract inequalities.

6 Functions and Graphing Functions

Learning objectives

In this chapter you will learn how to:

- Recognise that a function assigns a unique output to a given input
- Make use of function notation and understand the domain, co-domain and range of functions
- Use the vertical line test for functions
- Recognise surjective, injective and bijective functions
- Form composite functions and learn the notation required
- Find the inverse of a bijective function
- Sketch the graph of the inverse of a function given the graph of that function
- Investigate the concept of the limit of a function
- Informally explore limits and the continuity of functions
- Express quadratic functions in completed square form
- Use the completed square form of a quadratic function to
  - Find the roots and turning points
  - Sketch the function
- Recognise transformations of graphs.

Relations

A **relation** is a set of ordered pairs.

The set of all first elements of the ordered pair is called the **domain** of the relation (independent variable).

The set of all second elements of the ordered pair is called the **range** of the relation (dependent variable).

We can represent a relation with a mapping diagram, with set notation as a list of couples or a table of values, or with a set of points on the Cartesian plane.

Examples

The table shows the height and mass of five adults.

Height (cm) (independent variable)	Mass (kg)(dependent variable)
178	90
167	66
157	59
167	80
176	88

(a) Express the relation between the height and mass of the adults with a mapping diagram and a graphical representation.

(b) What are the domain and range of the relation?

Solutions

(a)

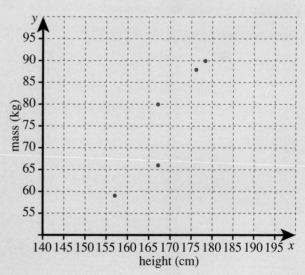

(b) Domain = $\{178, 167, 157, 167, 176\}$

Range = $\{90, 66, 59, 80, 88\}$

Functions

A **function** is a special relation.

We can think of a **function machine**. Each input value that is put into the function machine will give a unique output value.

The **domain** of values is the **set of input values** (what goes into the function machine).

The **range** of values is the **set of output values** (what actually comes out of the function machine).

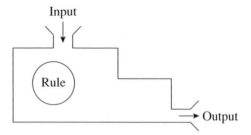

Input

Rule

Output

The **co-domain** of values is the **set of possible output values**.

So a function is a special relation where each element in the domain maps onto one and only one element in the range.

We can write a function in various forms:

$$f : x \rightarrow 2x^2$$

$$f(x) = 2x^2$$

$$y = 2x^2$$

Example

A and B are two non-empty sets where $A = \{2, 4, 6, 8\}$ and $B = \{a, b, c\}$.

Consider the following relations:

$R = \{(2, a), (4, b), (4, c), (6, c), (8, b)\}$

$S = \{(2, a), (4, b), (8, b)\}$

$T = \{(2, a), (4, b), (6, c), (8, b)\}$.

Which of these relations are functions? Give reasons for your answer.

Solution

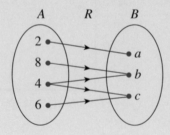

R is not a function, because R maps $4 \in A$ to both b and $c \in B$.

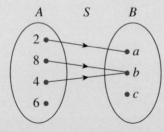

S is not a function, because S is not defined for all elements of A.

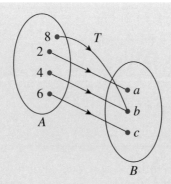

T is a function, because each element of the domain maps onto one and only one element in the range.

Examples

(a) A function f is given by $f: x \rightarrow 2x^2 - 4x + 5$, $x \in \mathbb{R}$.

Find **(i)** $f(1)$ **(ii)** $f(-1)$ **(iii)** $f(x+2)$ **(iv)** $f(-x)$.

(b) A graph of $f(x)$ is drawn in the diagram below.

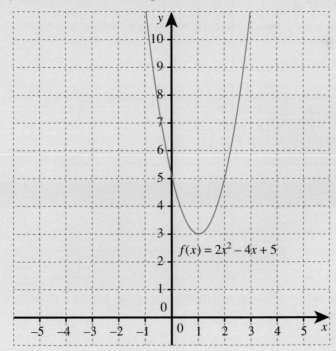

Draw a graph of $f(-x)$ and explain what transformation maps $f(x)$ onto $f(-x)$.

Solutions

(a)   **(i)** $f(1) = 2(1)^2 - 4(1) + 5 = 2 - 4 + 5 = 3$

    (ii) $f(-1) = 2(-1)^2 - 4(-1) + 5 = 2 + 4 + 5 = 11$

(iii) $f(x+2) = 2(x+2)^2 - 4(x+2) + 5$

$$= 2(x^2 + 4x + 4) - 4x - 8 + 5$$

$$= 2x^2 + 8x + 8 - 4x - 3$$

$$= 2x^2 + 4x + 5$$

(iv) $f(-x) = 2(-x)^2 - 4(-x) + 5$

$$= 2x^2 + 4x + 5$$

(b)

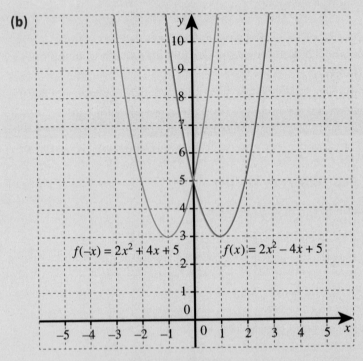

$f(x)$ is mapped onto $f(-x)$ by reflection in the y-axis.

Examples

(a) A function g is defined as $g: \mathbb{N} \rightarrow \mathbb{N}: x \rightarrow x^3$.

Find the domain, range and co-domain of the function.

Sketch $g(x)$ and $g(x) + 2$ using the same axes and scales.

Describe what transformation maps $g(x)$ onto $g(x) + 2$ where $x \in \mathbb{R}$.

(b) $h: \mathbb{R} \rightarrow \mathbb{R}: x \rightarrow x^2$

Find the domain, co-domain and range for this function.

Is $h(x) = h(-x)$?

Solutions

(a) Domain = $\mathbb{N}$, range = $\{1, 8, 27, 64, \ldots\}$, co-domain = $\mathbb{N}$.

Notice that the range is a subset of the co-domain.

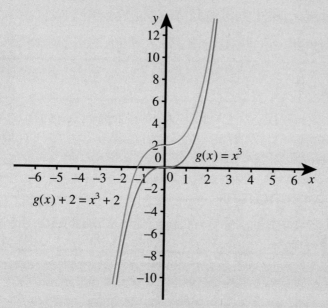

$g(x)$ is mapped onto $g(x) + 2$ by a vertical shift upwards of 2 units.

(b) Domain = $\mathbb{R}$, co-domain = $\mathbb{R}$, range = $[0, \infty)$.

$h(x) = x^2$, $h(-x) = (-x)^2 = x^2$

So $h(x) = h(-x)$. A function such as this is called an **even function**.

Point to note

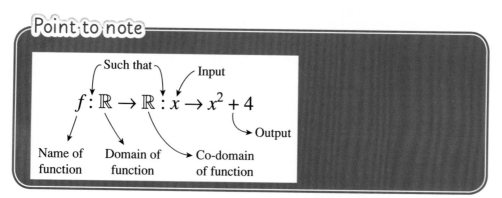

Remember

$\mathbb{R}^+$ = set of positive real numbers

$\mathbb{Z}^+$ = set of positive integers

$\mathbb{Q}^+$ = set of positive rational numbers

Point to note

A **closed interval** is an interval that includes the endpoints. It is denoted by square brackets [ ].

An open interval is an interval that does not include the endpoints. It is denoted by rounded brackets ( ).

Interval	Meaning
$[a, b]$	$\{x \in \mathbb{R} \mid a \leq x \leq b\}$ a and b are included
(a, b)	$\{x \in \mathbb{R} \mid a < x < b\}$ a and b are not included
$[a, b)$	$\{x \in \mathbb{R} \mid a \leq x < b\}$ a included, b not included
$(a, b]$	$\{x \in \mathbb{R} \mid a < x \leq b\}$ a not included, b included

Vertical line test for functions

If any **vertical line** that can be drawn intersects the graph **at most once**, then the graph represents a function.

Examples

State the domain and range of the following relations represented by the graphs and state which are functions using the vertical line test.

(a)

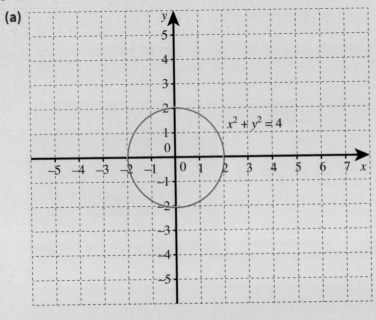

$x^2 + y^2 = 4$

(b)

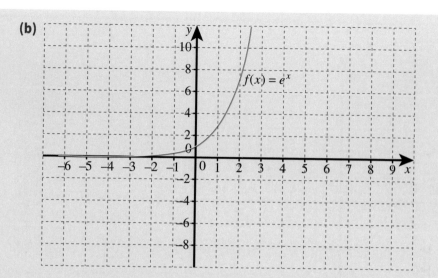

$f(x) = e^x$

(c)

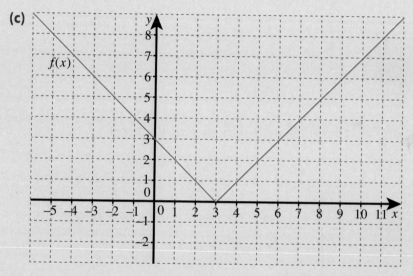

$f(x)$

(d)

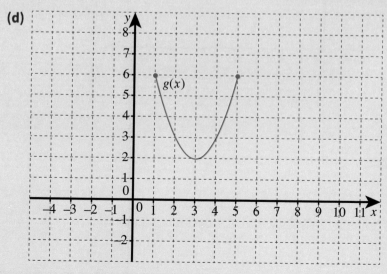

$g(x)$

Solutions

(a)

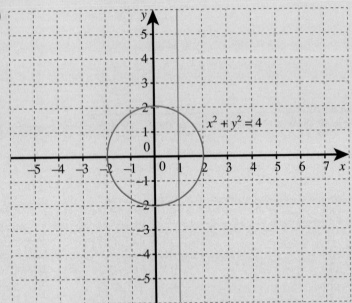

Domain = $[-2, 2]$

Range = $[-2, 2]$

Vertical line intersects the graph more than once, so this is not a function.

(b)

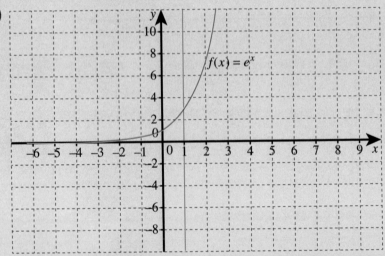

Domain = $\mathbb{R}$

Range = $\mathbb{R}^+$

Any vertical line will intersect the graph at most once, so this is a function.

(c)

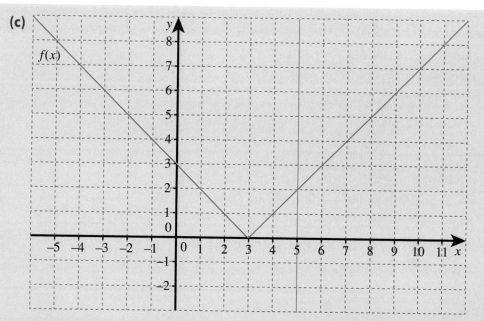

Domain = ℝ

Range = [0, ∞)

Any vertical line will intersect the graph at most once, so this is a function.

(d)

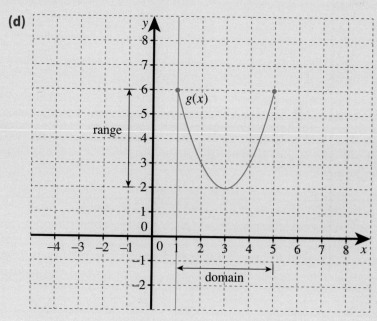

Domain = [1, 5]

Range = [2, 6]

Any vertical line will intersect the graph at most once for the closed interval [1, 5], so this is a function defined on [1, 5].

Examples

f is a function given by $f(x) = |x - 5| - 3$.

(a) Find the x and y intercepts of f.

(b) Find the domain and range of f.

(c) Sketch the graph of f.

Solution

(a) x intercept: $|x - 5| - 3 = 0 \Rightarrow |x - 5| = 3 \Rightarrow x - 5 = \pm 3$

$x = 2$ or $x = 8$, so the x intercepts are $(2, 0)$ and $(8, 0)$.

y intercept: $x = 0 \Rightarrow f(0) = |0 - 5| - 3 = 5 - 3 = 2$, so the y intercept is $(0, 2)$

(b) The domain of f is the set of all real numbers, $\mathbb{R}$.

The range of f is $[-3, \infty)$.

(c)

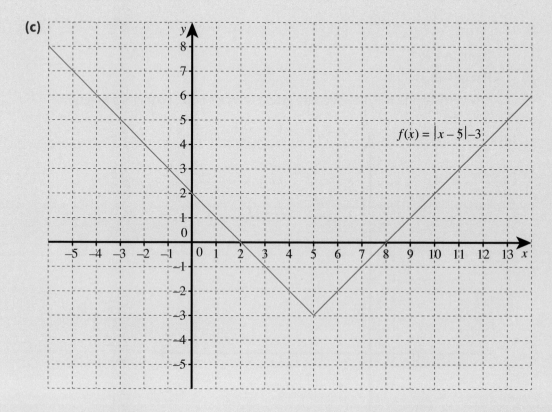

Types of function

The main types of function are listed in the table below.

Type of function	Properties	Diagram	Test
Injective (one to one)	No two inputs have the same output. Not necessary that every output in the co-domain has a corresponding input in the domain. $f(a) = f(b)$ $\Rightarrow a = b$	 A Input B Output	Horizontal line test: any horizontal line intersects graph of function at most once
Surjective (many to one)	Every output is possible. No output is left unused. Range and co-domain are equal.	 A Input B Output	Horizontal line test: any horizontal line intersects graph of function at least once
Bijective (exactly one to one)	Each input has a unique output. Both injective and surjective. A function has an inverse if, and only if, it is bijective.	 A Input B Output	

Horizontal line test

In the graph of an injective function, any horizontal line intersects the graph at most once.

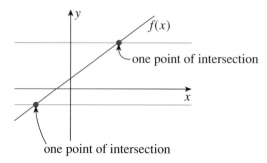

In the graph of a surjective function, any horizontal line intersects the graph at least once.

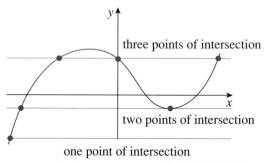

Examples

A is the closed interval $[0, 5]$. That is, $A = \{x \mid 0 \leq x < 5, x \in \mathbb{R}\}$.

The function f is defined on A by:

$f: A \rightarrow \mathbb{R}: x \rightarrow x^3 - 5x^2 + 3x + 5$.

(a) Find the maximum and minimum values of f.

(b) State whether f is injective. Give a reason for your answer.　　　(SEC 2014)

Solutions

(a) $f(x) = x^3 - 5x^2 + 3x + 5 \implies f'(x) = 3x^2 - 10x + 3$　　　Differentiate $f(x)$.

$\quad f'(x) = 0 \implies 3x^2 - 10x + 3 = 0$　　　Set the derivative to 0 and solve to find the turning points.

$\quad (3x - 1)(x - 3) = 0$

$\quad x = \dfrac{1}{3}$ or $x = 3$

Substitute the x values into $f(x)$ to find the y values.

$f\left(\frac{1}{3}\right) = \left(\frac{1}{3}\right)^3 - 5\left(\frac{1}{3}\right)^2 + 3\left(\frac{1}{3}\right) + 5 = 5\frac{13}{27}$ so $\left(\frac{1}{3}, 5\frac{13}{27}\right)$ is a turning point.

$f(3) = (3)^3 - 5(3)^2 + 3(3) + 5 = -4$ so $(3, -4)$ is a turning point.

$f(x)$ is defined on the closed interval $[0, 5]$.

$x = 0 \implies f(0) = (0)^3 - 5(0)^2 + 3(0) + 5 = 5$, so $(0, 5)$ is the starting point of the function.

$x = 5 \implies f(5) = (5)^3 - 5(2)^2 + 3(5) + 5 = 20$, so $(5, 20)$ is the finishing point of the function.

$(3, -4)$ is a turning point. This must be a local minimum, because the y value is lower than that of the start point, end point and other turning point.

Therefore, minimum value = –4 and maximum value = 20.

(b) We can use the horizontal line test to see if the function is injective.

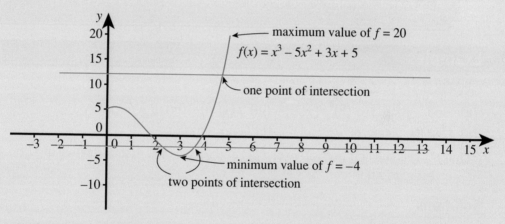

The function is not injective as there is a horizontal line that intersects the graph more than once.

Composition of functions

When we combine two or more functions we get **composite functions**.

If f and g are two functions, then we denote their composite functions by $f \circ g$ and $g \circ f$.

$f \circ g$ reads 'f after g', and means that we work with function g **first** and then apply f.

$g \circ f$ reads 'g after f' and means that we work with function f **first** and then apply g.

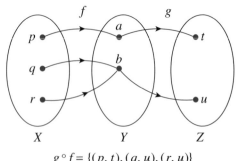

$$g \circ f = \{(p, t), (q, u), (r, u)\}$$

Point to note

$f \circ g(x) = f(g(x)), g \circ f(x) = g(f(x))$

Point to note

In general, if f and g are two functions, then $f(g(x)) \neq g(f(x))$.

Examples

Given that $f(x) = 2x - 5$ and $g(x) = x^2 - 2$:

(a) Find **(i)** $g(2)$ **(ii)** $f(g(2))$ **(iii)** $f(g(x))$ **(iv)** $g \circ f(x)$.

(b) Find the values of x for which $f(g(x)) = g(f(x))$.

(c) If $f'(x)$ is the first derivative of $f(x)$ and $g'(x)$ is the first derivative of $g(x)$, investigate whether $f \circ g'(x) = g \circ f'(x)$.

Solutions

(a) **(i)** $g(2) = (2)^2 - 2 = 4 - 2 = 2$

(ii) $f(g(2)) = f(2) = 2(2) - 5 = -1$

(iii) $f(g(x)) = f(x^2 - 2) = 2(x^2 - 2) - 5 = 2x^2 - 9$

(iv) $g \circ f(x) = g(f(x)) = g(2x - 5) = (2x - 5)^2 - 2$

$$= 4x^2 - 20x + 25 - 2$$

$$= 4x^2 - 20x + 23$$

(b) Use the expressions for $f(g(x))$ and $g(f(x))$ found in part (a)

$2x^2 - 9 = 4x^2 - 20x + 23$ Set the expressions equal to each other.

$2x^2 - 20x + 32 = 0$ Rearrange and solve for x.

$x^2 - 10x + 16 = 0$

$(x - 8)(x - 2) = 0$

$\therefore x = 8$ or $x = 2$

(c) $f'(x) = 2$, $g'(x) = 2x$ Find the first derivatives.

$f(g'(x)) = f(2x) = 2(2x) - 5 = 4x - 5$

$g(f'(x)) = g(2) = 2$

Therefore $f(g'(x)) \neq g(f'(x))$.

Inverse of functions

Consider the following mapping diagram.

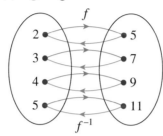

f is a function, and $f = \{(2, 5), (3, 7), (4, 9), (5, 11)\}$.

If we go backwards from output to input, we will reverse the couples.
This function is called the **inverse function**, denoted by f^{-1}.

$f^{-1} = \{(5, 2), (7, 3), (9, 4) \, (11, 5)\}$

f		f^{-1}	
Input	**Output**	**Input**	**Output**
2	5	5	2
3	7	7	3
4	9	9	4
5	11	11	5

If we plot the couples of the function f as points on a co-ordinate plane and
reflect the points in the line $y = x$, the image points are the couples of the
inverse function f^{-1}.

> **Point to note**
>
> A function has an inverse if and only if it is a bijective function. It must be
> an exactly one to one mapping, as in the table above – there are no gaps!

> **Point to note**
>
> If $f(g(x)) = g(f(x)) = x$, then f and g are inverse functions of each other.

Examples

If $f(x) = 3x - 5$:

(a) Find $f^{-1}(x)$.

(b) Find $f(2)$ and $f^{-1}(1)$.

(c) Show that $f \circ f^{-1}(x) = x$.

Point to note

To find $f^{-1}(x)$, express x in terms of y, then replace y with x. This is called **variable interchange**.

Solutions

(a) $f(x) = 3(x) - 5$

$y = 3x - 5 \implies 3x = y + 5$ Write in terms of x and y.

$x = \dfrac{y + 5}{3}$ Rearrange to make x the subject.

So $f^{-1}(x) = \dfrac{x + 5}{3}$ Replace y with x.

(b) $f(2) = 3(2) - 5 = 1$

$f^{-1}(1) = \dfrac{(1) + 5}{3} = 2$

We can see that f maps 2 onto 1 and then the inverse function reverses the mapping from 1 to 2.

(c) $f \circ f^{-1}(x) = f\left(\dfrac{x + 5}{3}\right) = 3\left(\dfrac{x + 5}{3}\right) - 5 = x + 5 - 5 = x$

Examples

Consider the function $g: x \rightarrow 4x + 5$.

(a) On the same axes, draw the graph of g and its inverse function, g^{-1}, a reflection of g in the line $y = x$.

(b) Find $g^{-1}(x)$ using **(i)** co-ordinate geometry and the slope of $g^{-1}(x)$ from (a) **(ii)** variable interchange.

Solutions

(a) g contains $(0, 5)$ and $(-1, 1)$.

g^{-1} contains $(5, 0)$ and $(1, -1)$, reverse couples of g.

Plot these points and join with straight lines.

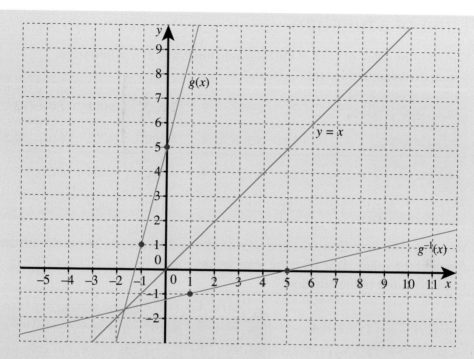

(b) **(i)** $m = \dfrac{y_2 - y_1}{x_2 - x_1} = \dfrac{-1 - 0}{1 - 5} = \dfrac{-1}{-4} = \dfrac{1}{4}$

Equation of line: $y - y_1 = m(x - x_1)$

$m = \dfrac{1}{4}$, $(x_1, y_1) = (5, 0)$

$y - 0 = \dfrac{1}{4}(x - 5)$

$y = g^{-1}(x) = \dfrac{x - 5}{4}$

(ii) $y = 4x + 5$ Express g in terms of x and y.

$4x + 5 = y$ Rearrange to make x the subject.

$4x = y - 5$

$x = \dfrac{y - 5}{4}$

$y = \dfrac{x - 5}{4}$ Replace y with x (variable interchange).

Limit of a function

Consider the value of each of the following functions as x approaches 2 from the left and the right.

x	1·9	1·99	1·999	2	2·0001	2·001	2·01	2·1
$f(x) = x + 2$	3·9	3·99	3·999	4	4·0001	4·001	4·01	4·1
$g(x) = \dfrac{x^2 - 4}{x - 2}$	3·9	3·99	3·999	4	4·0001	4·001	4·01	4·1
$h(x) = \dfrac{1}{x - 2}$	−10	−100	−1000		10 000	1000	100	10

We can see for functions $f(x)$ and $g(x)$ that as x approaches 2 from the left and the right the value of the function approaches a fixed value, which is 4. This is called the **limit** of the function.

$\lim\limits_{x \to 2} f(x) = \lim\limits_{x \to 2} (x + 2) = 4$

$\lim\limits_{x \to 2} g(x) = \lim\limits_{x \to 2} \left(\dfrac{x^2 - 4}{x - 2} \right) = 4$

The function $h(x)$ does not have a limit as x approaches 2.

Point to note

The limit of $f(x)$ as x approaches from the left is written as $\lim\limits_{x \to a^-} f(x)$.

The limit of $f(x)$ as x approaches from the right is written as $\lim\limits_{x \to a^+} f(x)$.

Examples

Evaluate the following limits, where they exist:

(a) $\lim\limits_{x \to 3} \dfrac{x^2 - 9}{x + 3}$

(b) $\lim\limits_{x \to 3} \dfrac{x^2 - 9}{x - 3}$.

Solutions

(a) $\lim\limits_{x \to 3} \dfrac{x^2 - 9}{x + 3} = \dfrac{(3)^2 - 9}{(3) + 3}$ Substitute in the value for which we want to find the limit.

$= \dfrac{0}{6} = 0$ Evaluate.

(b) $\lim\limits_{x \to 3} \dfrac{x^2 - 9}{x - 3} = \dfrac{(3)^2 - 9}{(3) - 3} = \dfrac{0}{0}$

$\dfrac{0}{0}$ is undefined, so factorise, simplify and then evaluate the limit.

$\lim\limits_{x \to 3} \dfrac{x^2 - 9}{x - 3} = \lim\limits_{x \to 3} \dfrac{(x - 3)(x + 3)}{(x - 3)} = \lim\limits_{x \to 3} (x + 3) = (3) + 3 = 6$

Continuous functions

Most of the functions on our course are **continuous functions**.

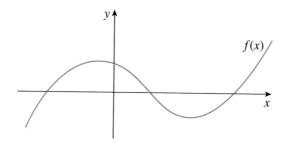

If a graph is continuous, we can trace the graph from left to right without the pen leaving the paper.

With functions that are not continuous there is a jump (or gap, or break, or hole) in the graph, so the pen leaves the paper when we trace the graph from left to right.

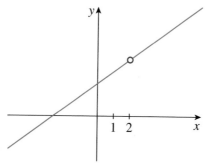

This diagram shows a graph with a 'hole'. The function is undefined at $x = 2$.

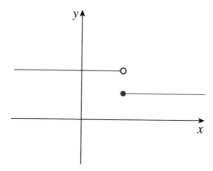

This diagram shows a **piecewise**, or **split**, function. There is a jump in the function, resulting in two distinct lines.

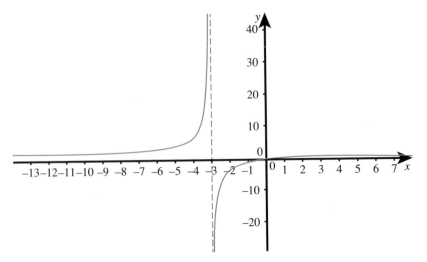

This diagram shows a graph with a vertical asymptote at $x = 3$. It is not continuous: the asymptote makes a gap in the graph.

A function is continuous at a point x_0 if it satisfies these three conditions:

- The function has a value at x_0
- The function has a limit at x_0
- The value and the limit are equal.

In mathematical notation, a function f is continuous at $x = a$ if $\lim\limits_{x \to a} f(x) = f(a)$.

Examples

In each case:

(i) Find $\lim\limits_{x \to x_0} f(x)$ if the limit exists.

(ii) Determine whether the function is defined at $x = x_0$.

(iii) Decide whether the function is continuous at the point $x = x_0$.

(a)

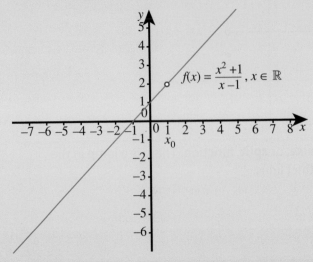

$$f(x) = \frac{x^2 + 1}{x - 1}, \ x \in \mathbb{R}$$

(b)

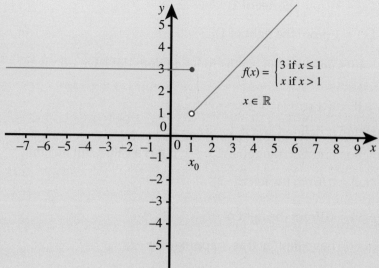

$$f(x) = \begin{cases} 3 \text{ if } x \le 1 \\ x \text{ if } x > 1 \end{cases}$$

$$x \in \mathbb{R}$$

(c)

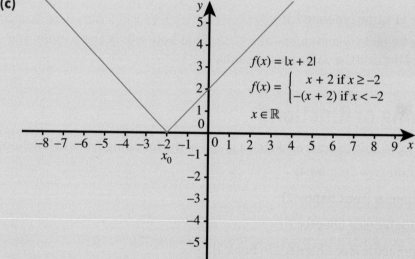

$$f(x) = |x + 2|$$

$$f(x) = \begin{cases} x + 2 \text{ if } x \ge -2 \\ -(x + 2) \text{ if } x < -2 \end{cases}$$

$$x \in \mathbb{R}$$

Solutions

(a) **(i)** $\lim\limits_{x \to 1^-} f(x) = 2$ (from the left of 1)

$\lim\limits_{x \to 1^+} f(x) = 2$ (from the right of 1)

The function has a limit of 2 as x approaches 1.

(ii) $f(1) = \dfrac{(1)^2 - 1}{(1) - 1} = \dfrac{0}{0}$

This is undefined, so the function is undefined at $x = 1$.

(iii) The function is not continuous at $x = 1$. It has a limit, but no value.

(b) **(i)** $\lim_{x \to 1^-} f(x) = 3$ (from the left of 1)

$\lim_{x \to 1^+} f(x) = 1$ (from the right of 1)

These values are different, so the function does not have a limit as x approaches 1.

(ii) $f(x) = 3$ if $x \le 1$ so $f(1) = 3$.

The function is defined at $x = 1$.

(iii) The function is not continuous at $x = 1$. It has a value, but no limit.

(c) **(i)** $\lim_{x \to -2^-} f(x) = 0$ (from the left of −2)

$\lim_{x \to -2^+} f(x) = 0$ (from the right of −2)

The function has a limit of 0 as x approaches −2.

(ii) $f(-2) = |-2 + 2| = |0| = 0$

The function is defined at $x = -2$.

(iii) The function is continuous at $x = -2$. It has both a limit and a value, and the limit and the value are the same.

Graphing of functions

You need to be able to draw or sketch a graph of the following types of functions:

- quadratic (see Chapter 4)
- exponential (see Chapter 2)
- logarithmic (see Chapter 2)
- trigonometric (see Chapter 1 in Book 2).

Top Tip

Use GeoGebra to draw graphs for different types of function. Learn the shapes of each type so that you can easily sketch them yourself.

Top Tip

Refer to the Student Area at www.projectmaths.ie, where you will find many digital resources to help you practise drawing and recognising graphs.

Quadratic functions in completed square form

Completing the square is a method for solving a quadratic that can't be factorised. The steps are as follows. A function in **completed square** form consists of a squared linear expression and a constant.

To write a function in completed square form:

1 Halve the x coefficient.

2 Square this number.

3 Add the squared number to the x^2 and x terms to form a perfect square.

4 Subtract the squared number from the constant to keep the function the same (you have added and subtracted the same number, so the overall value is the same).

5 Write the quadratic in completed square form, as a squared linear expression and a constant.

Example

Write the function $f(x) = x^2 - 4x + 6$ in completed square form.

Solution

The x coefficient is -4. Halve this to get -2, then square to get 4.

$f(x) = x^2 - 4x + 6 = x^2 - 4x + 4 + 6 - 4$

$\quad = (x - 2)^2 + 2$

The formula for completed square form is $y = a(x - h)^2 + k$. The following table shows the properties of some different completed square equations.

Equation in completed square form	Turning point	Shape of graph	Local max/min	Equation of axis of symmetry
$a(x - h)^2 + k$	(h, k)	$a > 0$ gives a U-shaped graph	Local minimum	$x = h$
		$a < 0$ gives a ∩-shaped graph	Local maximum	
$(x - 3)^2 + 2$	$(3, 2)$	U-shaped	Local minimum	$x = 3$
$2(x + 2)^2 - 4$	$(-2, -4)$	U-shaped	Local minimum	$x = -2$
$-(x - 5)^2 + 5$	$(5, 5)$	∩-shaped	Local maximum	$x = 5$

Examples

(a) Express the quadratic function $f(x) = 3x^2 + 12x + 4$ in completed square form.

(b) State the turning points of this function and write down the equation of the axis of symmetry.

(c) By considering the completed square form, find the roots of

$3x^2 + 12x + 4 = 0$, in the form $a \pm \dfrac{b\sqrt{c}}{d}$, where $a, b, c, d \in \mathbb{Z}$.

(d) Using the same scales and axes, draw the graphs of $f(x)$ and $g(x) = 4 - 4x$ in the domain $-6 \le x \le 1$, $x \in \mathbb{R}$.

(e) Use your graph to estimate the values of x for which $f(x) = g(x)$.

(f) Use your graph to estimate the values of x for which $f(x) \ge g(x)$.

Solutions

(a) $f(x) = 3x^2 + 12x + 4 = 3(x^2 + 4x) + 4$ — Take the common factor out of the first two terms.

$= 3(x^2 + 4x + 4) + 4 - 12$ — Halve and square the x coefficient to get 4. The added 4 is inside the brackets, so we need to subtract $3 \times 4 = 12$ from the constant to make the equation balance.

$= 3(x + 2)^2 - 8$

(b) The turning point is $(h, k) = (-2, -8)$. The equation of the axis of symmetry is $x = -2$.

(c) $3(x + 2)^2 - 8 = 0$ — Write the function in completed square form as an equation equal to 0.

$(x + 2)^2 = \dfrac{8}{3}$ — Add 8 to both sides, and then divide both sides by 3.

$x + 2 = \pm \sqrt{\dfrac{8}{3}}$ — Square root both sides.

$x + 2 = \pm \sqrt{\dfrac{24}{9}} = \pm \dfrac{\sqrt{4 \times 6}}{\sqrt{9}} = \pm \dfrac{2\sqrt{6}}{3}$ — Simplify the right-hand side.

$x = -2 \pm \dfrac{2\sqrt{6}}{3}$ — Subtract 2 from both sides to get the answer in the required form.

(d)

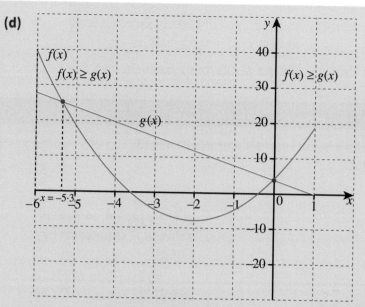

(e) $f(x) = g(x)$ at the points of intersection: $x = -5\cdot3$ (approximately) and $x = 0$.

(f) $f(x) \geq g(x)$ where the graph of $f(x)$ is higher than the graph of $g(x)$: $-6 \leq x \leq -5\cdot3$ or $0 \leq x \leq 1$.

Summary of graph transformations

Given the graph of $f(x)$, we can make the following transformations:

Shifts for $c > 0$	Translation
$f(x) + c$	Shift $f(x)$ up by c units
$f(x) - c$	Shift $f(x)$ down by c units
$f(x + c)$	Shift $f(x)$ left by c units
$f(x - c)$	Shift $f(x)$ right by c units

Stretches and compressions for $c > 1$	Scaling
$c f(x)$	Stretch $f(x)$ vertically by a factor of c
$\left(\frac{1}{c}\right) f(x)$	Compress $f(x)$ vertically by a factor of c
$f(cx)$	Compress $f(x)$ horizontally by a factor of c
$f\left(\frac{x}{c}\right)$	Stretch $f(x)$ horizontally by a factor of c

Reflections	
$-f(x)$	Reflect $f(x)$ in the x-axis
$f(-x)$	Reflect $f(x)$ in the y-axis

Example

Draw the graphs of $f(x) = x^2$, $g(x) = x^2 + 4$ and $h(x) = x^2 - 3$.
Comment on your graphs.

Solution

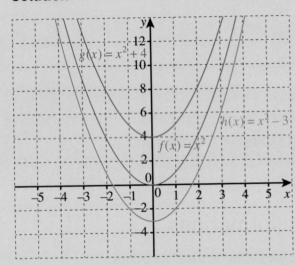

$g(x) = f(x) + 4$, so $g(x)$ is a shift of $f(x)$ upwards by 4 units.

$h(x) = f(x) - 3$ so $h(x)$ is a shift of $f(x)$ downwards by 3 units.

Example

Draw the graphs of $f(x) = x^2$, $g(x) = (x-2)^2$ and $h(x) = (x+4)^2$.
Describe the transformations that map $f(x)$ to $g(x)$ and $f(x)$ to $h(x)$.

Solution

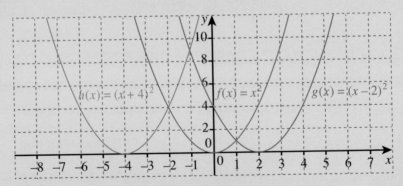

$g(x) = f(x - 2)$, so $g(x)$ is a shift of $f(x)$ right by 2 units.

$h(x) = f(x + 4)$ so $h(x)$ is a shift of $f(x)$ left by 4 units.

Example

Draw the graphs of $f(x) = x^3 - 3x$, $g(x) = \dfrac{x^3 - 3x}{2}$ and $h(x) = 2(x^3 - 3x)$.

Describe the transformations that map $f(x)$ to $g(x)$ and $f(x)$ to $h(x)$.

Solution

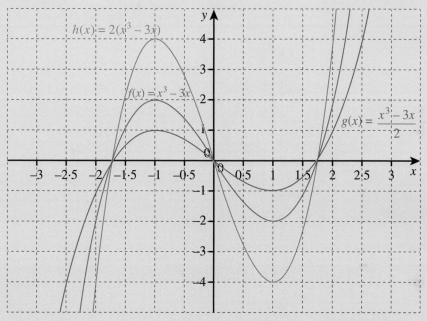

$g(x) = \dfrac{1}{2}f(x)$, so $g(x)$ is a compression of $f(x)$ vertically by a factor of 2.

$h(x) = 2f(x)$ so $h(x)$ is a stretch of $f(x)$ vertically by a factor of 2.

> **Point to note**
>
> For transformations of the form $c\,f(x)$:
> - points on the x-axis remain the same
> - points on the y-axis are multiplied by a factor of c.
>
> For transformations of the form $\dfrac{1}{c}\,f(x)$:
> - points on the x-axis remain the same
> - points on the y-axis are multiplied by a factor of $\dfrac{1}{c}$.

Examples

(a) Draw the graphs of $f(x) = \sin(x)$ and $g(x) = \sin\left(\frac{x}{2}\right)$. Comment on the transformation of $f(x)$ to $g(x)$.

(b) Draw the graphs of $f(x) = \sin(x)$ and $h(x) = \sin(2x)$. Comment on the transformation of $f(x)$ to $h(x)$.

Solutions

(a)

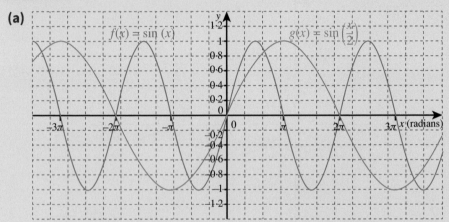

$g(x) = f\left(\frac{x}{2}\right)$, so $g(x)$ is a stretch of $f(x)$ horizontally by a factor of 2.

(b)

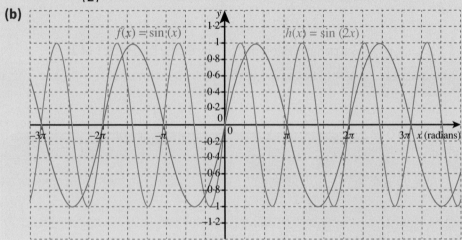

$h(x) = f(2x)$ so $h(x)$ is a compression of $f(x)$ horizontally by a factor of 2.

Point to note

The period of $f(x)$ is 2π.

The period of $f\left(\frac{x}{2}\right)$ is 4π.

The period of $f(2x)$ is π.

Point to note

For transformations of the form $f(cx)$:

- points on the x-axis are multiplied by a factor of $\frac{1}{c}$
- points on the y-axis remain the same.

For transformations of the form $f\left(\frac{x}{c}\right)$:

- points on the x-axis are multiplied by a factor of c
- points on the y-axis remain the same.

Examples

(a) Draw the graphs of $f(x) = e^x$ and $g(x) = -e^x$. Comment on the transformation of $f(x)$ to $g(x)$.

(b) Draw the graphs of $f(x) = 2^x$ and $h(x) = 2^{-x}$. Comment on the transformation of $f(x)$ to $h(x)$.

Solutions

(a)

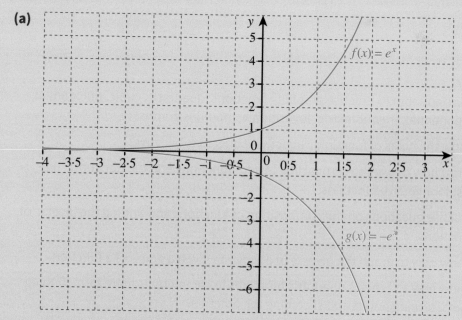

$g(x) = -f(x)$, so $g(x)$ is a reflection of $f(x)$ in the x-axis.

(b)

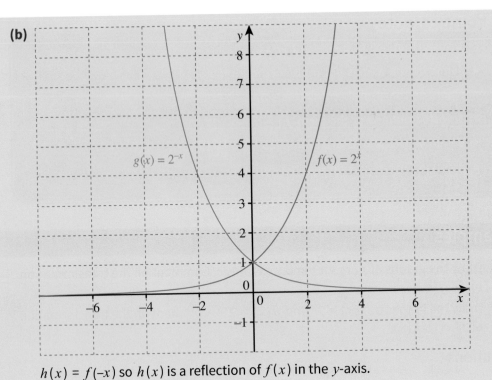

$h(x) = f(-x)$ so $h(x)$ is a reflection of $f(x)$ in the y-axis.

Checklist

✓ Use GeoGebra to practise graphing functions: quadratic, cubic, polynomial, exponential, trigonometric, logarithmic, modulus graphs.

✓ Know the types of functions: injective, surjective, bijective.

✓ Know how to use the vertical line test for functions and the horizontal line test for injective functions.

✓ Practise questions on the composition of functions and finding the inverse of functions.

✓ Know how to graph the inverse of a function given a graph of a function.

✓ Know how to express quadratic functions in completed square form, finding roots, turning points and sketching the function.

✓ Know how to find the limit of a function and show whether a function is continuous at a point.

✓ Know the effects of translations (horizontal and vertical), scaling (stretches and compressions), and reflections on a given graph.

Patterns

7

Learning objectives

In this chapter you will learn how to:

- Appreciate that processes can generate sequences of numbers or objects
- Investigate patterns among these sequences
- Use patterns to continue the sequence
- Generalise and explain patterns and relationships in algebraic form (linear, quadratic, cubic and exponential patterns and sequences).

Number patterns

A list of numbers which form a pattern is called a **sequence**. We can extend patterns to shapes, points, dots, and so on.

Tables, diagrams, graphs and formulae can all be used for representing and analysing patterns and sequences.

By examining number patterns we can find the **constant difference** between terms. This could be a **first difference (linear)**, **second difference (quadratic)** or **third difference (cubic)**.

> **Remember**
>
> The first differences are the differences between terms in the sequence.
>
> The second differences are the differences between the first differences.
>
> The third differences are the differences between the second differences.

Once we know the constant difference we can use a formula for the number pattern (linear, quadratic, cubic) and substitute in known terms. This will give us simultaneous equations (quadratic and cubic sequences) which we can solve to find a general formula for the pattern.

Linear patterns

The general term of a pattern with a **constant difference** a is $T_n = an + b$, where n is the term number.

> **Point to note**
>
> The terminology used for patterns and sequences is slightly different to that used when we come to arithmetic sequences.
>
> | Patterns | Sequences |
> |---|---|
> | a = constant difference | a = first term |
> | n = term number | n = term number |
> | b = adjustment term | |
> | | d = common difference |

Examples

Given the number pattern 3, 7, 11, 15, ...

(a) Find a formula for T_n and hence find the 10th term.

(b) Represent the pattern on a graph, and find the slope of the graph.

(c) Represent the pattern using squares measuring 4 mm × 4 mm, and find the area of the 10th pattern.

Solutions

(a) We can see that the constant difference is the first difference between terms.

Term	Term value	First difference
T_1	3	
T_2	7	4
T_3	11	4
T_4	15	4

The first difference, a, is +4.

$T_n = an + b \Rightarrow T_n = 4n + b$

We can find b by using one of the terms and substituting.

$T_1 = 4(1) + b = 3 \Rightarrow b = 3 - 4 = -1$ Substitute $n = 1$.

$T_n = 4n - 1$

$T_{10} = 4(10) - 1 = 39$

(b)

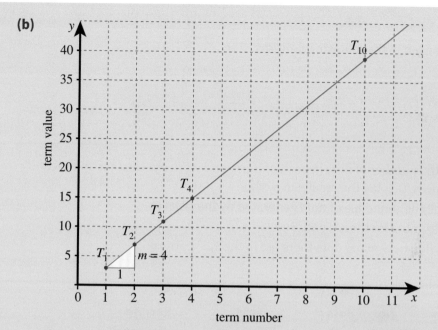

This is a linear graph. Constant difference = slope of linear graph = 4.

This is also an arithmetic sequence with common difference = 4.

(c)

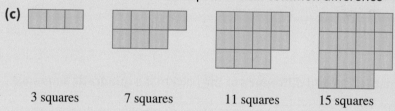

| 3 squares | 7 squares | 11 squares | 15 squares |

From part (a), we know that the 10th pattern will have 39 squares.

Area of 10th pattern = 39 × 4 × 4 = 624 mm².

Quadratic patterns

A **quadratic pattern** is non-linear. The difference between consecutive terms is not constant. **The difference between first differences (known as the second difference) is constant.**

The general term of a quadratic sequence with **second difference $2a$ is $T_n = an^2 + bn + c$.**

Point to note

First differences can be positive or negative.

Examples

Dots are arranged in the following patterns.

(a) Count the number of dots in each pattern, and work out the first and second differences. Display the results in a table.

(b) Describe the sequence of dots generated by the pattern.

(c) Find a formula for the nth pattern.

(d) Hence, find how many dots there are in the 12th pattern.

Solutions

(a)

Term	No. of dots = term value	First difference	Second difference
T_1	2		
T_2	7	5	
T_3	14	7	2
T_4	23	9	2

(b) There is a **constant second difference** so the pattern is a **quadratic sequence**.

(c) $T_n = an^2 + bn + c$

The second difference, $2a$, is 2, so $a = 1$.

$T_n = 1n^2 + bn + c$

We need to find the values of b and c. Substitute terms into T_n to form simultaneous equations and then solve.

The first term, $n = 1$, gives $T_1 = (1)^2 + b(1) + c = 2 \Rightarrow b + c = 1$.

The second term, $n = 2$, gives $T_2 = (2)^2 + b(2) + c = 7 \Rightarrow 2b + c = 3$.

Our simultaneous equations are

(A) $b + c = 1$

(B) $2b + c = 3$

We have two equations in two unknowns, so we can now solve for b and c.

$(B - A)\ b = 2$ Subtract (A) from (B).

$b + c = 1 \Rightarrow 2 + c = 1$ Substitute $b = 2$ into (A).

$\Rightarrow c = -1$

So $T_n = n^2 + 2n - 1$

(d) $T_{12} = 12^2 + 2(12) - 1 = 144 + 24 - 1 = 167$

There are 167 dots in the 12th pattern.

Shapes in the form of small equilateral triangles can be made using matchsticks of equal length. These shapes can be put together into patterns. The beginning of a sequence of these patterns is shown below.

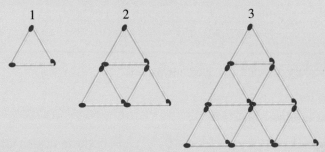

(a) **(i)** Draw the 4th pattern in the sequence.

(ii) The table below shows the number of small triangles in each pattern and the number of matchsticks needed to create each pattern. Complete the table.

Pattern	1st	2nd	3rd	4th
Number of small triangles	1		9	
Number of matchsticks	3	9		

(b) Write an expression in n for the number of triangles in the nth pattern in the sequence.

(c) Write an expression in n for the number of matchsticks needed to turn the $(n-1)^{th}$ pattern into the nth pattern.

(d) The number of matchsticks in the nth pattern in the sequence can be represented by the function $u_n = an^2 + bn$ where $a, b \in \mathbb{Q}$ and $n \in \mathbb{N}$. Find the value of a and the value of b.

(e) One of the patterns in the sequence has 4134 matchsticks. How many small triangles are in that pattern?   *(SEC 2013)*

Solutions

(a) **(i)**

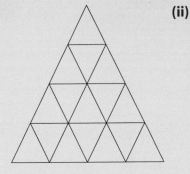

(ii)

Pattern	1st	2nd	3rd	4th
Number of small triangles	1	4	9	16
Number of matchsticks	3	9	18	30

(b)

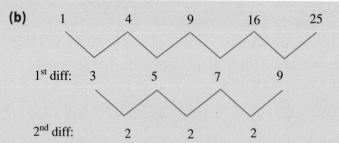

1   4   9   16   25

1st diff: 3   5   7   9

2nd diff: 2   2   2

Second difference constant $\Rightarrow$ quadratic pattern

$T_n = an^2 + bn + c$

$2a$ = constant difference = 2 $\Rightarrow a = 1$

$T_1 = (1)^2 + b(1) + c = 1 \Rightarrow b + c = 0$ Substitute values for T_1 and T_2.

$T_2 = (2)^2 + b(2) + c = 4 \Rightarrow 2b + c = 0$

The only way that both equations can be true is if $b = 0$ and $c = 0$.

Therefore, $T_n = n^2$.

> ## Top Tip
>
> You could reach the same result much quicker by noticing that the terms in the sequence are the square numbers.

(c)

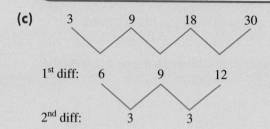

3   9   18   30

1st diff: 6   9   12

2nd diff: 3   3

Second difference constant $\Rightarrow$ quadratic pattern

$T_n = an^2 + bn + c$

$2a$ = constant difference = 3 $\Rightarrow a = \dfrac{3}{2}$

$T_1 = \dfrac{3}{2}(1)^2 + b(1) + c = 3 \Rightarrow b + c = \dfrac{3}{2}$ Substitute values for T_1 and T_2.

$T_2 = \dfrac{3}{2}(2)^2 + b(2) + c = 9 \Rightarrow 2b + c = 3$

Our simultaneous equations are

(A) $b + c = \dfrac{3}{2}$

(B) $2b + c = 3$

We have two equations in two unknowns, so we can now solve for b and c.

$(B - A)$ $b = \dfrac{3}{2}$ Subtract (A) from (B).

$b + c = \dfrac{3}{2} \Rightarrow \dfrac{3}{2} + c = \dfrac{3}{2}$ Substitute $b = \dfrac{3}{2}$ into (A).

$\Rightarrow c = 0$

So $T_n = \dfrac{3}{2}n^2 + \dfrac{3}{2}n$.

Now work out T_n and T_{n-1} and subtract.

$T_n = \dfrac{3}{2}n^2 + \dfrac{3}{2}n$

$T_{n-1} = \dfrac{3}{2}(n-1)^2 + \dfrac{3}{2}(n-1) = \dfrac{3}{2}(n^2 - 2n + 1) + \dfrac{3}{2}(n - 1)$

$T_n - T_{n-1} = \dfrac{3}{2}n^2 + \dfrac{3}{2}n - \dfrac{3}{2}(n^2 - 2n + 1) - \dfrac{3}{2}(n - 1)$

$\qquad = \dfrac{3}{2}n^2 + \dfrac{3}{2}n - \dfrac{3}{2}n^2 + 3n - \dfrac{3}{2} - \dfrac{3}{2}n + \dfrac{3}{2}$ Multiply out the brackets and simplify.

$\qquad = 3n$

$3n$ matchsticks are needed to turn the $(n-1)^{\text{th}}$ pattern into the nth pattern.

(d) Method one

$u_n = an^2 + bn$

$u_1 = a(1)^2 + b(1) = 3$ Substitute in values from first and second terms.

$u_2 = a(2)^2 + b(2) = 9$

Our simultaneous equations are

(A) $a + b = 3$

(B) $4a + 2b = 9$

Multiply (A) by 2, and subtract from (B).

$(2A)$ $2a + 2b = 6$

$(B - 2A)$ $2a = 3 \Rightarrow a = \dfrac{3}{2}$

$a + b = 3 \Rightarrow \dfrac{3}{2} + b = 3 \Rightarrow b = \dfrac{3}{2}$

Method two

$3, 9, 18, 30 = 3, 3 + 6, 3 + 6 + 9, 3 + 6 + 9 + 12$

These are the partial sums, $S_1, S_2, S_3, S_4 \ldots$ of the series $3 + 6 + 9 + 12 + \ldots$

$S_n = \dfrac{n}{2}[2a + (n-1)d]$ where $a = d = 3$

$\Rightarrow S_n = \dfrac{n}{2}[6 + (n-1)3]$

$\Rightarrow S_n = \dfrac{3n}{2}(n+1)$

Equating $an^2 + bn$ and $\dfrac{3n}{2}(n+1)$ gives $a = b = \dfrac{3}{2}$.

(e) $u_n = \frac{3}{2}n^2 + \frac{3}{2}n = 4134$

$\Rightarrow n^2 + n - 2756 = 0$

$\Rightarrow (n+53)(n-52) = 0$

$\Rightarrow n = -53$ or $n = 52$

We know that n must be positive, so the 52nd pattern uses 4134 matchsticks, and that pattern has $n^2 = 52^2 = 2704$ triangles.

> **Top Tip**
>
> If you can't quickly see how to factorise an equation like $n^2 + n - 2756 = 0$, use the quadratic formula instead.

Cubic patterns

A **cubic pattern** is non-linear. The first differences are not constant, and neither are the second differences. **The difference between the second differences, known as the third difference, is constant**.

The general term of a cubic sequence with **third difference 6 a** is $T_n = an^3 + bn^2 + cn + d$.

Examples

The first five terms of a sequence are 5, 16, 41, 86, 157.

(a) Draw a graph to illustrate this sequence.

(b) Determine, using a table or other method, whether the sequence is quadratic or cubic. Give a reason for your answer.

(c) Find the nth term for the sequence.

(d) Another sequence has the first five terms 16, 41, 86, 157, 260. Plot this sequence on the same graph as part (a). Find the nth term for this sequence.

Solutions

(a)

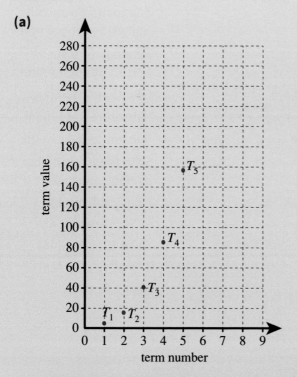

(b)

Sequence	First difference	Second difference	Third difference
5			
16	11		
41	25	14	
86	45	20	6
157	71	26	6

The sequence is a cubic sequence as the third difference is constant.

(c) $T_n = an^3 + bn^2 + cn + d$

Third difference $= 6a = 6 \implies a = 1$

$T_1 = (1)^3 + b(1)^2 + c(1) + d = 5$

(A) $b + c + d = 4$

$T_2 = (2)^3 + b(2)^2 + c(2) + d = 16$

(B) $4b + 2c + d = 8$

$T_3 = (3)^3 + b(3)^2 + c(3) + d = 41$

(C) $9b + 3c + d = 14$

We have three simultaneous equations with three unknowns.

$3b + c = 4$ Eliminate d from (A) and (B) by subtraction.

$5b + c = 6$ Eliminate d from (B) and (C) by subtraction.

$2b = 2 \Rightarrow b = 1$ Solve by eliminating c.

$b + c + d = 4 \Rightarrow (1) + c + d = 4 \Rightarrow c + d = 3$ Substitute $b = 1$ in (A).

$4b + 2c + d = 8 \Rightarrow 4(1) + 2c + d = 8 \Rightarrow 2c + d = 4$ Substitute $b = 1$ in (B).

$c = 1$ Solve these equations by eliminating d.

$b + c + d = 4 \Rightarrow (1) + (1) + d = 4 \Rightarrow d = 2$ Finally substitute $b = c = 1$ in (A).

$T_n = an^3 + bn^2 + cn + d \Rightarrow T_n = n^3 + n^2 + n + 2$ Substitute in values $a = 1, b = 1, c = 1, d = 2$.

(d)

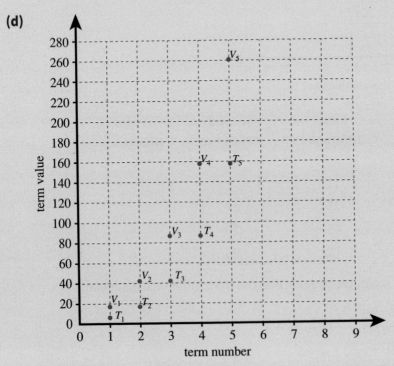

Compare the sequences in a table, and see the comparison on the graph.

Term number	First sequence term value	Second sequence term value
1	5	16
2	16	41
3	41	86
4	86	157
5	157	260
n	$n^3 + n^2 + n + 2$	

We can see from the table that the second term value of the first sequence is the same as the first term value of the second sequence.

T_2 (first sequence) $= T_1$ (second sequence)

$\Rightarrow T_{n+1}$ (first sequence) $= T_n$ (second sequence)

T_n (second sequence) $= (n+1)^3 + (n+1)^2 + (n+1) + 2$

We can see from the graph that point T_2 is translated one unit to the left to V_1, and the same translation applies to the points T_3, T_4 and T_5.

If $f(x)$ was modelled on the first cubic sequence then a translation one unit to the left would give another cubic function $f(x+1)$.

Exponential sequences

An **exponential sequence** is a sequence where the ratio of consecutive terms is a constant. These sequences can be decreasing or increasing, depending on the value of the ratio.

All exponential sequences are **geometric**.

Point to note

An exponential sequence is **discrete** while an exponential function is **continuous**.

Discrete means that the sequence has values only at distinct points (1st term, 2nd term, etc.).

Continuous means that the function has values for all possible values of x.

Examples

Find the common ratio (r) for each of the following sequences and find the next two terms.

(a) $2, 4, 8, 16$

(b) $2, 1, \frac{1}{2}, \frac{1}{4}$

(c) $100, 10, 1, \frac{1}{10}$

(d) Complete the table for the sequence in part (a).

Point to note

In an exponential sequence we denote the first term by a and the common ratio by r.

Term	Term value	First term: $a = 2$ Common ratio: $r = 2$	Pattern in terms of a and r
T_1	2	2×2^0	$a \times r^0 = a$
T_2	4		
T_3	8		
T_4	16		

Solutions

(a) Divide the second term by the first term to find the common ratio: $r = \frac{4}{2} = 2$.
   The next two terms are 32 and 64. (The values increase since $r > 1$.)

(b) $r = \frac{1}{2}$; the next two terms are $\frac{1}{8}$ and $\frac{1}{16}$. (The values decrease since $r < 1$.)

(c) $r = \frac{10}{100} = \frac{1}{10}$; the next two terms are $\frac{1}{100}, \frac{1}{1000}$.

(d)

Term	Term value	First term: $a = 2$ Common ratio: $r = 2$	Pattern in terms of a and r
T_1	2	2×2^0	$a \times r^0 = a$
T_2	4	2×2^1	$a \times r^1 = ar$
T_3	8	2×2^2	$a \times r^2 = ar^2$
T_4	16	2×2^3	$a \times r^3 = ar^3$

We can see from this table that the general term for this sequence is
$T_n = 2(2)^{n-1} = 2^n$.

Point to note

The general term for any geometric sequence is $T_n = ar^{n-1}$, where a = first term and r = common ratio.

A ball is dropped from an initial height h_0.

Each time it rebounds, its new height is 40% of its previous height.

(a) What are the first four rebound heights after being dropped from a height of $h_0 = 15$ m?

(b) If the initial height is A metres, what are the first four rebound heights in terms of A? Use your answers to fill in the following table.

Rebound number	Height (in terms of A)
1	
2	
3	
4	

(c) Find the nth rebound height. What type of sequence is the sequence of rebound heights?

(d) Graph the first four rebound heights of the bouncing ball when $A = 20$ m.

(e) Hence, find the equation of an exponential function which models the rebound heights when $n \geq 0$. How high does the ball bounce on the 6th bounce to the nearest cm?

Solutions

(a) $h_1 = 15 \times 0\cdot4 = 6$ m

$h_2 = 6 \times 0\cdot4 = 2\cdot4$ m

$h_3 = 2\cdot4 \times 0\cdot4 = 0\cdot96$ m

$h_4 = 0\cdot96 \times 0\cdot4 = 0\cdot384$ m

(b)

Rebound number	Height (in terms of A)
1	$0\cdot4^1 A$
2	$0\cdot4^2 A$
3	$0\cdot4^3 A$
4	$0\cdot4^4 A$

(c) $T_n = A(0\cdot4)^n$

This is a decreasing exponential (or geometric) sequence.

(d)

Rebound	Height (metres)
1	$0.4(20) = 8$
2	$0.4^2(20) = 3.2$
3	$0.4^3(20) = 1.28$
4	$0.4^4(20) = 0.512$

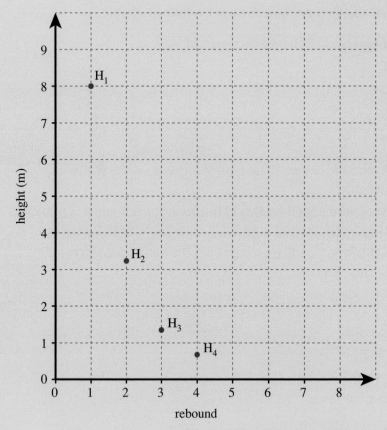

(e) $f(n) = 20(0.4)^n \implies f(6) = 20(0.4)^6 = 0.08192$ m $= 8$ cm to the nearest cm.

Checklist

✓ Know about the constant difference for linear, quadratic and cubic sequences.

✓ Practise using tables, diagrams and formulae for these sequences.

✓ Know how to recognise exponential sequences/geometric sequences.

Arithmetic and Geometric Sequences and Series

8

Learning objectives

In this chapter you will learn how to:

- Recognise whether a sequence is arithmetic, geometric or neither
- Find the sum to n terms of an arithmetic series
- Investigate geometric sequences and series
- Find by inspection the limits of sequences such as $\lim\limits_{n \to \infty} \dfrac{n}{n+1}$ and $\lim\limits_{n \to \infty} r^n,\ |r| < 1$
- Derive the formula for the sum to infinity of geometric series by considering the limit of a sequence of partial sums
- Solve problems involving finite and infinite geometric series including applications such as recurring decimals and financial problems.

Notation for sequences

A **number sequence** is a sequence of numbers connected by a rule. The notation used to describe the terms of a sequence is shown in the table below.

First term	U_1	T_1
Second term	U_2	T_2
Third term	U_3	T_3
$\vdots$	$\vdots$	$\vdots$
$(n-1)^{\text{th}}$ term	U_{n-1}	T_{n-1}
n^{th} term	U_n	T_n

Point to note

If we know the nth term, or **general term**, of a sequence then we can find any term in that sequence.

Examples

Write down the first five terms of the following sequences, given the nth term (T_n) in each case. Is each sequence increasing or decreasing?

(a) $T_n = 6n - 4$

(b) $T_n = (n - 1)^2$

(c) $T_n = n^3 - 2$

(d) $T_n = \dfrac{n}{n + 1}$

(e) $T_n = 2^n$

(f) $T_n = \left(\dfrac{1}{2}\right)^n$

(g) $T_n = (-3)^n$

Solutions

	T_n	T_1	T_2	T_3	T_4	T_5	Increasing/decreasing
(a)	$6n - 4$	1	8	14	20	26	Increasing
(b)	$(n - 1)^2$	0	1	4	9	16	Increasing
(c)	$n^3 - 2$	-1	6	25	62	123	Increasing
(d)	$\dfrac{n}{n + 1}$	$\dfrac{1}{2}$	$\dfrac{2}{3}$	$\dfrac{3}{4}$	$\dfrac{4}{5}$	$\dfrac{5}{6}$	Increasing very slowly to a limit
(e)	2^n	2	4	8	16	32	Increasing
(f)	$\left(\dfrac{1}{2}\right)^n$	$\dfrac{1}{2}$	$\dfrac{1}{4}$	$\dfrac{1}{8}$	$\dfrac{1}{16}$	$\dfrac{1}{32}$	Decreasing to a limit
(g)	$(-3)^n$	-3	9	-27	81	-243	Oscillating between positive and negative values

Arithmetic sequences

A sequence where the difference between consecutive terms is constant is called an **arithmetic sequence**. The difference between terms is called the **common difference**.

Consider the sequence: 2, 8, 14, 20, 26, ... The first term is 2, and the common difference is 6.

We can see a pattern connecting the first term, the common difference and the term number.

T_1	2	$2 + 0(6)$
T_2	8	$2 + 1(6)$
T_3	14	$2 + 2(6)$
T_4	20	$2 + 3(6)$
T_5	26	$2 + 4(6)$
T_n		$a + (n - 1)d$

Point to note

We use the following notation when talking about arithmetic sequences:

- a = first term
- n = term number ($n \in \mathbb{N}$)
- d = common difference.

The formula for the nth term of an arithmetic sequence is on page 22 of the *Formulae and Tables* booklet:

n^{th} term or $T_n = a + (n - 1)d$

An arithmetic sequence is sometimes called an **arithmetic progression (AP)**.

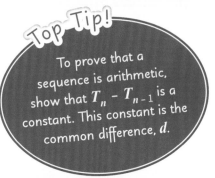

Top Tip!

To prove that a sequence is arithmetic, show that $T_n - T_{n-1}$ is a constant. This constant is the common difference, d.

Point to note

If $T_n > T_{n-1} \Rightarrow T_n - T_{n-1} > 0$, then the sequence is **increasing**.

If $T_n < T_{n-1} \Rightarrow T_n - T_{n-1} < 0$, then the sequence is **decreasing**.

Examples

The nth term of a sequence is given by $T_n = 6n + 4$.

(a) Verify that the sequence is arithmetic.

(b) Investigate whether the sequence is increasing or decreasing.

Solutions

(a) $T_{n-1} = 6(n - 1) + 4 = 6n - 6 + 4 = 6n - 2$

$T_n - T_{n-1} = 6n + 4 - (6n - 2) = 6n + 4 - 6n + 2 = 6$ (a constant)

Therefore the sequence is arithmetic.

(b) $T_n - T_{n-1} = 6 > 0$

Therefore the sequence is increasing.

If we are given a problem involving three consecutive terms in an AP, we can label the middle term as m and the other terms as $m - d$ and $m + d$.

Example

Three numbers are in an arithmetic sequence. The sum of the consecutive terms is 30 and the product of the terms is 977·5. Find the three numbers.

Solution

Let the three consecutive terms be $m - d$, m, $m + d$.

Sum of three terms = $m - d + m + m + d = 30$

$\Rightarrow 3m = 30 \Rightarrow m = 10$

Product of three terms = $(m - d)(m)(m + d) = 977\cdot5$

$(10 - d)(10)(10 + d) = 977\cdot5$ Substitute in $m = 10$.

$100 - d^2 = \dfrac{977\cdot5}{10} = 97\cdot75$

$100 - 97\cdot75 = d^2$

$2\cdot25 = d^2$

$d = \pm\sqrt{2\cdot25} = \pm1\cdot5$

The three numbers are 8·5, 10 and 11·5.

Limit of a sequence

Consider the following two sequences.

Sequence A: 2, 4, 6, 8 ,10, 12, …

Sequence B: $\dfrac{1}{2}, \dfrac{2}{3}, \dfrac{3}{4}, \dfrac{4}{5}, \dfrac{5}{6}, \ldots$

From the graph of the two sequences we can clearly see that sequence A is increasing and will continue to increase. Sequence A is divergent.

Sequence B is increasing very slowly and is approaching a limit. From the graph we can see that the sequence is approaching 1. Sequence B is convergent, as the nth term of the sequence converges to a certain number.

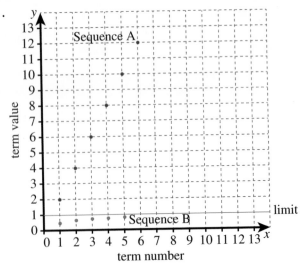

Arithmetic series

An **arithmetic series** is the sum of the terms of an arithmetic sequence. The sum of the first n terms is denoted S_n.

Point to note

$S_n = \dfrac{n}{2}(2a + (n - 1)d)$, where a is the first term and d is the common difference. This formula is on page 22 of the *Formulae and Tables booklet*

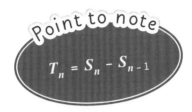

Point to note

$$T_n = S_n - S_{n-1}$$

Example

Find the sum of the arithmetic series $4 + 7 + 10 + \ldots + 151$.

Solution

First, find the number of terms.

$a = 4$, $d = 3$

$T_n = a + (n - 1)d = 4 + (n - 1)3 = 4 + 3n - 3$

$T_n = 3n + 1 = 151$

$3n = 150$

$n = 50$

Next, find the sum of the series.

$S_n = \dfrac{n}{2}[2a + (n - 1)d]$, $a = 4$, $d = 3$, $n = 50$

$S_{50} = \dfrac{50}{2}[2(4) + (50 - 1)(3)]$

$\phantom{S_{50}} = 25[8 + 49(3)]$

$\phantom{S_{50}} = 25(155)$

$\phantom{S_{50}} = 3875$

Examples

The nth term of a sequence is $T_n = \ln a^n$, where $a > 0$ and a is a constant.

(a) (i) Show that T_1, T_2 and T_3 are in arithmetic sequence.

(ii) Prove that the sequence is arithmetic and find the common difference.

(b) Find the value of a for which $T_1 + T_2 + T_3 + \ldots + T_{98} + T_{99} + T_{100} = 10\,100$.

(c) Verify that, for all values of a,

$$(T_1 + T_2 + T_3 + \ldots + T_{10}) + 100\,d = (T_{11} + T_{12} + T_{13} + \ldots + T_{20}),$$ where d is the common difference of the sequence.

(SEC 2014)

Solutions

(a) (i) $T_1 = \ln a$, $T_2 = \ln a^2 = 2\ln a$, $T_3 = \ln a^3 = 3\ln a$ Evaluate the first three terms.

$T_2 - T_1 = 2\ln a - \ln a = \ln a$ Find the difference between the first term and the second term.

$T_3 - T_2 = 3\ln a - 2\ln a = \ln a$ Find the difference between the second term and the third term.

$T_3 - T_2 = T_2 - T_1$. Hence the terms are in arithmetic sequence.

(ii) $T_n = \ln a^n = n\ln a$

$T_{n-1} = \ln a^{n-1} = (n-1)\ln a$

$T_n - T_{n-1} = n\ln a - (n-1)\ln a = \ln a$

$\ln a$ is a constant, so the sequence is arithmetic and the common difference is $\ln a$.

(b) $T_1 + T_2 + T_3 + \ldots + T_{98} + T_{99} + T_{100} = 10\,100$

$\Rightarrow \ln a + 2\ln a + 3\ln a + \ldots + 100\ln a = 10\,100$

$\Rightarrow \dfrac{100}{2}[2\ln a + (100 - 1)\ln a] = 10\,100$

$\Rightarrow 50[101\ln a] = 10\,100$

$\Rightarrow 5050\ln a = 10\,100$

$\Rightarrow \ln a = 2$

$\Rightarrow a = e^2 = 7{\cdot}389$

(c) **Method one**

$(T_1 + T_2 + T_3 + \ldots + T_{10}) + 100\,d$

$= (T_1 + 10d) + (T_2 + 10d) + (T_3 + 10d) + \ldots + (T_{10} + 10d)$

$= T_{11} + T_{12} + T_{13} + \ldots + T_{20}$

Method two

$(T_1 + T_2 + T_3 + ... + T_{10}) + 100d = (\ln a + 2 \ln a + 3 \ln a + ... + 10 \ln a) + 100 \ln a$

$$= \frac{10}{2}(2 \ln a + (10 - 1) \ln a) + 100 \ln a$$

$$= 5(11 \ln a) + 100 \ln a$$

$$= 155 \ln a$$

$(T_{11} + T_{12} + T_{13} + ... + T_{20}) = 11 \ln a + 12 \ln a + 13 \ln a + ... + 20 \ln a$

$$= \frac{10}{2}(22 \ln a + (10 - 1) \ln a)$$

$$= 5(31 \ln a)$$

$$= 155 \ln a$$

Hence, left-hand side = right-hand side.

Example

A small theatre begins to fill up in a certain pattern. After the first minute 4 people arrive, after the second minute 6 people arrive and after the third minute 8 people arrive.

The theatre is half full after 6 minutes. After how many minutes is the theatre full?

Solution

The arithmetic series is $4 + 6 + 8 + ...$

$a = 4$, $d = 2$

After 6 minutes, the total number in the theatre

is $S_6 = \frac{6}{2}[2(4) + (6 - 1)(2)] = 3(8 + 10) = 54$.

The theatre is half full after 6 minutes so the capacity of the theatre is $2 \times 54 = 108$.

Now we need to solve for the number of minutes (n).

$108 = \frac{n}{2}[2a + (n - 1)d]$

$\Rightarrow 108 = \frac{n}{2}[2(4) + (n - 1)(2)]$

$\Rightarrow 108 = \frac{n}{2}[8 + 2n - 2]$

$\Rightarrow 108 = \frac{n}{2}[6 + 2n]$

$\Rightarrow 216 = 6n + 2n^2$

$\Rightarrow 2n^2 + 6n - 216 = 0$

$\Rightarrow n^2 + 3n - 108 = 0$

$\Rightarrow (n + 12)(n - 9) = 0$ Factorise and solve.

$n = -12, n = 9$

We know that n must be positive, so the answer is that the theatre is full after 9 minutes.

Geometric sequences

A **geometric sequence** or **geometric progression** is a sequence of the form

$a, ar, ar^2, ar^3, ar^4, ..., ar^{n-1}$.

The nth term of the sequence is $T_n = ar^{n-1}$ (*Formulae and Tables* booklet page 22) where a is the first term and r is the common ratio.

> **Point to note**
>
> $r = $ common ratio $= \dfrac{\text{term}}{\text{previous term}}$

> **Point to note**
>
> To prove a sequence is geometric, show that $\dfrac{T_n}{T_{n-1}} = $ a constant (this is the common ratio).

A **geometric series** is the sum of the first n terms of a geometric sequence.

It is given by $S_n = \dfrac{a(1 - r^n)}{1 - r}$ (*Formulae and Tables* booklet page 22). The proof for this formula is covered in Chapter 16.

> **Top Tip**
>
> If $r > 1$ it is easier to use the formula $S_n = \dfrac{a(r^n - 1)}{r - 1}$.

> **Remember**
>
> $T_n = S_n - S_{n-1}$

Examples

The second term of a geometric progression is 4 and the fifth term is $8\sqrt{2}$.

Find:

(a) The common ratio

(b) The 10th term

(c) The sum of the first 9 terms in the form $a + b\sqrt{c}$, where $a, b, c \in \mathbb{N}$.

Solutions

(a) $T_2 = ar$, $T_5 = ar^4$

$$\frac{ar^4}{ar} = \frac{8\sqrt{2}}{4}$$

$$r^3 = 2\sqrt{2} = 2^{\frac{3}{2}}$$

$$r = \sqrt[3]{2^{\frac{3}{2}}} = \sqrt{2}$$

The common ratio is $\sqrt{2}$.

Form the two given terms into an equation and solve for r.

(b) $ar = 4$

$$a(\sqrt{2}) = 4 \implies a = \frac{4}{\sqrt{2}} = 2\sqrt{2}$$

$$T_{10} = ar^9 = 2\sqrt{2}\left(\sqrt{2}\right)^9 = 2^6 = 64$$

Use the common ratio and the formula for the second term to find the first term.

Substitute a and r into the formula for the 10th term.

(c) We want to find S_9, and $r > 1$. Use the formula $S_n = \dfrac{a(r^n - 1)}{r - 1}$, with $a = 2\sqrt{2}$, $r = \sqrt{2}$, $n = 9$.

$$S_9 = \frac{\left(2\sqrt{2}\right)\left(\left(\sqrt{2}\right)^{(9)} - 1\right)}{\left(\sqrt{2}\right) - 1} = \frac{2\sqrt{2}\left(16\sqrt{2} - 1\right)}{\sqrt{2} - 1}$$

$$= \frac{64 - 2\sqrt{2}}{\sqrt{2} - 1} = 60 + 62\sqrt{2}$$

Examples

(a) Find the nth term of the sequence $3, 6, 12, 24, \ldots$

(b) Find the first term in the sequence to exceed 1000.

Solutions

(a) $T_n = ar^{n-1}$, $a = 3$, $r = 2$

$$T_n = ar^{n-1} = 3\left(2^{n-1}\right)$$

Substitute values for a and r into the formula for the nth term.

(b) We need to find n such that $3\left(2^{n-1}\right) > 1000$.

$$2^{n-1} > \frac{1000}{3}$$

Rearrange to put n on the left.

$$n - 1 > \log_2 \frac{1000}{3}$$

Use logs to find the value of n.

$$n - 1 > 8 \cdot 38$$

$$n > 9 \cdot 38$$

$$n = 10$$

The 10th term is the first one to exceed 1000.

Example

John placed €500 in an investment bond on 1st January each year for 5 consecutive years. He earned 2% interest per annum for this period of time.

Calculate the amount of savings he had at the end of the 5th year. Give your answer to the nearest euro.

Solution

This forms a geometric series, with $a = $ €500 × 1·02 = €510, $r = 1·02$, $n = 5$.

At the end of the 5th year, total amount of savings $= S_5 = \dfrac{510\,(1·02^5 - 1)}{1·02 - 1}$

$S_5 = $ €2654 to the nearest euro.

Examples

$x + 2$, x and $2x - 3$ are three consecutive terms in a geometric sequence, where $x \in \mathbb{R}$.

(a) Find two possible values of x.

(b) Hence, write down the next two terms of each sequence.

Solutions

(a) For a geometric progression, the ratio of consecutive terms is equal.

$$\frac{x}{x + 2} = \frac{2x - 3}{x}$$

$x^2 = (x + 2)(2x - 3)$

$x^2 = 2x^2 + x - 6$

$x^2 + x - 6 = 0$

$(x + 3)(x - 2) = 0$ Factorise and solve for x.

$x = -3$ or $x = 2$

(b) Using $x = -3$, $r = \dfrac{(-3)}{(-3) + 2} = 3$.

The first three terms are −1, −3, −9 and the next two terms are −27 and −81.

Using $x = 2$, $r = \dfrac{(2)}{(2) + 2} = \dfrac{1}{2}$.

The first three terms are 4, 2, 1. The next two terms are $\dfrac{1}{2}$ and $\dfrac{1}{4}$.

Sigma notation

Σ is the Greek symbol 'sigma'. In mathematics, it is used to mean 'the sum of'. We can express the sum of a series using sigma notation.

The initial value, or starting value, of the unknown is written underneath the sigma and the highest value of the unknown is written on top. The general term of the series is written after the sigma symbol.

The following table shows some examples of sigma notation.

Sigma notation	Meaning	Series
highest value $\displaystyle\sum$ general term $n =$ starting value		$S_n = T_1 + T_2 + \dots + T_n$ (finite series) $S_\infty = T_1 + T_2 + \dots$ (infinite series)
$\displaystyle\sum_{n=1}^{8} 2^n$	Sum of the first eight terms of 2^n	$2 + 4 + 8 + 16 + \dots + 256$ Finite geometric series; use formula to find sum.
$\displaystyle\sum_{r=1}^{n} \left(\frac{1}{2}\right)^{r-1}$	Sum of the first n terms of $\left(\frac{1}{2}\right)^{r-1}$	$1 + \frac{1}{2} + \frac{1}{4} + \dots + \left(\frac{1}{2}\right)^{n-1}$ Finite geometric series; use formula to find sum.
$\displaystyle\sum_{n=1}^{9} (4n - 1)$	Sum of the first nine terms of $4n - 1$	$3 + 7 + 11 + \dots + 35$ Finite arithmetic series; use formula to find sum.
$\displaystyle\sum_{n=1}^{\infty} (3x)^{n-1}$	Sum to infinity of $(3x)^{n-1}$	$1 + 3x + (3x)^2 + \dots$ Infinite geometric series; use formula to find sum to infinity. $a = 1, r = 3x$ $S_\infty = \dfrac{a}{1-r} = \dfrac{(1)}{1-(3x)}$ S_∞ will exist if $-1 < r < 1$ $\Rightarrow -1 < 3x < 1$ $\Rightarrow \dfrac{-1}{3} < x < \dfrac{1}{3}$

Infinite geometric series

Consider the sums of two infinite series and their graphs.

1 $S_n = 2 + 4 + 8 + 16 + 32 + \ldots$

The first five partial sums are

$S_1 = 2$

$S_2 = 2 + 4 = 6$

$S_3 = 2 + 4 + 8 = 14$

$S_4 = 2 + 4 + 8 + 16 = 30$

$S_5 = 2 + 4 + 8 + 16 + 32 = 62$

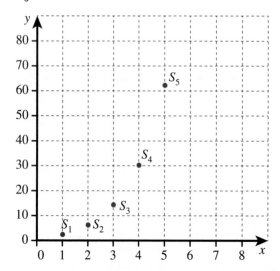

In this infinite series, the series is getting bigger. It is a **divergent series**; it has no sum to infinity.

2 $S_n = 1 + \dfrac{1}{2} + \dfrac{1}{4} + \dfrac{1}{8} + \ldots$

The first four partial sums are

$S_1 = 1$

$S_2 = 1 + \dfrac{1}{2} = \dfrac{3}{2} = 1{\cdot}5$

$S_3 = 1 + \dfrac{1}{2} + \dfrac{1}{4} = \dfrac{7}{4} = 1{\cdot}75$

$S_4 = 1 + \dfrac{1}{2} + \dfrac{1}{4} + \dfrac{1}{8} = \dfrac{15}{8} = 1{\cdot}875$

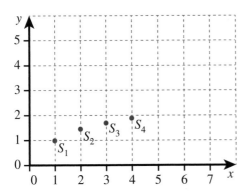

In this infinite series, the series is converging to a constant, 2.

What determines whether a series is convergent or divergent is the common ratio, r.

Point to note

A geometric series converges if the common ratio is between -1 and 1.

Point to note

Note that $\lim_{n \to \infty} r^n = 0$ when $-1 < r < 1$ (i.e. $|r| < 1$).

The sum to infinity of a geometric series is calculated using the formula $S_\infty = \dfrac{a}{1 - r}$, where $|r| < 1$. This is on page 22 of the *Formulae and Tables* booklet.

We can prove this formula using the limit of a sequence of partial sums.

$$\lim_{n \to \infty} S_n = \lim_{n \to \infty} \left(\frac{a(1 - r^n)}{1 - r} \right)$$

$$= \lim_{n \to \infty} \left(\frac{a}{1 - r} \right) - \lim_{n \to \infty} \left(\frac{ar^n}{1 - r} \right)$$

We know that $\lim_{n \to \infty} r^n = 0$, where $|r| < 1$.

Hence

$$\lim_{n \to \infty} S_n = \lim_{n \to \infty} \left(\frac{a(1 - r^n)}{1 - r} \right) = \frac{a}{1 - r}$$

Example

Find the sum to infinity of the geometric series $1 + \dfrac{3}{5} + \left(\dfrac{3}{5} \right)^2 + \left(\dfrac{3}{5} \right)^3 + \ldots$

Solution

$a = 1, r = \dfrac{3}{5}$

$S_\infty = \dfrac{a}{1 - r} = \dfrac{1}{1 - \dfrac{3}{5}} = \dfrac{1}{\dfrac{2}{5}} = \dfrac{5}{2}$

Example

By writing the recurring part as an infinite geometric series, express the following number as a fraction of integers:

$5 \cdot \dot{2}\dot{1} = 5 \cdot 2121212121...$

(SEC 2012)

Solution

$$5 \cdot \dot{2}\dot{1} = 5 + \frac{21}{100} + \frac{21}{10\,000} + \frac{21}{1\,000\,000} + ...$$

This is the same as $5 +$ a geometric series with $a = \frac{21}{100}$ and $r = \frac{1}{100}$.

$$5 \cdot \dot{2}\dot{1} = 5 + \frac{\frac{21}{100}}{1 - \frac{1}{100}}$$

$$= 5 + \frac{21}{100 - 1} = 5\frac{21}{99} = 5\frac{7}{33}$$

Checklist

✓ Practise using the formulae for arithmetic sequences and series.

✓ Know how to prove that a sequence is arithmetic.

✓ Practise using the formulae for geometric sequences and series, both finite and infinite.

✓ Know how to prove that a sequence is geometric.

✓ Know how to derive the formula for the sum to infinity of a geometric series using the limit of a sequence of partial sums.

✓ Practise questions on applications of geometric series. There are more examples in Chapter 9.

Financial Maths and Arithmetic

Learning objectives

In this chapter you will learn how to:

- Calculate percentage error and tolerance
- Solve problems that involve
  - Mark up and margin
  - Compound interest, depreciation (reducing balance method), income tax and net pay (including other deductions)
- Use finite geometric series in financial applications
- Use present value when solving problems involving loan repayments and investments
- Derive the formula for a mortgage repayment.

Relative and percentage error

The **error** in a measurement or estimate is the difference between the true value and the estimated value. It is always positive.

The **relative error** is the ratio of the error to the true value.

$$\text{Relative error} = \frac{\text{error}}{\text{true value}}$$

The **percentage error** expresses the relative error as a percentage.

$$\text{Percentage error} = \frac{\text{error}}{\text{true value}} \times 100$$

Tolerance interval

The error in a measurement may be represented by a tolerance interval.

Tolerance involves a small error. Machines used in making products have a tolerance interval, or range, in which product measurements will be accepted before they are considered flawed.

Examples

A rectangle has a tolerance interval of $15 \cdot 5 \pm 0 \cdot 5$ cm for the length and a tolerance of $20 \cdot 3 \pm 0 \cdot 5$ cm for the width.

(a) Find the maximum perimeter and minimum area of the rectangle.

(b) Find the percentage error for the length of the rectangle. Give your answer to 2 decimal places.

(c) Is a perimeter of 80 cm allowed for this rectangle?

Solutions

(a) Here we have an accumulation of error, since we have two measurements for perimeter.

Smallest possible value for length is $15 \cdot 5 - 0 \cdot 5 = 15$ cm.

Largest possible value for length is $15 \cdot 5 + 0 \cdot 5 = 16$ cm.

Smallest possible value for width is $20 \cdot 3 - 0 \cdot 5 = 19 \cdot 8$ cm.

Largest possible value for width is $20 \cdot 3 + 0 \cdot 5 = 20 \cdot 8$ cm.

Maximum perimeter of rectangle is

2 (maximum length + maximum width) = $2 (16 + 20 \cdot 08) = 2 (36 \cdot 8) = 73 \cdot 6$ cm.

Minimum area is minimum length × minimum width = $15 \times 19 \cdot 8 = 297$ cm^2.

(b) Percentage error for length $= \dfrac{\text{error}}{\text{true value}} \times 100 = \dfrac{0 \cdot 5}{15 \cdot 5} \times 100 = 3 \cdot 23\%$

(c) The largest possible perimeter of the rectangle is $73 \cdot 6$ cm (from part (a)). Therefore a rectangle with perimeter 80 cm is outside the tolerance interval allowed.

Percentage profit and loss

The **profit** on a product is calculated as selling price – cost price. If the profit is negative, it is called a **loss**.

The **percentage profit**, or **mark up**, is the profit as a percentage of the cost price.

$$\text{Percentage profit} = \dfrac{\text{profit}}{\text{cost price}} \times 100$$

Similarly, the **percentage loss** is the loss as a percentage of the cost price.

$$\text{Percentage loss} = \dfrac{\text{loss}}{\text{cost price}} \times 100$$

The **margin** is the profit as a percentage of the selling price.

$$\text{Margin} = \dfrac{\text{profit}}{\text{selling price}} \times 100$$

Income tax

Tax is charged by the government on all employment-related income. It is charged at two different rates: **standard rate**, which is the lower rate, and **higher rate**.

Each employee is given a **standard rate cut off point (SRCOP)**. All income up to and including the SRCOP is taxed at the standard rate. Any income above this amount is taxed at the higher rate.

Each employee is also given a **tax credit**, which is a reduction in the amount of tax they have to pay. The **gross tax** is the amount of tax calculated before the tax credit is deducted.

Gross income is the total amount of income earned before any deductions are taken away.

There are two other statutory deductions on income. These are **pay-related social insurance (PRSI)** and **universal social charge (USC)**.

Non-statutory (optional) deductions include pensions, trade union fees, health insurance and salary protection.

> **Point to note**
>
> Tax payable = gross tax − tax credit
>
> Net income = gross income − deductions

To calculate income tax where gross income ≤ SRCOP

1 Calculate gross tax: Gross income × standard rate = gross tax
2 Calculate tax payable: Gross tax − tax credit = tax payable

To calculate income tax where gross income > SRCOP

1 Calculate gross tax:
  SRCOP × standard rate + (gross income − SRCOP) × higher rate = gross tax
2 Calculate tax payable: Gross tax − tax credit = tax payable

> **Point to note**
>
> Gross income − SRCOP is called the **balance of income**.

Examples

Alan pays income tax, a universal social charge (USC) and pay-related social insurance (PRSI) on his gross wages. His gross weekly wages are €510.

(a) Alan pays income tax at the rate of 20%. He has weekly tax credits of €63. How much income tax does he pay?

(b) Alan pays the USC at the rate of 2% on the first €193, 4% on the next €115 and 7% on the balance. Calculate the amount of USC Alan pays.

(c) Alan also pays PRSI. His total weekly deductions amount to €76·92. How much PRSI does Alan pay?

(SEC OL 2012)

Solutions

(a) Total tax: $510 \times 0·2 = €102$

Multiply gross weekly wage by 20% = 0·2 to find the total tax.

Tax paid: $102 - 63 = €39$

Subtract the tax credits from the total tax to find the tax paid.

(b) $193 \times 0·02 = €3·86$

2% on the first €193.

$115 \times 0·04 = €4·60$

4% on the next €115.

$510 - (193 + 115) = €202$

Calculate the balance.

$202 \times 0·07 = €14·14$

7% on the balance.

USC: $3·86 + 4·60 + 14·14 = €22·60$

(c) PRSI: $76·92 - (39 + 22·60) = €15·32$

Subtract the tax and USC from the total deductions to find the PRSI.

Present value and future value

Which would you prefer to receive as a gift: €100 today or €100 in one year's time?

If I invest €100 today it might be worth more than €100 in one year's time, because it has the potential to earn interest. If I receive €100 in one year's time it will not have the same value as €100 now.

We can say that the **future value** of €100 received now is **more** than €100.

The **present value** of €100 received next year is **less** than €100.

The formulae for future value and present value are on page 30 of the *Formulae and Tables* booklet.

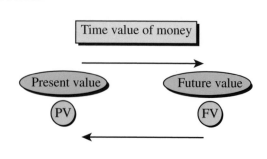

Time value of money

Present value · PV

Future value · FV

Remember

Future value: $F = P(1 + i)^t$

Present value: $P = \dfrac{F}{(1 + i)^t}$

F = future or final value

P = principal

i = rate of interest (expressed as a decimal)

t = time in years

Examples

(a) A person invests €100 at an interest rate of 5% per annum. What is the future value of this investment in 5 years' time?

(b) What is the present value of €127·63 received 5 years from now?

Solutions

(a) Use $F = P(1 + i)^t$, where P = €100, i = 5% = 0·05, t = 5.

$F = (100)(1 + (0·05))^{(5)}$ Substitute the values for P, i and t into the formula.

$F = 100(1·05)^5$

F = €127·63

(b) Use $P = \dfrac{F}{(1 + i)^t}$, where F = €127·63, i = 5% = 0·05, t = 5.

$P = \dfrac{(127·63)}{(1 + (0·05))^{(5)}} = \dfrac{127·63}{1·05^5} = €100$

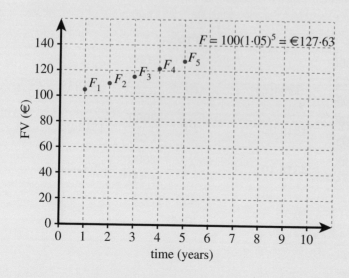

Top-Tip

When working with savings, use the future value formula.

When working with loans, use the present value formula.

The **net present value (NPV)** is the present value of all cash inflows minus the present value of all cash outflows.

Point to note

NPV = present value of all cash inflows − present value of cash outflows.

We use the NPV to decide if a project or proposal is a good investment (in other words, if it is likely to be profitable).

If NPV > 0, the investment will yield a profit so we should invest in the project.
If NPV ≤ 0, the investment will yield a loss so we should not invest in the project.

Example

Catherine is presented with a short-term investment project as shown in the table below. All figures are in euros.

Year	0	1	2	3
Project X: Cash flow	−5000	−2000	2000	5000
Project Y: Cash flow	−3000	−1000	2000	3000

Using present values, advise Catherine on which project is profitable, given that the discount rate is 5%.

Solution

Year	Project X	Project Y
0	$PV = -5000$	$PV = -3000$
1	$PV = \dfrac{-2000}{(1 \cdot 05)^1} = -1904 \cdot 76$	$PV = \dfrac{-1000}{(1 \cdot 05)^1} = -952 \cdot 38$
2	$PV = \dfrac{2000}{(1 \cdot 05)^2} = 1814 \cdot 06$	$PV = \dfrac{2000}{(1 \cdot 05)^2} = 1814 \cdot 06$
3	$PV = \dfrac{5000}{(1 \cdot 05)^3} = 4319 \cdot 19$	$PV = \dfrac{3000}{(1 \cdot 05)^3} = 2591 \cdot 51$
NPV	−771·51	453·19
Advice	Reject	Invest

Compound interest

We can use the formula $F = P(1 + i)^t$ to calculate the final value F after t years of a sum of money P (the principal) which grows at an annual interest rate of i.

Point to note

The annual equivalent rate (AER) is used for savings and investments.

The equivalent annual rate (EAR) and the compound annual rate (CAR) are the same as the AER.

The annual percentage rate (APR) is used for loans and mortgages.

Examples

(a) Find the future value of €4000 at 3% (AER) per annum, compounded annually for 4 years. Find the interest earned over the period.

(b) An investment offers a return of 12% if invested for 5 years. Calculate the AER for the investment correct to 1 decimal place.

(c) How much would Jonathan need to invest now at a rate of 2·5% per annum to have €5000 two years from now?

(d) Find the number of years it will take an investment of €6000 to grow to €15 000 if the AER is 4·5% compounded annually. Give your answer to 2 decimal places.

Solutions

Top Tip

All these questions require the same formula, $F = P(1 + i)^t$.
You need to find a different unknown in each case.

(a) Use the formula $F = P(1 + i)^t$, where $P = $ €4000, $i = 3\% = 0.03$, $t = 4$.

$F = (4000)(1 + (0.03))^{(4)} = 4000(1.03)^4$

$F = $ €4502·04

Interest $= F - P = $ €4502·04 $-$ €4000 $= $ €502·04   Subtract the final value from the principal to find the interest earned.

(b) The investment will give a return of 12% after 5 years. $12\% = 0.12$.

If $P = $ principal then after 5 years $F = 1.12P$.

$F = P(1 + i)^t \Rightarrow 1.12P = P(1 + i)^5$

$\Rightarrow 1.12 = (1 + i)^5$ Divide both sides by P.

$\Rightarrow 1 + i = \sqrt[5]{1.12}$

$\Rightarrow 1 + i = 1.02292$

$\Rightarrow i = 0.02292 = 2.3\%$

The AER is 2·3%, correct to 1 decimal place.

(c) Use $F = P(1 + i)^t$, with $F = €5000$, $i = 2.5\% = 0.025$, $t = 2$. We want to find P.

$(5000) = P(1 + (0.025))^{(2)}$

$\dfrac{5000}{(1.025)^2} = P$

$P = €4759.07$

Jonathan would need to invest €4759.07 now.

(d) Use $F = P(1 + i)^t$, with $F = €15\,000$, $P = €6000$, $i = 4.5\% = 0.045$. We want to find t.

$(15\,000) = (6000)(1 + (0.045))^t$

$\dfrac{15\,000}{6000} = 1.045^t$

$2.5 = 1.045^t$

$\ln(2.5) = \ln(1.045)^t$ Use logs to solve for t.

$t\ln(1.045) = \ln(2.5)$

$t = \dfrac{\ln(2.5)}{\ln(1.045)} = 20.82$ years

It will take 20.82 years for the investment to grow to €15 000.

Depreciation

An asset (such as a car, computer or machine) that a company buys will lose value over a period of time. This is due to wear and tear over time, assets becoming obsolete due to advances in technology, and so on. This is called **depreciation**.

The value of the asset at the end of a period is called the **net book value (NBV)**, or sometimes called the **later value**. Companies can deduct the cost of these assets as business expenses.

We use the **reducing balance method** to calculate the value of an asset after t years.

The formula for depreciation is on page 30 of the *Formulae and Tables* booklet.

$F = P(1 - i)^t$ where F = future value, P = initial value, t = time in years and i = depreciation rate.

> **Point to note**
>
> The depreciation formula looks very similar to the compound interest formula. Notice the key difference: the depreciation rate is subtracted from 1, instead of added, because it represents a decrease in value.

Examples

A new car is purchased by a company for €20 000. The car depreciates in value by 15% in the first 2 years and by 10% each year after that on a reducing balance method.

Find the NBV of the car after **(a)** 2 years **(b)** 5 years.

Solutions

(a) P = initial value = €20 000, i = 15% = 0·15, t = 2. We want to find F.

$$F = P(1 - i)^t$$
$$= (20\,000)(1 - (0·15))^{(2)}$$
$$= 20\,000\,(0·85)^2$$
$$F = €14\,450$$

(b) At the start of the third year, P = €14 450, i = 10% = 0·1, t = 3. We want to find F.

$$F = P(1 - i)^t$$
$$= (14\,450)(1 - (0·1))^{(3)}$$
$$= 14\,450\,(0·9)^3$$
$$F = €10\,534·05$$

Examples

A machine was bought for €25 000 and depreciates to a scrap value of €600 in 12 years.

Calculate:

(a) The annual rate of depreciation

(b) The value of the machine at the end of the fourth year.

Solutions

(a) Use $F = P(1 - i)^t$, where F = €600, P = €25 000, t = 12. We want to find i.

$$(600) = (25\,000)(1 - i)^{(12)}$$
$$\frac{600}{25\,000} = (1 - i)^{12}$$
$$0·024 = (1 - i)^{12}$$
$$1 - i = (0·024)^{\frac{1}{12}} = 0·7329$$
$$i = 1 - 0·7329 = 0·2671 = 26·71\%$$

(b) Use $F = P(1 - i)^t$, where P = €25 000, i = 0·2671, t = 4. We want to find F.

$$F = (25\,000)(1 - (0·2671))^{(4)}$$
$$F = 25\,000(0·7329)^4 = €7213·05$$

Interest periods and rates

Interest periods can be varied, such as per annum (annually), per year (yearly), six months, three months (quarterly), monthly. For example, 5% per annum, 1·2% quarterly, 0·3% monthly.

Interest can also be compounded over varied periods. This is called the **compounding period**. For example, 3% per annum, compounded monthly. Here, the interest period is one year and the compounding period is one month.

Other examples are 5·6% per annum, compounded annually, or 3·4% per annum. In these examples the interest period is one year and the compounding period is also one year.

Is a monthly rate of 1·5% interest equivalent to an annual rate of $(1·5 \times 12) = 18\%$?

We will see later that this is not the case. It is approximately equal, but not equivalent.

Converting between annual and monthly interest rates

The following table shows some examples of conversions from annual to monthly interest rates.

Annual rate	$1 + i$	Equivalent monthly rate
i		$(1 + i)^{\frac{1}{12}} - 1$
$5\% = 0·05$	$1 + 0·05 = 1·05$	$(1·05)^{\frac{1}{12}} - 1 = 0·40741\%$
$8\% = 0·08$	$1 + 0·08 = 1·08$	$(1·08)^{\frac{1}{12}} - 1 = 0·6434\%$
$9·3\% = 0·093$	$1 + 0·093 = 1·093$	$(1·093)^{\frac{1}{12}} - 1 = 0·7438\%$

Examples

(a) Find the monthly rate of interest equivalent to an annual rate of 7·5%.

(b) Dermot says that an annual rate of interest of 18% is equivalent to a monthly rate of 1·5%. Sheila disagrees and says that the monthly rate is lower. Is Sheila right? Give a reason for your answer.

(c) A loan company advertises an APR of 16·9%. If the loan is compounded monthly, what is the rate of interest charged per month? Give your answer correct to 1 decimal place.

Solutions

(a) $i = 7·5\% = 0·075$, $1 + i = 1·075$

Equivalent monthly rate $= (1 + i)^{\frac{1}{12}} - 1 = (1·075)^{\frac{1}{12}} - 1 = 0·6045\%$

(b) Sheila is right.

$i = 18\% = 0·18$, $1 + i = 1·18$

Equivalent monthly rate $= (1·18)^{\frac{1}{12}} - 1 = 0·013888 = 1·388\% \approx 1·4\%$

(c) $i = 16·9\% = 0·169$, $1 + i = 1·169$

Equivalent monthly rate $= (1·169)^{\frac{1}{12}} - 1 = 0·0130974 = 1·309\% \approx 1·3\%$

The following table shows some examples of conversions from monthly to annual interest rates.

Monthly rate i	$1 + i$	Equivalent annual rate $(1 + i)^{12} - 1$
$1\% = 0·01$	$1 + 0·01 = 1·01$	$(1·01)^{12} - 1 = 0·12685 = 12·6825\%$
$1·5\% = 0·015$	$1 + 0·015 = 1·015$	$(1·015)^{12} - 1 = 0·195618 = 19·5618\%$

Point to note

A bank might advertise an APR for a car loan of 8·8% per annum, compounded monthly. Notice that the interest period and compounding period are different.

If we convert the annual rate to a monthly rate we get

$(1·088)^{\frac{1}{12}} - 1 = 0·007053 = 0·7053\%$ monthly.

If we multiply 0·7053% by 12 we get $8·4636 \approx 8·5\%$. We can see there is a difference between the two rates: an APR of 8·8% and an annual rate of 8·5%.

We call 8·5% the **annual nominal rate of interest**. The APR can be used to compare the annual interest on loans or savings that compound over different periods.

Point to note

We can use the formula on page 32 of the *Formulae and Tables* booklet to convert to an annual rate from other compounding periods.

$i = \left(1 + \dfrac{r}{m}\right)^m - 1$, where i = APR or AER, r = nominal annual rate (as a decimal) and m = number of compounding periods.

Using the previous example of $r = 8·5\% = 0·085$, $m = 12$,

$APR = \left(1 + \dfrac{0·085}{12}\right)^{12} - 1 = 0·08839 \approx 8·8\%$.

Savings and investments

We can apply geometric series to savings and investments questions. Remember the formula for a geometric series:

$$S_n = \frac{a(1 - r^n)}{1 - r} \text{ for } r < 1 \text{ or } S_n = \frac{a(r^n - 1)}{r - 1} \text{ for } r > 1.$$

Example

Sean wants to start a savings plan with a certain bank. He wants to save €50 each year, starting now, for 4 years. Find the future value of his savings if the AER is 10% compounded annually.

Solution

Method one

$P = €50$, $i = 10\% = 0.1$

Year 1	Year 2	Year 3	Year 4	Future value $F = P(1 + i)^t$
50 ————————————————————————→				$50(1.1)^4 = 73.21$
	50 ——————————————————→			$50(1.1)^3 = 66.55$
		50 ——————————→		$50(1.1)^2 = 60.50$
			50 →	$50(1.1)^1 = 55.00$
At the end of 4 years, the sum of future values is				€255.26

We can see from the table that the total future value is €255.26.

Method two

Use a geometric series. Remember the formula:

$$S_n = \frac{a(1 - r^n)}{1 - r} \text{ or } \frac{a(r^n - 1)}{r - 1}.$$

The geometric series is $50(1.1) + 50(1.1)^2 + 50(1.1)^3 + 50(1.1)^4$

Here, $a = 50(1.1)$, $r = 1.1$, $n = 4$

$$S_4 = \frac{50(1.1)[(1.1)^4 - 1]}{1.1 - 1} = €255.26$$

It's possible that the specified compounding period will be different to the interest period. For example, interest of 7% annually, compounded monthly. In this case, you have two options.

Option 1: Use the annual interest rate, but change the time periods to fractions (so 2 years = $\frac{24}{12}$ months, etc.).

Option 2: Convert the annual interest rate to a monthly interest rate, and change the time periods to a whole number of months (so 2 years = 24 months, etc.).

Point to note

Remember to check whether the payments are made at the start or the end of the time period. If it is the end, then the values of n in the geometric series will start at 0 and end at one less than the number of time periods.

For example, if a payment is made at the end of each year for 5 years, the values for n will be 0, 1, 2, 3, 4. If the payments were at the start of each year then the values for n would be 1, 2, 3, 4, 5.

Example

Joe is interested in saving for a holiday. He wants to invest €400 at the end of each month into a savings account in his local bank. The account pays an AER of 6% compounded monthly.

What will be the final amount in Joe's account after 4 years?

Solution

In this question we have two options regarding the compounding period and interest period.

We can leave the AER as 6% = 0·06 and adjust t (time) to fractions: $\frac{47}{12}, \frac{46}{12}$, etc.

We can adjust the AER to a monthly rate and leave t (time) as whole numbers: 1, 2, 3, etc.

Also, the money is invested at the end of the month so we must be careful with time periods.

For this example, we will leave the AER as 6% = 0·06 and adjust t to fractional units of time. Since the money is invested at the end of the month, t will be $\frac{47}{12}, \frac{46}{12}, \dots, \frac{1}{12}$. The last payment in will just be €400 on its own.

Payment	Future value $F = P(1+i)^t$
First €400	$F = 400(1 + 0.06)^{\frac{47}{12}}$
Second €400	$F = 400(1 + 0.06)^{\frac{46}{12}}$
$\vdots$	$\vdots$
Second last €400	$F = 400(1 + 0.06)^{\frac{1}{12}}$
Last €400	$F = 400$

We can find the future value of the savings by using a geometric series.

Sum of all future values $= 400 + 400(1 \cdot 06)^{\frac{1}{12}} + \dots + 400(1 \cdot 06)^{\frac{47}{12}}$

$a = 400, r = (1 \cdot 06)^{\frac{1}{12}}, n = 48$

$$S_n = \frac{a(r^n - 1)}{r - 1} = \frac{400\left[(1 \cdot 06)^{\frac{48}{12}} - 1\right]}{(1 \cdot 06)^{\frac{1}{12}} - 1} = €21\,569 \cdot 53$$

Loans and mortgages

We pay off loans and mortgages to a bank in a series of equal regular monthly repayments. Such loans are called **amortised loans**. Each payment made will reduce some of the principal and some of the interest on the loan. At the start of a mortgage, most of each repayment will pay for the interest and just a small portion of the repayment will reduce the principal.

The graph shows the monthly interest and principal payments on a fixed-rate mortgage of €100 000 at 6% over 30 years.

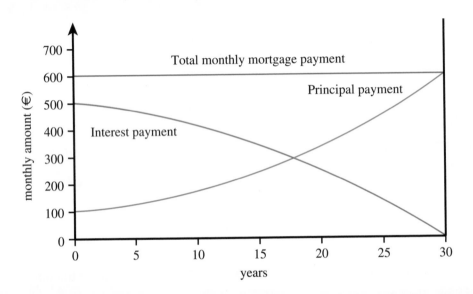

Example

Andrew takes a loan of €5000 for 5 years at an APR of 10%. How much should the annual repayments be if the loan is repaid in 5 equal instalments over the 5 years?

Solution

The first instalment is paid one year after the loan is taken out. We can write the sum of the present values as a geometric series, where A = annual repayment amount.

Present value	Year 1	Year 2	Year 3	Year 4	Year 5
$\dfrac{A}{1\cdot1}$	$\longleftarrow P_1$				
$\dfrac{A}{(1\cdot1)^2}$	$\longleftarrow\qquad P_2$				
$\dfrac{A}{(1\cdot1)^3}$	$\longleftarrow\qquad\qquad P_3$				
$\dfrac{A}{(1\cdot1)^4}$	$\longleftarrow\qquad\qquad\qquad P_4$				
$\dfrac{A}{(1\cdot1)^5}$	$\longleftarrow\qquad\qquad\qquad\qquad P_5$				
€5000	Sum of present values = loan amount				

$$S_n = \frac{a(1 - r^n)}{1 - r}$$

$$a = \frac{A}{1\cdot1}, \ r = \frac{1}{1\cdot1} = \frac{10}{11}, \ n = 5$$

$$S_5 = \frac{\dfrac{A}{1\cdot1}\left(1 - \left(\dfrac{10}{11}\right)^5\right)}{1 - \dfrac{10}{11}} = \frac{A\left(1 - \left(\dfrac{10}{11}\right)^5\right)}{(1\cdot1)\left(\dfrac{1}{11}\right)}$$

Loan amount = sum of present values = sum of series

$$5000 = \frac{A\left(1 - \left(\dfrac{10}{11}\right)^5\right)}{(1\cdot1)\left(\dfrac{1}{11}\right)}$$

$$A = \frac{5000}{10\left(1 - \left(\dfrac{10}{11}\right)^5\right)} = €1318\cdot99$$

Andrew must pay €1318·99 at the end of each year.

Amortisation formula

We can use an **amortisation formula** to find the repayment amount each period for a loan. It applies to mortgages and other loans that are made up of equal repayments at equal intervals.

The formula is on page 31 of the *Formulae and Tables* booklet.

$$A = P\left[\frac{i(1 + i)^t}{(1 + i)^t - 1}\right]$$

A = annual repayment amount, P = principal, i = interest rate

Note that payments start one period (usually month) after the loan is made.

The proof of this formula is part of the course, and it is based on the sum of the present values and a geometric series as in the previous example.

Let the annual repayment amount = A, and the sum borrowed = the present value of all the regular repayments = P.

$$P = \frac{A}{(1 + i)^1} + \frac{A}{(1 + i)^2} + \frac{A}{(1 + i)^3} + \ldots + \frac{A}{(1 + i)^t}$$

$$= A\left(\frac{1}{(1 + i)^1} + \frac{1}{(1 + i)^2} + \frac{1}{(1 + i)^3} + \ldots + \frac{1}{(1 + i)^t}\right)$$

$$= A\left(\text{sum of a geometric series with } a = \frac{1}{1 + i}, r = \frac{1}{1 + i}, n = t\right)$$

$$= A\left(\frac{a(1 - r^n)}{1 - r}\right) = A\left[\frac{\left(\frac{1}{1 + i}\right)\left(1 - \left(\frac{1}{1 + i}\right)^t\right)}{\left(1 - \frac{1}{1 + i}\right)}\right]$$

$$= \frac{\frac{1}{1 + i} - \frac{1}{(1 + i)^{t+1}}}{\left(\frac{1 + i - 1}{1 + i}\right)} \quad \text{Multiply above and below by } (1 + i)^{t+1}.$$

$$P = A\left[\frac{(1 + i)^t - 1}{i(1 + i)^t}\right]$$

Hence $A = P\left[\frac{i(1 + i)^t}{(1 + i)^t - 1}\right]$

Example

A bank offers a car loan to customers at an APR of 12·99% for car loans under €10 000.

A customer wants to buy a car for €5000 and wants to get a short-term loan over 5 years. The customer wishes to make monthly repayments in equal instalments over this period. The first payment is one month after the loan is taken out. How much will the monthly repayments be?

Solution

Use the amortisation formula $A = P\dfrac{i(1 + i)^t}{(1 + i)^t - 1}$ with $P = 5000$,
$t = 5$ years = 60 months.

Convert the APR to a monthly rate:

12·99% = 0·1299

Monthly rate = $(1 + 0·1299)^{\frac{1}{12}} - 1 = 0·01022939393 = i$ Hold this number in the calculator memory as ANS.

$$A = P\frac{i(1 + i)^t}{(1 + i)^t - 1} = 5000\frac{ANS(1 + ANS)^{60}}{(1 + ANS)^{60} - 1} = €111·92$$

(a) Niamh has saved to buy a car. She saved an equal amount at the beginning of each month in an account that earned an annual equivalent rate (AER) of 4%.

  (i) Show that the rate of interest, compounded monthly, which is equivalent to an AER of 4% is 0·327%, correct to 3 decimal places.

  (ii) Niamh has €15 000 in the account at the end of 36 months. How much has she saved each month, correct to the nearest euro?

(b) Conall borrowed to buy a car. He borrowed €15 000 at a monthly interest rate of 0·866%. He made 36 equal monthly payments to repay the entire loan. How much, to the nearest euro, was each of his monthly payments?

(SEC 2013)

Solutions

(a) (i) **Method one**

Convert 4% to a monthly rate.

$(1 + i)^{12} = 1·04 \Rightarrow 1 + i = \sqrt[12]{1·04} = 1·003274 \Rightarrow i = 0·003274$

Hence, $r = 0·327\%$ to 3 decimal places.

Method two

Convert 0·327% to an annual rate.

$(1·00327)^{12} = 1·039953481$

$\qquad\qquad\quad = 1·0400$

Hence, $r = 4\%$.

(ii) **Method one**

Write the payments as the sum of a geometric series.

$15\,000 = P(1·00327^{36} + 1·00327^{35} + ... + 1·00327^2 + 1·00327)$

$\Rightarrow P\left[\dfrac{1·00327(1·00327^{36} - 1)}{1·00327 - 1}\right] = 15\,000$

$\Rightarrow P[38·26326387] = 15\,000$

$\Rightarrow P = 392·02 = €392$

Method two

Use the amortisation formula.

$P = \dfrac{F}{(1 + i)^t} = \dfrac{15\,000}{(1·04)^3} = 13\,334·95$ Find the present value of the €15 000 saved.

$A = \dfrac{(13334·95)(0·00327)(1·00327)^{36}}{1·00327^{36} - 1}$ Use the present value as the principal in the amortisation formula.

$\qquad = €393·25 = €393$ to the nearest euro

(b) Method one

Use the amortisation formula.

$$A = P\frac{i(1 + i)^t}{(1 + i)^t - 1}$$

$$= 15\,000\left[\frac{0.00866(1.00866)^{36}}{1.00866^{36} - 1}\right] = 486.77$$

The monthly payment is €487.

Method two

Use the formula for the sum of a geometric series.

$$15\,000 = P\left(\frac{1}{1.00866} + \frac{1}{1.00866^2} + \dots + \frac{1}{1.00866^{36}}\right)$$

$$\Rightarrow P\left[\frac{\frac{1}{1.00866}\left(1 - \frac{1}{1.00866^{36}}\right)}{1 - \frac{1}{1.00866}}\right] = 15\,000$$

$$\Rightarrow P[30.8151777] = 15\,000$$

$$\Rightarrow P = 486.77$$

The monthly payment is €487.

Examples

Most lottery games in the USA allow winners of the jackpot prize to choose between two forms of the prize: an annual-payments option or a cash-value option. In the case of the New York Lotto, there are 26 annual payments in the annual-payments option, with the first payment immediately, and the last payment in 25 years' time. The payments increase by 4% each year. The amount Y advertised as the jackpot prize is the total amount of these 26 payments. The cash-value option pays a smaller amount than this.

(a) If the amount of the first annual payment is A, write down, in terms of A, the amount of the second, third, fourth and 26th payments.

(b) The 26 payments form a geometric series. Use this fact to express the advertised jackpot prize in terms of A.

(c) Find, correct to the nearest dollar, the value of A that corresponds to an advertised jackpot prize of $215 million.

(d) A winner who chooses the cash-value option receives, immediately, the total of the present values of the 26 annual payments. The interest rate used for the present value calculations is 4·78%. We want to find the cash value of the prize referred to in part (c).

(i) Complete the table below to show the actual amount and the present value of each of the first three annual payments.

Payment number	Time to payment (years)	Actual amount	Present value
1	0		
2	1		
3	2		

(ii) Write down, in terms of n, an expression for the present value of the nth annual payment.

(iii) Find the amount of prize money payable under the cash-value option. That is, find the total of the present values of the 26 annual payments.

Give your answer in millions, correct to 1 decimal place.

(e) The jackpot described in parts (c) and (d) above was won by an Irish woman earlier this year.

She chose the cash-value option. After tax, she received $7·9 million. What percentage of tax was charged on her winnings? *(SEC 2011)*

Solutions

(a) First payment (now) = A

Second payment = $A(1·04)$

Third payment = $A(1·04)^2$

Fourth payment = $A(1·04)^3$

26th payment = $A(1·04)^{25}$

(b) Prize $= A[1 + 1·04 + 1·04^2 + \ldots + 1·04^{25}]$

$$= A\left[\frac{1(1·04^{26} - 1)}{(1·04 - 1)}\right] = 44·31174462A$$

Keep as many decimal places as possible, as this will be used in the next calculation.

(c) $44·31174462A = 21\,500\,000$

$A = \$485\,199$ to the nearest dollar

(d) (i)

Payment number	Time to payment (years)	Actual amount	Present value
1	0	485 199	485 199
2	1	504 606·96	481 587·10
3	2	524 791·24	478 002·02

(ii) $\dfrac{485\,199(1{\cdot}04)^{n-1}}{(1{\cdot}0478)^{n-1}}$ or $485\,199\left(\dfrac{1{\cdot}04}{1{\cdot}0478}\right)^{n-1}$

(iii) $S_{26} = 485\,199 + 485\,199\left(\dfrac{1{\cdot}04}{1{\cdot}0478}\right) + \ldots + 485\,199\left(\dfrac{1{\cdot}04}{1{\cdot}0478}\right)^{26-1}$

$$= 485\,199\left[\dfrac{1 - \left(\dfrac{1{\cdot}04}{1{\cdot}0478}\right)^{26}}{1 - \left(\dfrac{1{\cdot}04}{1{\cdot}0478}\right)}\right]$$

$$= \$11{\cdot}5 \text{ million}$$

(e) Tax: $11{\cdot}5$ million $- 7{\cdot}9$ million $= \$3{\cdot}6$ million

Percentage tax: $\dfrac{3{\cdot}6}{11{\cdot}5} \times 100 = 31{\cdot}3\%$

Checklist

✓ Read the question carefully. Is it asking for the future value or the present value?

✓ Check the APR and AER – do you need to change to a monthly rate?

✓ Check the time period – do you use fractional units or whole numbers?

✓ Check whether the repayment period is at the start or end of the month.

✓ Practise using the amortisation formula and practise using a calculator to evaluate repayments.

✓ Know the proof for the amortisation formula.

✓ Know how to use a geometric series to answer a question.

Nets, Length, Area and Volume

10

Learning objectives

In this chapter you will learn how to:

- Investigate the nets of prisms, cylinders and cones
- Recognise the length of the perimeter and the area of plane figures: disc, triangle, rectangle, square, parallelogram, trapezium, sectors of discs
- Recognise properties of solid figures: rectangular block, cylinder, right cone, triangular-based prism (right-angled, isosceles and equilateral), sphere, hemisphere.

Glossary of terms

Term	Explanation	Diagram
Circumference	Length of the perimeter of a circle	*Circumference*
Cone	A solid shape with an elliptical or circular base, a curved surface and one vertex	l = slant height h = perpendicular height r = radius $l^2 = h^2 + r^2$

Term	Explanation	Diagram
Cube	A prism with six congruent faces	
Cylinder	A solid shape with two congruent circular or elliptical bases and one curved surface	
Edge	Straight line where two faces of a 3D shape meet	Edge
Face	Plane surface of a 3D shape	Face
Net	Plan of a 3D object	
Parallelogram	A quadrilateral with both pairs of opposite sides parallel • opposite sides are equal • opposite angles are equal • diagonals bisect each other	

Term	Explanation	Diagram
Perimeter	Sum of the length of the sides of a plane figure or shape	 Perimeter = 3 + 7 + 3 + 7 = 20
Polygon ('many corners/ angles')	2D closed shape made up of straight edges	Triangle 3-sided polygon Quadrilateral 4-sided polygon Pentagon 5-sided polygon Hexagon 6-sided polygon Octagon 8-sided polygon
Polyhedron ('many faces')	3D solid made of flat surfaces	
Prism	3D solid made up of two identical polygons at opposite ends, joined up by parallel lines Prisms are named after the shape of their base, e.g. rectangular prism, triangular prism	Hexagonal prism Triangular prism
Pyramid	3D solid with a polygon as a base and triangular faces that meet at the top (apex)	

Term	Explanation	Diagram
Quadrilateral	Shape with four sides	
Rectangle	Quadrilateral with four right angles <ul><li>opposite sides are equal</li><li>diagonals bisect each other</li></ul>	
Rhombus	Parallelogram with four equal sides <ul><li>opposite angles are equal</li><li>diagonals bisect each other at right angles</li><li>diagonals bisect angles of the rhombus</li></ul>	
Sphere	3D solid with one curved surface Every point on the surface is equidistant from the sphere's centre	
Square	Special rectangle with all sides equal and all angles right angles <ul><li>diagonals bisect each other at right angles</li><li>diagonals bisect angles of the square</li></ul>	

Term	Explanation	Diagram
Trapezium	Quadrilateral with only one pair of parallel sides	
Triangle	Three-sided shape • Equilateral triangle has three sides of equal length and all angles are 60° • Isosceles triangle has two sides of equal length and two equal angles • Scalene triangle has three different length sides and three different angles	
Vertex	A point or corner on a 2D shape where two sides meet A point or corner on a 3D shape where two or more edges meet	

Nets of prisms, cylinders and cones

The nets of some common 3D shapes are shown below.

Rectangular prism (cuboid)

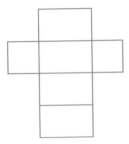

Triangular prism

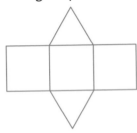

Cone

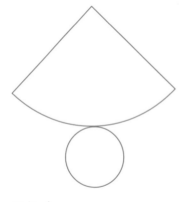

Cylinder

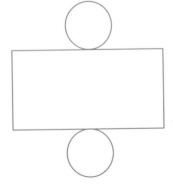

Properties of 3D shapes

Name of 3D shape	Faces	Edges	Vertices
Cube	6 square faces	12	8
Cylinder	3 (1 curved face, 2 circular faces)	2	0
Cone	2 (1 curved face, 1 circular face)	1	1
Cuboid	6 rectangular faces	12	8
Sphere	1 curved face	0	0
Triangular-based prism	5 (2 triangular faces, 3 rectangular faces)	9	6
Square pyramid	5 (1 square face, 4 triangular faces)	8	5

Length and area formulae

The following formulae are on pages 8 and 9 of the *Formulae and Tables* booklet. In all cases, A represents the area.

Parallelogram

$A = ah = ab \sin C$

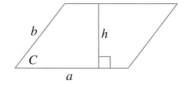

Trapezium

$A = \left(\dfrac{a + b}{2}\right)h$

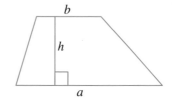

Circle/disc

l = circumference = $2\pi r$

$A = \pi r^2$

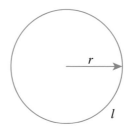

Arc/sector

When θ is in radians, $l = r\theta$, $A = \dfrac{1}{2}r^2\theta$.

When θ is in degrees, $l = 2\pi r\left(\dfrac{\theta}{360°}\right)$, $A = \pi r^2\left(\dfrac{\theta}{360°}\right)$.

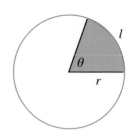

There are examples of using the arc/sector formula in Chapters 1 and 2 of Book 2.

Triangle

$A = \dfrac{1}{2}ah$

$= \dfrac{1}{2}ab\sin C$

$= \sqrt{s(s-a)(s-b)(s-c)}$, taking $s = \dfrac{a+b+c}{2}$.

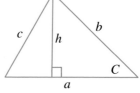

The trapezoidal rule is on page 12 of the *Formulae and Tables* booklet.

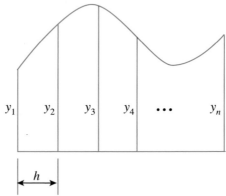

$A \approx \dfrac{h}{2}[y_1 + y_n + 2(y_2 + y_3 + \dots + y_{n-1})]$

There are examples of using the trapezoidal rule in Chapter 14.

Surface area and volume

The following formulae are on pages 10 and 11 of the *Formulae and Tables* booklet. In all cases, A represents the curved surface area and V represents the volume.

Point to note

Note that A represents only the *curved* surface area of each shape. To find the total surface area you need to add on the areas of the flat faces.

Cylinder

$A = 2\pi r h$

$V = \pi r^2 h$

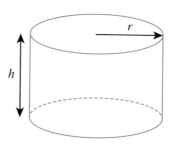

Cone

$A = 2\pi r l$

$V = \dfrac{1}{3}\pi r^2 h$

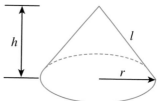

Sphere

$A = 4\pi r^2$

$V = \dfrac{4}{3}\pi r^3$

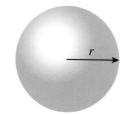

Frustum of cone

$A = \pi(r + R)l$

$V = \dfrac{1}{3}\pi h (R^2 + Rr + r^2)$

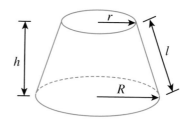

Solid cross-section (prism)

$V = Bh$, where B is the area of the base.

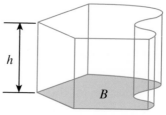

Pyramid on any base

$V = \dfrac{1}{3}Bh$, where B is the area of the base.

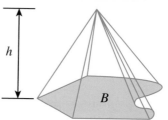

A company has to design a rectangular box for a new range of jellybeans. The box is to be assembled from a single piece of cardboard, cut from a rectangular sheet measuring 31 cm by 22 cm. The box is to have a capacity (volume) of 500 cm³.

The net for the box is shown below. The company is going to use the full length and width of the rectangular piece of cardboard. The shaded areas are flaps of width 1 cm which are needed for assembly. The height of the box is h cm, as shown on the diagram.

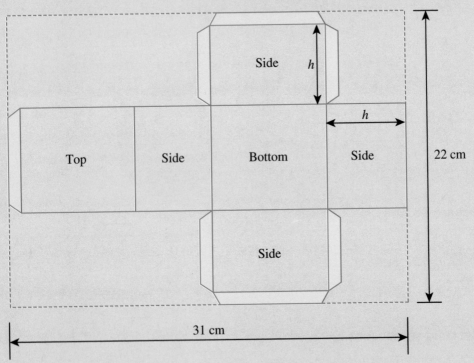

(a) Write the dimensions of the box, height, length and width, in centimetres, in terms of h.

(b) Write an expression for the capacity of the box in cubic centimetres, in terms of h.

(c) Show that the value of h that gives a box with a square bottom will give the correct capacity.

(d) Find, correct to 1 decimal place, the other value of h that gives a box of the correct capacity.

(e) The client is planning a special '10% extra free' promotion and needs to increase the capacity of the box by 10%. The company is checking whether they can make this new box from a piece of cardboard the same size as the original one (31 cm by 22 cm). They draw the graph below to represent the box's capacity as a function of h. Use the graph to explain why it is not possible to make the larger box from such a piece of cardboard.

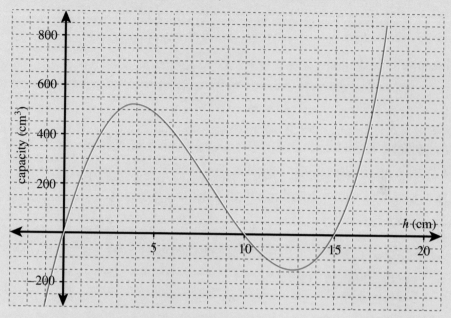

(SEC Sample 2014)

Solutions

(a) Start by labelling the dimensions in the diagram.

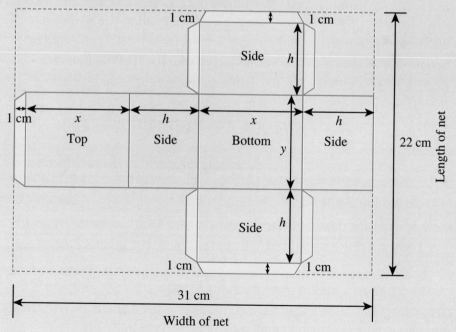

Let x be the width of the box, and y be the length of the box.

We already know that height $= h$ cm.

From the diagram, $2 + 2h + y = 22$

$$\Rightarrow 2h + y = 20$$
$$\Rightarrow y = 20 - 2h$$

Also from the diagram, $2x + 2h + 1 = 31$

$$\Rightarrow 2x + 2h = 30$$
$$\Rightarrow 2x = 30 - 2h$$
$$\Rightarrow x = 15 - h$$

So height $= h$ cm, length $= 20 - 2h$ cm and width $= 15 - h$ cm.

(b) $V = l \times b \times h = (20 - 2h)(15 - h)(h)$

(c) In a box with a square bottom, length = width.

$$\Rightarrow 20 - 2h = 15 - h$$
$$\Rightarrow 20 - 15 = 2h - h$$
$$\Rightarrow h = 5 \text{ cm}$$
$$\Rightarrow V = (20 - 2(5))(15 - (5))(5)$$
$$= (10)(10)(5)$$
$$= 500 \text{ cm}^3, \text{ as required.}$$

(d) $V = l \times b \times h = 500$

$(20 - 2h)(15 - h)(h) = 500$

$(20h - 2h^2)(15 - h) = 500$ Multiply out the first and third brackets.

$2h^3 - 50h^2 + 300h - 500 = 0$ Multiply out the final brackets and rearrange to get a cubic equation equal to zero.

We know that $h = 5$ is a solution, so $h - 5$ is a factor of the cubic. We can equate coefficients to find the other factor, which will be a quadratic.

$2h^3 \div h = 2h^2$ and $500 \div 5 = 100$. Use k to represent the middle term.

$(h - 5)(2h^2 + kh + 100) = 2h^3 - 50h^2 + 300h - 500 - 5kh + 100h$

$= 300h$ Equate h terms on left and right.

$\Rightarrow -5k + 100 = 300$

$\Rightarrow -5k = 200 \Rightarrow k = -40$ Substitute this into the quadratic factor and solve for h.

$2h^2 - 40h + 100 = 0$

Solving using the quadratic formula gives $h = 10 \pm 5\sqrt{2} \Rightarrow h = 17 \cdot 07$ or $h = 2 \cdot 93$.

$h = 17 \cdot 07$ will give a negative length and width, so the other correct value of h is $2 \cdot 9$ cm.

(e) A 10% increase in volume gives a volume of $500 \times 1 \cdot 1 = 550$ cm^3.

From the graph, a volume of 550 cm^3 requires h to be about 17·3 cm. This is not possible, as it would give a length of $20 - 2(17 \cdot 3) = -14 \cdot 6 < 0$.

Examples

The graph below shows a circular sheet of tin of radius 6 cm.

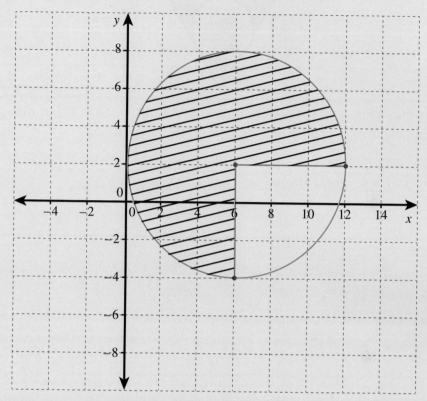

The shaded region is cut from the sheet to form an open cone.

(a) Find the surface area of the cone in terms of π.

(b) Hence, find the radius and height of the cone.

(c) How much liquid will the cone hold in terms of π?

Solutions

(a) The surface area of the cone is $\frac{3}{4}$ of the circle so surface area $= \frac{3}{4}\pi(6)^2 = 27\pi$ cm^2.

(b) Surface area of cone $\pi r l = 6\pi r = 27\pi$ so $r = \frac{27}{6}$

$$= 4{\cdot}5 \text{ cm.}$$

$$r^2 + h^2 = 36 \implies h^2 = 36 - 4{\cdot}5^2 = 15{\cdot}75$$

$$\text{so } h = \sqrt{15{\cdot}75} = 3{\cdot}97 \text{ cm.}$$

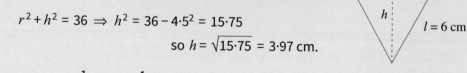

(c) Volume $= \frac{1}{3}\pi r^2 h = \frac{1}{3}\pi(4{\cdot}5)^2(3{\cdot}97) = 26{\cdot}8\pi$ cm^3.

The cone will hold $26{\cdot}8\pi$ cm^3 of liquid.

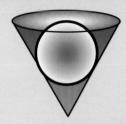

A sphere fits exactly into the open cone from the example on page 163. The diagram below shows the cross-section of the sphere inside the cone.

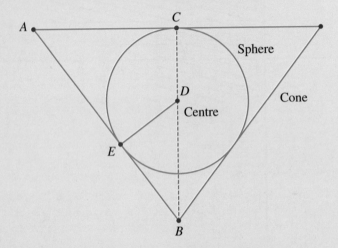

(a) Find two similar triangles, giving reasons for your answer.

(b) Hence find the radius of the sphere in the form $\dfrac{a\sqrt{b}}{c}$, where $a, b, c \in \mathbb{N}$.

(c) Hence show that $r = \dfrac{2a}{p}$, where r is the radius of the incircle, a is the area of the triangle and p is the perimeter of the triangle shown in the diagram.

(d) Find the volume of the sphere in terms of π.

(e) What is the ratio of the volume of the cone to the volume of the sphere? Express your answer in its simplest form $a:b$ where $a, b \in \mathbb{N}$.

Solutions

(a) Triangles DEB and ABC are similar.

Reasons: $\angle DEB$ is a right angle because AB is a tangent to the sphere at E. $\angle BCA$ is also a right angle. $\angle CBA$ is common to both triangles. If two angles are the same, then the third angle must also be the same, so the triangles are similar.

(b)

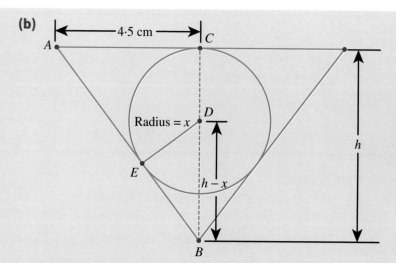

Let x = radius length.

Because triangles DEB and ABC are similar, the ratios of their sides are the same. That is, $\dfrac{|BD|}{|DE|} = \dfrac{|AB|}{|AC|}$.

$|DE| = |DC|$ = radius of sphere = x.

$|AC|$ = radius of cone = 4·5 cm (from previous example).

$|BC|$ = height of cone = $\sqrt{15\cdot75}$ (from previous example) = $\sqrt{(2\cdot25)(7)} = 1\cdot5\sqrt{7} = h$.

$|BD| = h - x = 1\cdot5\sqrt{7} - x$.

$|AB|$ = slant height of cone = 6 cm (from previous example).

$$\frac{1\cdot5\sqrt{7} - x}{x} = \frac{6}{4\cdot5}$$

$$6x = 4\cdot5(1\cdot5\sqrt{7} - x)$$

$$6x = 6\cdot75\sqrt{7} - 4\cdot5x$$

$$10\cdot5x = 6\cdot75\sqrt{7}$$

$$x = \frac{9\sqrt{7}}{14} \text{ cm}$$

The answer is in the required form.

(c) Note that this will check your answer to part (b).

Area of triangle = $\dfrac{1}{2}$ base × height = $\dfrac{1}{2}(9)(1\cdot5\sqrt{7}) = 6\cdot75\sqrt{7}$

Perimeter of triangle = $6 + 6 + 9 = 21$

$$r = \frac{2a}{p} = \frac{2(6\cdot75\sqrt{7})}{21} = \frac{27\sqrt{7}}{42} = \frac{9\sqrt{7}}{14} \text{ cm}$$

(d) Volume of sphere $= \frac{4}{3}\pi r^3$

$$= \frac{4}{3} \times \pi \times \left(\frac{9\sqrt{7}}{14}\right)^3$$

$$= \frac{243}{98}\sqrt{7}\,\pi \text{ cm}^3$$

(e) Volume of cone $= \frac{1}{3}\pi r^2 h$

$$= \frac{1}{3}\pi(4{\cdot}5)^2(1{\cdot}5\sqrt{7})$$

$$= \frac{81}{8}\sqrt{7}\,\pi \text{ cm}^3$$

Volume of cone : Volume of sphere $= \dfrac{81}{8}\sqrt{7}\,\pi : \dfrac{243}{98}\sqrt{7}\,\pi$

$$= \frac{81}{8} : \frac{243}{98}$$

$$= \frac{1}{4} : \frac{3}{49}$$

$$= 49 : 12$$

Checklist

✓ Know the nets of prisms, cylinders and cones.

✓ Practise solving problems involving length and area of plane figures and combinations of these figures.

✓ Practise solving problems involving surface area and volume of solid figures and combinations of these figures.

✓ Practise using the trapezoidal rule to approximate area (covered in Chapter 14).

Differentiation 1

11

Learning objectives

In this chapter you will learn how to:

- Understand the concept of differentiation and link it to graphs of motion
- Understand the meaning of first derivative (instantaneous rate of change of one quantity with respect to another)
- Understand the concept of a limit
- Differentiate linear and quadratic functions from first principles
- Recognise notation for differentiation and evaluate derivatives
- Differentiate by rule the following function types
  - Polynomial
  - Exponential
  - Trigonometric
  - Rational powers
  - Inverse functions
  - Logarithms
- Find the derivatives of sums, differences, products, quotients and compositions of functions of the above forms.

Introduction

Differentiation (or **differential calculus**) is the branch of mathematics that deals with the rate of change of one quantity with respect to another quantity.

If we have a function $y = f(x)$ with an independent variable x, the derivative of $f(x)$ is written as $\dfrac{dy}{dx}$ or $f'(x)$.

Linear motion graphs

Linear motion refers to the motion (distance, displacement, speed, velocity, etc.) of an object in a straight line. A **linear motion graph** shows motion on the y-axis against time taken on the x-axis. We can use these graphs to see the varying quantity of distance, speed, acceleration, and so on with respect to time.

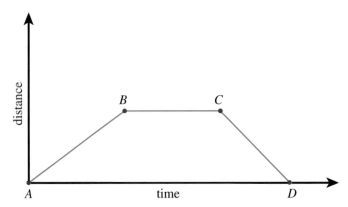

Consider the graph above. It shows a car leaving home and travelling at a steady, or constant, speed. The car stops for a period of time, perhaps at traffic lights (shown by the horizontal line), and then returns home at a constant speed.

Point to note

$$\text{Speed} = \frac{\text{distance}}{\text{time}} = \frac{\text{rise}}{\text{run}} = \text{slope of line.}$$

Speed is the rate of change of distance with respect to time. It is measured in metres per second (m/s). Speed is a scalar quantity, that is, it has no direction.

The rate of change of speed is acceleration/deceleration.

Examples

Consider the linear motion graph of speed/time of an object starting at A and finishing at E.

(a) Comment on the stages of the linear motion graph. Refer to the slope, acceleration and speed of the object.

(b) Explain the difference between stages AB and CD of the graph.

(c) Find the total distance travelled by the object.

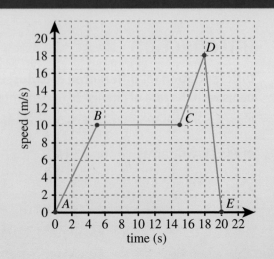

Solutions

(a) Between A and B the slope of the graph is $\dfrac{10}{5} = 2$. The object accelerates at a constant rate of 2 m/s².

Between B and C the slope of the graph is 0. The object travels at a constant speed of 10 m/s; it is not accelerating.

Between C and D the slope of the graph is $\dfrac{8}{3} = 2\cdot67$. The object accelerates at a constant rate of 2·67 m/s².

Between D and E the slope of the graph is $-\dfrac{18}{2} = -9$. The object decelerates at a constant rate of -9 m/s².

(b) CD has a steeper slope than AB so the object has higher acceleration at stage CD.

(c) The total distance travelled is given by the area under the graph. (This is an application of integration, which gives the area under a curve.)

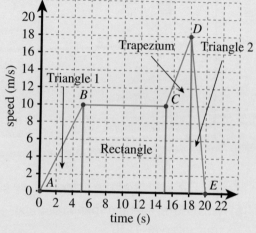

Area of first triangle

$= \dfrac{1}{2}bh = \dfrac{1}{2}(5)(10) = 25$

Area of rectangle $= (10)(10) = 100$

Area of trapezium

$= \left(\dfrac{a+b}{2}\right)h = \left(\dfrac{10+18}{2}\right)3 = 42$

Area of second triangle $= \dfrac{1}{2}bh = \dfrac{1}{2}(18)(2) = 18$

Total distance $= 25 + 100 + 42 + 18 = 185$ m

Top Tip

The area under a speed–time graph gives the distance.

Average rate of change vs instantaneous rate of change

In the previous example the rate of change was constant at each stage of the graph. In reality, speed and acceleration change at each moment. We can get an average speed for a journey over a certain interval or over the whole journey, but it is more difficult to find the instantaneous rate of change at a certain point in the journey. The speedometer in a car gives the instantaneous rate of change at any stage of the journey.

Examples

An object is thrown into the air 4 metres above the ground and the path of the object is modelled by the function $f(x) = 4 + 15x - 3x^2$ as shown in the diagram.

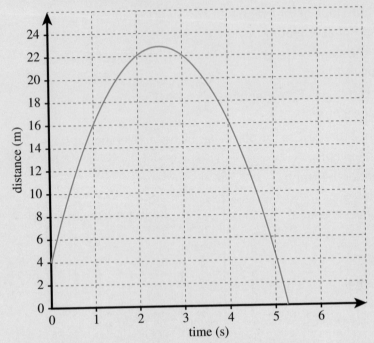

(a) At what time does the object hit the ground?

(b) What is the average speed (average rate of change) of the object for the time interval $[1, 3]$?

(c) What is the instantaneous rate of change of the object at 1 second?

Solutions

(a) The x-axis represents time and the y-axis represents the height of the object. Notice that graph is a curve, so **the rate of change is not constant** for the path of the object.

The object hits the ground at the point where the curve intersects the x-axis. We can read an approximate value for this point from the graph, or solve the quadratic for a more accurate answer.

Using the quadratic formula, $f(x) = 0$ when $x = 5\cdot25$ or $x = -0\cdot25$. The negative value is not possible here, because x represents time taken and must be positive, so the object reaches ground after $5\cdot25$ seconds.

(b)

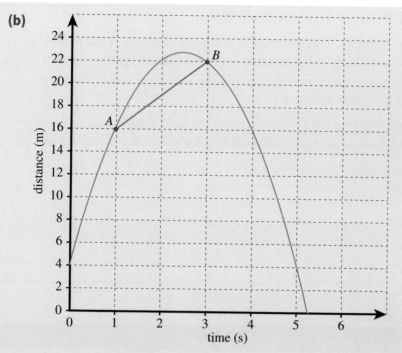

Average rate of change = average speed = slope of secant AB = $\dfrac{\text{rise}}{\text{run}}$

$$= \frac{22 - 16}{3 - 1} = \frac{6}{2} = 3 \text{ m/s.}$$

(c) If we take a sequence of shorter secants about the interval [1, 3] and find their corresponding slopes we notice a pattern. Eventually the secant will become **a tangent to the curve** at the point (1, 16). This is the instantaneous rate of change of the object at $t = 1$ second.

Secant	Slope = rate of change $= \dfrac{f(b) - f(a)}{b - a}$
AB	$\dfrac{22 - 16}{3 - 1} = 3$
AB_1	$\dfrac{22 - 16}{2 - 1} = 6$
AB_2	$\dfrac{19 \cdot 75 - 16}{1 \cdot 5 - 1} = 7 \cdot 5$
AB_3	$\dfrac{16 \cdot 87 - 16}{1 \cdot 1 - 1} = 8 \cdot 7$

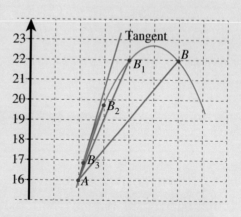

We can see that the value of the slope is increasing towards 9 and the gap between the points is getting smaller and smaller.

Slope of tangent at (1, 16) = 9, so the instantaneous rate of change or speed at $t = 1$ second is 9 m/s.

Differentiation by first principles

In the previous example, we saw how the value of the slopes of the secants of $f(x)$ get closer and closer to the instantaneous rate of change at a point as the interval gets closer to that point. We can use this idea to derive a formula for differentiation from first principles.

Suppose we want to find the rate of change of $f(x)$ at a point $(x, f(x))$. Choose a second point, $(x + h, f(x + h))$. Then the slope of the secant is given by

$$\frac{y_2 - y_1}{x_2 - x_1} = \frac{f(x + h) - f(x)}{(x + h) - x} = \frac{f(x + h) - f(x)}{h}.$$

As h gets closer to zero (i.e. as the second point gets closer to the first), this function will get closer to the true tangent at the first point. Therefore,

$$f'(x) = \lim_{h \to 0} \frac{f(x + h) - f(x)}{h}.$$

Example

Differentiate $4 + 15x - 3x^2$ with respect to x from first principles.

Solution

$f(x) = 4 + 15x - 3x^2$

$f(x + h) = 4 + 15(x + h) - 3(x + h)^2$

$\qquad = 4 + 15x + 15h - 3(x^2 + 2xh + h^2)$

$\qquad = 4 + 15x + 15h - 3x^2 - 6xh - 3h^2$

$f(x + h) - f(x) = 15h - 6xh - 3h^2$

$\dfrac{f(x + h) - f(x)}{h} = \dfrac{15h - 6xh - 3h^2}{h} = 15 - 6x - 3h$

$\displaystyle\lim_{h \to 0} \frac{f(x + h) - f(x)}{h} = \lim_{h \to 0} 15 - 6x - 3h = 15 - 6x$

Point to note

Differentiation from first principles can only be asked for linear and quadratic functions in the exam.

Evaluating derivatives

To evaluate a derivative, differentiate the function and substitute the value of x (the independent variable) into the derivative function (slope function). The result gives the slope of the tangent to the function for that value of x.

Example

Evaluate the derivative of the function $f(x) = x^3 - 3x^2 + 4x$ at $x = 1$ and hence find the equation of the tangent to the curve when $x = 1$.

Solution

$f'(x) = 3x^2 - 6x + 4$

$f'(1) = 3(1)^2 - 6(1) + 4 = 3 - 6 + 4 = 1$ This gives us the slope of the tangent, 1.

$f(1) = (1)^3 - 3(1)^2 + 4 = 1 - 3 + 4 = 2$ Find the value of y when $x = 1$.

Use the equation of a straight line formula, $y - y_1 = m(x - x_1)$, with $(x_1, y_1) = (1, 2)$ and $m = 1$.

Equation of tangent: $y - y_1 = m(x - x_1) \Rightarrow y - 2 = 1(x - 1) \Rightarrow y = x + 1$

Differentiation by rule

Polynomials and rational powers

The rule for polynomials and rational powers is on page 25 of the *Formulae and Tables* booklet.

$f(x) = x^n,\ f'(x) = nx^{n-1}$

Product rule: $y = uv \Rightarrow \dfrac{dy}{dx} = u\dfrac{dv}{dx} + v\dfrac{du}{dx}$

Quotient rule: $y = \dfrac{u}{v} \Rightarrow \dfrac{dy}{dx} = \dfrac{v\dfrac{du}{dx} - u\dfrac{dv}{dx}}{v^2}$

Examples

Differentiate:

(a) $f(x) = 2x^3 - 4x^2 - 6x + 2$

(b) $g(x) = \sqrt{x}(1 - x^2)$. Give your answer in the form $\dfrac{a - bx^2}{c\sqrt{x}}$, where $a, b, c \in \mathbb{N}$.

Solutions

(a) $f'(x) = 6x^2 - 8x - 6$

(b) We can use the product rule here, or simplify the function into rational powers of x and then differentiate as normal.

Using the product rule

$$u = \sqrt{x} = x^{\frac{1}{2}} \Rightarrow \frac{du}{dx} = \frac{1}{2}x^{-\frac{1}{2}} = \frac{1}{2\sqrt{x}}$$

$$v = 1 - x^2 \Rightarrow \frac{dv}{dx} = -2x$$

$$f'(x) = u\frac{dv}{dx} + v\frac{du}{dx} = \left(\sqrt{x}\right)(-2x) + (1 - x^2)\left(\frac{1}{2\sqrt{x}}\right)$$

That's the hard work done. Now just simplify to the required from.

$$f'(x) = \frac{\left(-2x\sqrt{x}\right)\left(2\sqrt{x}\right) + (1 - x^2)}{2\sqrt{x}} \qquad \text{Multiply first set of terms by } \frac{2\sqrt{x}}{2\sqrt{x}}.$$

$$= \frac{-4x^2 + 1 - x^2}{2\sqrt{x}} = \frac{1 - 5x^2}{2\sqrt{x}}$$

Simplifying the function

$$g(x) = \sqrt{x}(1 - x^2) = \sqrt{x} - \left(\sqrt{x}\right)(x^2)$$

$$= x^{\frac{1}{2}} - x^{\frac{5}{2}} \qquad \text{We now have a function in rational powers of } x \text{ and can differentiate as normal.}$$

$$g'(x) = \frac{1}{2}x^{-\frac{1}{2}} - \frac{5}{2}x^{\frac{3}{2}}$$

$$= \frac{1}{2}x^{-\frac{1}{2}} - \frac{5}{2}(x^2)\left(x^{-\frac{1}{2}}\right) \qquad \text{Use rules of indices to convert } x^{\frac{3}{2}} \text{ to the required form.}$$

$$= \frac{1 - 5x^2}{2\sqrt{x}}$$

> **Top Tip**
>
> Always use brackets when working with the product rule and quotient rule. This will help you to avoid mistakes.

Composite functions

The rule for differentiating composite functions is also known as the **chain rule**.

$$y = f(x) = (\text{function})^n \Rightarrow \frac{dy}{dx} = f'(x) = n(\text{function})^{n-1}(\text{derivative of function})$$

Differentiate:

(a) $f(x) = (2x^2 - x)^4$

(b) $g(x) = \dfrac{1}{\sqrt{x} - 4}$.

Solutions

(a) The derivative of $2x^2 - x$ is $4x - 1$. So, using the chain rule,
$$f'(x) = 4(2x^2 - x)^3 (4x - 1).$$

(b) $g(x) = \dfrac{1}{\sqrt{x} - 4} = \dfrac{1}{(x - 4)^{\frac{1}{2}}} = (x - 4)^{-\frac{1}{2}}$

This is now a function, $x - 4$, to a rational power.

$$g'(x) = -\frac{1}{2}(x - 4)^{-\frac{1}{2} - 1}(1) = -\frac{1}{2}(x - 4)^{-\frac{3}{2}}$$

$$g'(x) = -\frac{1}{2(x - 4)^{\frac{3}{2}}} = -\frac{1}{2(\sqrt{x} - 4)^3}$$

Simplify using rules of indices.

Trigonometric functions

These formulae are on page 25 of the *Formulae and Tables* booklet.

Standard trigonometric functions:

$f(x)$	$f'(x)$
$\cos(x)$	$-\sin(x)$
$\sin(x)$	$\cos x$
$\tan(x)$	$\sec^2(x)$

Top Tip

Don't take it for granted that you know the derivatives of the trig functions. Always check in the *Formulae and Tables* booklet. It could save you marks in the exam, especially when you might have to integrate these trig functions as well.

Composite trigonometric functions:

Again, these are based on the derivatives of standard trigonometric functions.

$f(x)$	$f'(x)$
$\cos(function)$	$-\sin(function)(derivative\ of\ function)$
$\sin(function)$	$\cos(function)(derivative\ of\ function)$
$\tan(function)$	$\sec^2(function)(derivative\ of\ function)$

Examples

(a) Differentiate $f(x) = \sin(4x) + \cos(3x)$.

(b) Find the derivative of $\sqrt{\sin(t)}$ with respect to t.

(c) $f(\theta) = \dfrac{\cos\theta}{1 + \sin\theta}$. Find $f'(\theta)$. Express your answer in the form $\dfrac{a}{1 + b\sin(\theta)}$ where $a, b \in \mathbb{Z}$ and $a, b \neq 0$. Hence, evaluate $f'\left(\dfrac{\pi}{2}\right)$.

Solutions

(a) $f'(x) = (\cos(4x))(4) - (\sin(3x))(3) = 4\cos(4x) - 3\sin(3x)$

(b) $y = \sqrt{\sin(t)} = (\sin(t))^{\frac{1}{2}}$ Express the function as a rational power of t.

> **Top Tip**
>
> When differentiating functions involving square roots we must express the function as a rational power of the independent variable first. That is, express the square root as power of a half. Then we can differentiate the function.

$$\frac{dy}{dt} = \frac{1}{2}(\sin(t))^{-\frac{1}{2}}(\cos(t)) = \frac{\cos(t)}{2(\sin(t))^{\frac{1}{2}}} = \frac{\cos(t)}{2\sqrt{\sin(t)}}$$

(c) Use the quotient rule to differentiate the function, then simplify it using trigonometric identities.

$u = \cos\theta, \qquad u' = \dfrac{du}{d\theta} = -\sin\theta$

$v = 1 + \sin\theta, \quad v' = \dfrac{dv}{d\theta} = \cos\theta$

$$f'(\theta) = \frac{vu' - uv'}{v^2} = \frac{(1 + \sin\theta)(-\sin\theta) - (\cos\theta)(\cos\theta)}{(1 + \sin\theta)^2}$$

$$= \frac{-\sin\theta - \sin^2\theta - \cos^2\theta}{(1 + \sin\theta)^2}$$

Now simplify the differentiated function.

The obvious next step would be to expand the brackets in the denominator. Don't do this! Use the trigonometric identity $\sin^2\theta + \cos^2\theta = 1$ to rearrange the numerator. This gives a common factor of $1 + \sin\theta$ that can be cancelled out.

$$= \frac{-(\sin\theta + \sin^2\theta + \cos^2\theta)}{(1 + \sin\theta)^2} = \frac{-(1 + \sin\theta)}{(1 + \sin\theta)^2} = -\frac{1}{1 + \sin\theta}$$

$$f'\left(\frac{\pi}{2}\right) = -\frac{1}{1 + \sin\dfrac{\pi}{2}} = -\frac{1}{1 + 1} = -\frac{1}{2}$$

Top Tip

Don't forget to simplify the answer if possible, or if asked in the question.

Inverse trigonometric functions

These formulae are on page 25 of the *Formulae and Tables* booklet.

Standard inverse trigonometric functions:

$f(x)$	$f'(x)$
$\cos^{-1}\left(\dfrac{x}{a}\right)$	$-\dfrac{1}{\sqrt{a^2 - x^2}}$
$\sin^{-1}\left(\dfrac{x}{a}\right)$	$\dfrac{1}{\sqrt{a^2 - x^2}}$
$\tan^{-1}\left(\dfrac{x}{a}\right)$	$\dfrac{a}{a^2 + x^2}$

a is a constant. If $a = 1$ there are three important inverse trigonometric functions and their derivatives.

$f(x)$	$f'(x)$
$\cos^{-1}(x)$	$-\dfrac{1}{\sqrt{1 - x^2}}$
$\sin^{-1}(x)$	$\dfrac{1}{\sqrt{1 - x^2}}$
$\tan^{-1}(x)$	$\dfrac{1}{1 + x^2}$

The derivatives of composite trig functions are based on their standard derivatives.

$f(x)$	$f'(x)$
$\cos^{-1}(function)$	$-\dfrac{1}{\sqrt{1 - (function)^2}}(derivative\ of\ function)$
$\sin^{-1}(function)$	$\dfrac{1}{\sqrt{1 - (function)^2}}(derivative\ of\ function)$
$\tan^{-1}(function)$	$\dfrac{1}{1 + (function)^2}(derivative\ of\ function)$

(a) Differentiate $y = \cos^{-1}\left(\frac{x}{2}\right) + \tan^{-1} x$.

(b) If $g(x) = \sin^{-1}(x + 5)$ and $h(x) = \sin^{-1}(\cos(x))$, find $g'(x)$ and $h'(x)$.
Hence, find $g'(-5)$ and $h'(5)$.

Solutions

(a) $\dfrac{dy}{dx} = -\dfrac{1}{\sqrt{4 - x^2}} + \dfrac{1}{1 + x^2}$

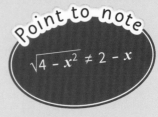

Point to note

$\sqrt{4 - x^2} \neq 2 - x$

(b) $g'(x) = \dfrac{1}{\sqrt{1 - (x + 5)^2}} \, (1) = \dfrac{1}{\sqrt{1 - (x + 5)^2}}$

$h'(x) = \dfrac{1}{\sqrt{1 - \cos^2(x)}} \, (-\sin(x)) = -\dfrac{\sin(x)}{\sqrt{\sin^2(x)}} = -1$ $h'(x)$ is a constant for all possible values of x.

$g'(-5) = \dfrac{1}{\sqrt{1 - (-5 + 5)^2}} = \dfrac{1}{\sqrt{1 - 0}} = 1$

$h'(5) = -1$

Exponential functions

The formulae for differentiating exponential functions are on page 25 of the *Formulae and Tables* booklet.

Standard exponential functions:

$f(x) = e^x \Rightarrow f'(x) = e^x$

$f(x) = e^{ax} \Rightarrow f'(x) = ae^{ax}$

Composite exponential functions:

$y = e^{function} \Rightarrow \dfrac{dy}{dx} = e^{function} \, \textbf{(\textit{derivative of function})}$

Differentiate:

(a) $y = e^{5x + 4} - 2e^{3x}$

(b) $f : x \rightarrow e^{\sin^2 x}$.

Remember

$\sin^2(x) = (\sin(x))^2$

Solutions

(a) $\dfrac{dy}{dx} = e^{5x + 4} \, (5) - 2e^{3x} \, (3)$

$= 5e^{5x + 4} - 6e^{3x}$

Use the formula for composite exponential functions on each term.

(b) $f(x) = e^{\sin^2(x)} = e^{(\sin(x))^2}$

$f'(x) = e^{(\sin(x))^2} \, 2\sin(x)\cos(x) = 2e^{\sin^2(x)}\sin(x)\cos(x)$

Example

Find the co-ordinates of the point at which the slope of the tangent to the curve
$f(x) = \dfrac{e^x - 1}{e^x + 1}$ is $\dfrac{1}{2}$.

Solution

Use the quotient rule to differentiate the function.

$u = e^x - 1$, $u' = e^x$

$v = e^x + 1$, $v' = e^x$

$$f'(x) = \frac{vu' - uv'}{v^2} = \frac{(e^x + 1)(e^x) - (e^x - 1)(e^x)}{(e^x + 1)^2}$$

$$= \frac{e^{2x} + e^x - e^{2x} + e^x}{(e^x + 1)^2}$$

$$= \frac{2e^x}{(e^x + 1)^2}$$

$\dfrac{2e^x}{(e^x + 1)^2} = \dfrac{1}{2}$ \qquad Slope of tangent $= \dfrac{1}{2}$ so $f'(x) = \dfrac{1}{2}$.

$4e^x = (e^x + 1)^2$

$4e^x = e^{2x} + 2e^x + 1$

$e^{2x} - 2e^x + 1 = 0$

$(e^x - 1)(e^x - 1) = 0$ \qquad Factorise and solve for x.

$e^x - 1 = 0$

$e^x = 1$

$\ln(e^x) = \ln(1)$

$x = 0$

$f(0) = \dfrac{e^0 - 1}{e^0 + 1} = \dfrac{1 - 1}{1 + 1} = 0$ \qquad Substitute $x = 0$ in $f(x)$.

The slope of the tangent is $\dfrac{1}{2}$ at $(0, 0)$.

General exponential functions

These formulae are on page 25 of the *Formulae and Tables* booklet.

$f(x) = a^x \Rightarrow f'(x) = a^x \ln a$

As we have seen in other examples, the composite function derivative is based on the standard derivative.

$f(x) = a^{function} \Rightarrow f'(x) = a^{function} \ln a \, (\textbf{\textit{derivative of function}})$

Examples

Find the slope function of:

(a) $y = 4^x$

(b) $y = 5^{\sin(x) + \cos(x)}$.

Solutions

(a) $\dfrac{dy}{dx} = 4^x \ln 4$

(b) $\dfrac{dy}{dx} = 5^{\sin(x) + \cos(x)} \ln 5 \big(\cos(x) - \sin(x) \big)$

> **Remember**
>
> $f(x) = \sin(x) + \cos(x) \Rightarrow f'(x) = \cos(x) - \sin(x)$

Natural logarithm

These formulae are on page 25 of the *Formulae and Tables* booklet.

Standard natural log function:

$f(x) = \ln(x) \Rightarrow f'(x) = \dfrac{1}{x}$

Composite natural log functions:

The derivative of a composite natural log function is based on the standard derivative.

ln(function) $= \dfrac{1}{\text{function}}$ **(derivative of function)**

Examples

Differentiate:

(a) $y = x \ln(x)$

(b) $f(x) = \ln(4x^2 - 1)$.

Solutions

(a) Notice that this is a product of two functions, so we must use the product rule.

$u = x, \ u' = 1$

$v = \ln x, \ v' = \dfrac{1}{x}$

$\dfrac{dy}{dx} = uv' + vu' = x\left(\dfrac{1}{x}\right) + \ln(x)(1) = 1 + \ln(x)$

(b) Use the chain rule for composite natural log functions.

$f'(x) = \dfrac{1}{4x^2 - 1}(8x) = \dfrac{8x}{4x^2 - 1}$

Examples

(a) Find the derivative of $\ln(\cos^2\theta)$. Express your answer in its simplest form.

(b) A light aircraft takes off above sea level and its altitude in feet at time t minutes is given by the function $h(t) = 2010\ln(t + 2)$.

Find the altitude of the aircraft before take-off and at $t = 5$ minutes.

What is the rate of change of altitude at $t = 3$ minutes?

Solutions

(a) First find the derivative of $\cos^2\theta$. Notice that this is the same as $(\cos\theta)^2 = (\cos\theta)(\cos\theta)$, so we can use the product rule.

$u = \cos\theta$, $u' = -\sin\theta$

$v = \cos\theta$, $v' = -\sin\theta$

$uv' + vu' = (\cos\theta)(-\sin\theta) + (\cos\theta)(-\sin\theta) = -2\cos\theta\sin\theta$

Now use this in the formula for the derivative of composite log functions.

$$f'(\theta) = \frac{1}{\cos^2\theta}(-2\cos\theta\sin\theta) = \frac{-2\cos\theta\sin\theta}{\cos^2\theta} = -\frac{2\sin\theta}{\cos\theta} = -2\tan\theta$$

(b) At take-off, $t = 0$. Substitute this into the function.

$$h(0) = 2010\ln(0 + 2) = 2010\ln(2) = 1393$$

The aircraft took off at approximately 1393 feet above sea level.

$$h(5) = 2010\ln(5 + 2) = 2010\ln(7) = 3911$$

After 5 minutes, the aircraft was approximately 3911 feet above sea level.

To find the rate of change at $t = 3$ minutes, differentiate the function then substitute in $t = 3$.

$$\frac{dh}{dt} = 2010\frac{1}{t + 2}(1) = \frac{2010}{t + 2}$$

At 3 minutes, $\dfrac{dh}{dt} = \dfrac{2010}{(3) + 2} = \dfrac{2010}{5} = 402$ feet/minute

We can use properties of logs to simplify more complicated log functions before we differentiate them.

$\ln XY = \ln X + \ln Y$

$\ln \dfrac{X}{Y} = \ln X - \ln Y$

$\ln X^p = p\ln X$

Example

Prove that $f'(x) = \sec(x)$ for the function $f(x) = \ln\sqrt{\dfrac{1 + \sin(x)}{1 - \sin(x)}}$.

Solution

$$\ln\sqrt{\frac{1 + \sin(x)}{1 - \sin(x)}} = \ln\left(\frac{1 + \sin(x)}{1 - \sin(x)}\right)^{\frac{1}{2}} = \frac{1}{2}\ln\left(\frac{1 + \sin(x)}{1 - \sin(x)}\right) \qquad \text{Simplify using } \ln X^{p} = p\ln X.$$

$$= \frac{1}{2}\left[\ln(1 + \sin(x)) - \ln(1 - \sin(x))\right] \qquad \text{Simplify using } \ln\frac{X}{Y} = \ln X - \ln Y.$$

Now we're ready to differentiate!

$$f'(x) = \frac{1}{2}\left[\frac{1}{1 + \sin(x)}(\cos(x)) - \frac{1}{1 - \sin(x)}(-\cos(x))\right] = \frac{1}{2}\left[\frac{\cos(x)}{1 + \sin(x)} + \frac{\cos(x)}{1 - \sin(x)}\right]$$

$$= \frac{1}{2}\left[\frac{\cos(x)(1 - \sin(x)) + \cos(x)(1 + \sin(x))}{1 - \sin^2(x)}\right]$$

$$= \frac{1}{2}\left[\frac{\cos(x) - \cos(x)\sin(x) + \cos(x) + \cos(x)\sin(x)}{\cos^2(x)}\right]$$

$$= \frac{1}{2}\left[\frac{2\cos(x)}{\cos^2(x)}\right] = \frac{\cos(x)}{\cos^2(x)} = \frac{1}{\cos(x)} = \sec(x)$$

Top Tip

Make sure that you are comfortable using trigonometric identities and manipulating trigonometric formulae.

Checklist

✓ Practise differentiating different types of functions.

✓ Practise evaluating derivatives and finding slopes of tangents to curves and equations of tangents to curves.

✓ Practise differentiating composite functions of various types.

✓ Know how to use the product and quotient rules for differentiation: label functions carefully, and don't mix up u and v.

✓ Simplify functions if possible before differentiation, especially natural log functions.

✓ Practise steps for differentiating from first principles for linear and quadratic functions. This will give you easy marks if it appears in the exam.

Differentiation 2

Learning objectives

In this chapter you will learn how to:

- Understand when a function is increasing, decreasing or constant in terms of the rate of change
- Associate derivatives with slopes and tangent lines
- Apply differentiation to
  - Maxima and minima
  - Curve sketching (including the point of inflection)
- Match a function with graphs of its first and second derivatives.

Increasing and decreasing functions

The sign of the slope of a function depends on whether that function is increasing, decreasing or constant. **Increasing** means that the graph of the function slopes **upwards**, **decreasing** means that it slopes **downwards** and **constant** means that there is **no slope**, i.e. the graph is horizontal.

Function	Slope function
$f(x)$ or y	$f'(x)$ or $\dfrac{dy}{dx}$
Increasing	Positive
Decreasing	Negative
Neither increasing nor decreasing (stationary)	Zero

Point to note

Always read a graph from left to right.

Examples

(a) Find the values of $x \in \mathbb{R}$ for which the curve $y = x^2 + 3$ is

    (i) increasing   (ii) decreasing.

(b) Determine where the curve is neither increasing nor decreasing and comment on this point.

(c) Hence draw a rough sketch of the curve $y = f(x)$.

Solutions

(a) (i) $y = x^2 + 3 \implies \dfrac{dy}{dx} = 2x$

      Increasing function $\implies \dfrac{dy}{dx} > 0 \implies 2x > 0 \implies x > 0$

  (ii) Decreasing function $\implies \dfrac{dy}{dx} < 0 \implies 2x < 0 \implies x < 0$

(b) The curve is neither increasing nor decreasing when $\dfrac{dy}{dx} = 0 \implies 2x = 0 \implies x = 0$.

    Find the corresponding y value by substitution: $x = 0 \implies y = (0)^2 + 3 = 3$.

    $(0, 3)$ is a stationary point.

(c)

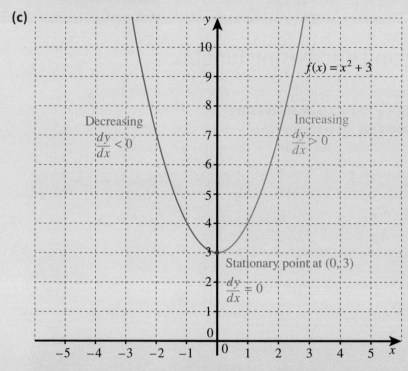

(a) Determine the values of $x \in \mathbb{R}$ for which the curve $f(x) = -2x^2 + 4x$ is decreasing using the graph below. Check your answer using another method.

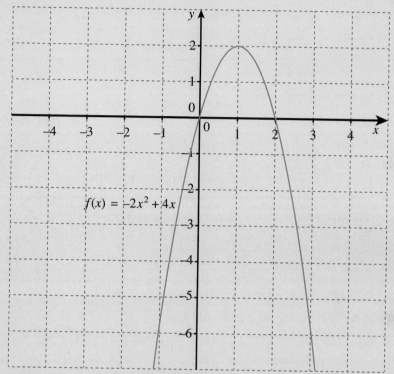

$f(x) = -2x^2 + 4x$

(b) What is the slope of the tangent at $(2, 0)$?

Solutions

(a) From the graph $f(x)$ is decreasing for $x > 1$.

Using differentiation, $f'(x) = -4x + 4$. The curve is decreasing if $f'(x) < 0 \implies -4x + 4 < 0 \implies -4x < -4 \implies x > 1$.

(b) The slope of the tangent at a point $= f'(x)$ at that point.

At $x = 2$, $f'(x) = f'(2) = -4(2) + 4 = -8 + 4 = -4$

Examples

(a) Prove that the curve $y = \dfrac{x + 3}{x - 1}$ is decreasing for all $x \in \mathbb{R}$, $x \neq 1$.

(b) $g(x) = x^3 - x^2 - 8x + 11$

    (i) Find the slope of the tangent to the curve when $x = -2$.

    (ii) For what values of x is the function increasing?

Solutions

(a) Use quotient rule for differentiation: $\dfrac{dy}{dx} = \dfrac{vu' - uv'}{v^2}$

$u = x + 3 \implies u' = 1$

$v = x - 1 \implies v' = 1$

$\dfrac{dy}{dx} = \dfrac{(x - 1)(1) - (x + 3)(1)}{(x - 1)^2} = \dfrac{x - 1 - x - 3}{(x - 1)^2} = \dfrac{-4}{(x - 1)^2}$

If the curve is decreasing then $\dfrac{dy}{dx} < 0$. We must show that $\dfrac{dy}{dx} < 0$ for all values of $x \in \mathbb{R}$, $x \neq 1$.

$-4 < 0$ and $(x - 1)^2 > 0$ for all $x \in \mathbb{R}$, $x \neq 1$.

$\dfrac{\text{negative}}{\text{positive}} = \text{negative}$

So the curve is decreasing for all $x \in \mathbb{R}$, $x \neq 1$.

(b) (i) $g'(x) = 3x^2 - 2x - 8 \implies g'(-2) = 3(-2)^2 - 2(-2) - 8 = 3(4) + 4 - 8 = 8$

    Slope of tangent at $x = -2$ is 8.

(ii) The function is increasing where $g'(x) > 0 \implies 3x^2 - 2x - 8 > 0$

> **Remember**
>
> Recall the method for solving a quadratic inequality from Chapter 5.

$(3x + 4)(x - 2) = 0 \implies x = -\dfrac{4}{3}$ or $x = 2$ Factorise the quadratic and find the roots.

The sign in the inequality is >, so the solution set is outside the roots.

$x < \dfrac{-4}{3}$ or $x > 2$.

Stationary points

Stationary points are points on a graph where the slope of the tangent $= 0$

$\implies \dfrac{dy}{dx} = 0$.

There are three types of stationary points: **local maximum** point, **local minimum** point and **point of inflection**.

To check for these types of points we need to examine the slope at either side of the stationary points.

Turning points are points on the curve where the function changes from increasing to decreasing or decreasing to increasing. All stationary points are turning points, but not all turning points are stationary points.

Consider the graph shown. The turning point at A is a local maximum point, and the turning point at B is a local minimum point.

How do we know if a stationary point is a local maximum or a local minimum? Use the **first derivative test**.

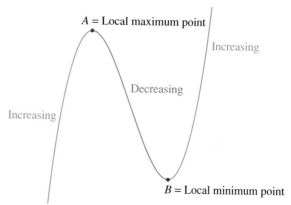

1 Find $\dfrac{dy}{dx}$ (first derivative of the function).

2 Let $\dfrac{dy}{dx} = 0$. Solve the equation and find the corresponding y values. This gives you the stationary points.

3 Test the x values to the left and right of the stationary points in the first derivative.

If $\dfrac{dy}{dx}$ changes from **positive** to **negative** the point is a **local maximum** point.

If $\dfrac{dy}{dx}$ changes from **negative** to **positive** the point is a **local minimum** point.

Example

Find the stationary points for the curve $y = 4x^3 + 2x^2$ and determine the nature of these turning points. Hence draw a rough sketch of the curve.

Solution

$\dfrac{dy}{dx} = 12x^2 + 4x$

$12x^2 + 4x = 0 \Rightarrow 3x^2 + x = 0 \Rightarrow x(3x + 1) = 0 \Rightarrow x = 0$ or $x = -\dfrac{1}{3}$

By substitution, $x = 0 \Rightarrow y = 4(0)^3 + 2(0)^2 = 0$, i.e. $(0, 0)$ is a stationary point.

By substitution, $x = -\dfrac{1}{3} \Rightarrow y = 4\left(-\dfrac{1}{3}\right)^3 + 2\left(-\dfrac{1}{3}\right)^2 = -\dfrac{4}{27} + \dfrac{2}{9} = \dfrac{2}{27}$, i.e. $\left(-\dfrac{1}{3}, \dfrac{2}{27}\right)$ is a stationary point.

Try x values in the region of $(0, 0)$.

x	$-0{\cdot}1$	0	$0{\cdot}1$
$\dfrac{dy}{dx} = 12x^2 + 4x$	$-0{\cdot}28$	0	$0{\cdot}52$
Shape of tangent			

The first derivative changes from negative to positive, so $(0, 0)$ is a local minimum.

Try x values in the region of $\left(-\dfrac{1}{3}, \dfrac{2}{27}\right)$.

Point to note

The table above is called a **nature table**.

x	$-\dfrac{2}{3}$	$-\dfrac{1}{3}$	$-\dfrac{1}{4}$
$\dfrac{dy}{dx} = 12x^2 + 4x$	$\dfrac{8}{3}$	0	$-\dfrac{1}{4}$
Shape of tangent			

The first derivative changes from positive to negative, so $\left(-\dfrac{1}{3}, \dfrac{2}{27}\right)$ is a local maximum.

The curve $y = 4x^3 + 2x^2$ cuts the y-axis at $(0, 0)$.

Find the roots to find out where the curve cuts the x-axis.

$4x^3 + 2x^2 = 0 \Rightarrow 2x^3 + x^2 = 0 \Rightarrow x^2(2x + 1) = 0 \Rightarrow x = 0$ or $x = -\dfrac{1}{2}$.

To sketch the graph, plot the stationary points and roots found above, and join with a smooth curve in the shape of a positive x^3 graph.

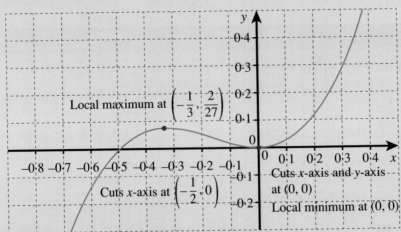

Point of inflection

A **point of inflection** is a stationary point on the curve where the curve changes from concave to convex or vice versa.

Imagine driving along a winding curve, moving the steering wheel as you go. The instant when the steering wheel is straight is the point of inflection.

At a point of inflection, the tangent cuts the curve. The curve is either increasing $\left(\dfrac{dy}{dx} > 0\right)$ on both sides of the point or decreasing $\left(\dfrac{dy}{dx} < 0\right)$ on both sides of the point.

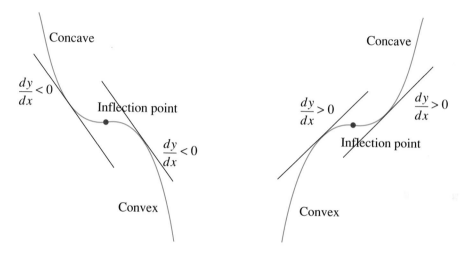

A graph is concave when the second derivative is positive.

A graph is convex when the second derivative is negative.

> **Top-Tip**
>
> If a curve looks like it can hold water then it is concave.
> If it looks like it will spill water then it is convex.

Examples

(a) The equation of a function is $y = 2x^3 - 6x^2 + 6x - 5$.

  (i) Find the co-ordinates of the stationary point of this function.

  (ii) Determine the nature of the stationary point.

(b) The diagram below shows the curve $f(x) = \sin(x)$ in the interval $[0, 2\pi]$.

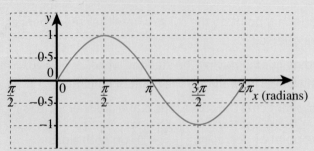

Indicate on the graph where the curve is concave and convex.

Hence indicate on the graph the point of inflection.

Prove your answer using the first derivative test.

Solutions

(a) (i) $\dfrac{dy}{dx} = 6x^2 - 12x + 6 = 0 \implies x^2 - 2x + 1 = 0$ Take out the common factor of 6.

$\implies (x - 1)(x - 1) = 0 \implies x = 1$

By substitution, $x = 1 \implies y = 2(1)^3 - 6(1)^2 + 6(1) - 5 = 2 - 6 + 6 - 5 = -3$

The stationary point is at $(1, -3)$.

(ii) Use the first derivative test to check nature of point. Select suitable values for x to the left and right of $x = 1$ and check the sign of the first derivative.

$x = 0 \implies f'(0) = 6(0)^2 - 12(0) + 6 = 6 > 0$

$x = 2 \implies f'(2) = 6(2)^2 - 12(2) + 6 = 6 > 0$

Since $f'(x)$ is positive on both sides of the stationary point, this must be a point of inflection.

(b)

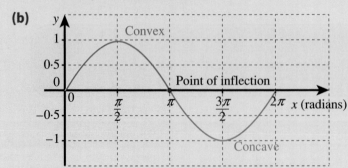

$f(x) = \sin(x) \implies f'(x) = \cos(x)$

Test x values to left and right of $x = \pi$ in the first derivative and check the sign.

$$f'\left(\frac{3\pi}{4}\right) = \cos\left(\frac{3\pi}{4}\right) = -\frac{\sqrt{2}}{2}$$

$$f'\left(\frac{5\pi}{4}\right) = \cos\left(\frac{5\pi}{4}\right) = \frac{-\sqrt{2}}{2}$$

Since $f'(x)$ is negative on both sides of the point, this must be a point of inflection.

Second derivative test for turning points

If $\dfrac{dy}{dx} = 0$ and $\dfrac{d^2y}{dx^2} < 0$ at a point (x_1, y_1) then that point is a local maximum.

If $\dfrac{dy}{dx} = 0$ and $\dfrac{d^2y}{dx^2} > 0$ at a point (x_1, y_1) then that point is a local minimum.

If $\dfrac{d^2y}{dx^2} = 0$ at a point (x_1, y_1) then that point is a point of inflection. The value

of the second derivative changes sign as the curve passes through this point.

Examples

(a) Find the turning points A and B of the curve $y = x^3 - x$, where A is a local maximum and B is a local minimum. Give your answers correct to 2 decimal places.

(b) How many distinct real roots does the curve have?

(c) Does the function have a point of inflection? Justify your answer.

Solutions

(a) Find the co-ordinates of the turning points using the first derivative.

$$\frac{dy}{dx} = 3x^2 - 1 = 0 \implies x^2 = \frac{1}{3} \implies x = \pm\frac{1}{\sqrt{3}} = \pm 0.58$$

Find the corresponding y values by substitution.

$x = 0.58 \implies y = x^3 - x = (0.58)^3 - (0.58) = -0.38$

$x = -0.58 \implies y = 0.38$

The turning points are $(0.58, -0.38)$ and $(-0.58, 0.38)$.

We can use the second derivative test to check the nature of the turning points.

$$\frac{d^2y}{dx^2} = 6x$$

$x = 0.58 \implies \dfrac{d^2y}{dx^2} = 6(0.58) = 3.48 > 0$ so the point is a local minimum.

$x = -0.58 \implies \dfrac{d^2y}{dx^2} = 6(-0.58) = -3.48 < 0$ so the point is a local maximum.

$A = (-0.58, 0.38)$, $B = (0.58, -0.38)$

(b) Plot A and B on a graph.

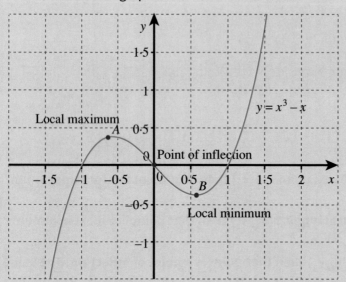

The local maximum and local minimum are on different sides of the x-axis, so the curve has three distinct roots.

(c) Use the second derivative test for a point of inflection.

$\dfrac{d^2y}{dx^2} = 6x = 0 \implies x = 0$

Find the corresponding y value by substitution.

$x = 0 \implies y = x^3 - x = (0)^3 - (0) = 0$

So $(0, 0)$ is a point of inflection.

We can justify this answer by taking x values to the left and right of $x = 0$ and checking if there is a change in sign of the second derivative.

$x = -0.5 \implies \dfrac{d^2y}{dx^2} = 6(-0.5) = -3 < 0$

$x = 0.5 \implies \dfrac{d^2y}{dx^2} = 6(0.5) = 3 > 0$

There is a change in sign, so $(0, 0)$ is a point of inflection.

Example

The function $g(x) = ax^3 + bx^2 + c$ has turning points at $(0, 1)$ and $(1, 0)$.
Find the values of a, b and c where $a > 0$.

Solution

We have to be careful with this type of question. We need to consider both $g(x)$ and $g'(x)$.

Both points are on the curve $g(x)$. We can use this fact to get to equations using a, b and c.

$g(0) = 1 \implies a(0)^3 + b(0)^2 + c = 1 \implies c = 1$

$g(1) = 0 \implies a(1)^3 + b(1)^2 + c = 0 \implies a + b + c = 0 \implies a + b + 1 = 0$

We know that $g'(x) = 0$ for turning points.

$g'(x) = 3ax^2 + 2bx$

$g'(1) = 3a(1)^2 + 2b(1) = 0 \implies 3a + 2b = 0.$

We now have two simultaneous equations with two unknowns.

$a + b = -1$ and $3a + 2b = 0$

$a = -1 - b \implies 3(-1 - b) + 2b = 0 \implies -3 - 3b + 2b = 0 \implies b = -3$

By substitution, $a + b = -1 \implies a - 3 = -1 \implies a = 2.$

So $a = 2$, $b = -3$ and $c = 1$.

Curve sketching

To draw a sketch of a curve, we need to find enough points on the curve to determine the shape. We can use differentiation to find the turning points and points of inflection, which will give a good idea of what the curve looks like. We can also find the y intercepts and x intercepts.

- To find the x intercept, let $y = 0$ and solve for x.

- To find the y intercept, let $x = 0$ and solve or evaluate for y.

- To find the local maxima and minima, and the points of inflection, use the first or second derivative tests.

Top Tip

Finding the x intercepts can sometimes be tricky. If you are having trouble then skip this part and use the other information to sketch the curve.

Example

Sketch the curve $f(x) = x^4 - 4x^3$, showing intercepts, local maxima and minima, and points of inflection.

Solution

Find the intercepts.

$y = 0 \Rightarrow x^4 - 4x^3 = 0$

$\Rightarrow x^3(x - 4) = 0$

$\Rightarrow x^3 = 0$ or $x - 4 = 0$

$\Rightarrow x = 0$ or $x = 4$

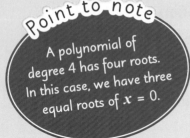

Point to note

A polynomial of degree 4 has four roots. In this case, we have three equal roots of $x = 0$.

The graph intersects the x-axis at $x = 0$ and $x = 4$.

$x = 0 \Rightarrow y = (0)^4 - 4(0)^3 = 0$

The graph intercepts the y-axis at $(0, 0)$.

Find the stationary points by setting the derivative equal to zero and solving for x.

$f'(x) = 4x^3 - 12x^2$

$f'(x) = 0 \Rightarrow 4x^3 - 12x^2 = 0$

$\Rightarrow x^2(x - 3) = 0$

$\Rightarrow x = 0$ or $x = 3$

There are stationary points at $x = 0$ and $x = 3$. Find the corresponding y values by substitution.

$x = 0 \Rightarrow f(0) = 0$ (We already calculated this when finding the intercepts.)

$x = 3 \Rightarrow y = (3)^4 - 4(3)^3 = 81 - 108 = -27$

$(0, 0)$ and $(3, -27)$ are stationary points.

Test for local maximum or minimum using the second derivative test.

$f''(x) = 12x^2 - 24x$

$x = 0 \Rightarrow f''(x) = 12(0)^2 - 24(0) = 0$, so $x = 0$ is not a maximum or a minimum.

Try values either side of 0.

$x = 0.5 \Rightarrow f''(x) = 12(0.5)^2 - 24(0.5) = -9$

$x = -0.5 \Rightarrow f''(x) = 12(-0.5)^2 - 24(-0.5) = 15$

There is a change in sign, so $(0, 0)$ is a point of inflection.

$x = 3 \implies f''(x) = 12(3)^2 - 24(3) = 36 > 0$

This means that $(3, -27)$ is a local minimum point and there is no local maximum point.

Check for another point of inflection (i.e. another point where $f''(x) = 0$).

$f''(x) = 12x^2 - 24x = 0 \implies x^2 - 2x = 0 \implies x(x - 2) = 0$

$\implies x = 0$ or $x = 2$.

This means that there is a second point of inflection at $x = 2$.

Find the corresponding y value by substitution:

$x = 2 \implies y = (2)^4 - 4(2)^3 = 16 - 32 = -16$

There is a second point of inflection at $(2, -16)$.

Summary:

x intercepts: $(0, 0)$ and $(4, 0)$

y intercepts: $(0, 0)$

Local maximum: none

Local minimum: $(3, -27)$

Points of inflection: $(0, 0)$ and $(2, -16)$

Shape of graph: polynomial of degree 4 (quartic) with leading coefficient positive, so both arms of the graph are up.

Plot relevant points, and calculate a point to the left of $x = 0$ if necessary for accuracy.

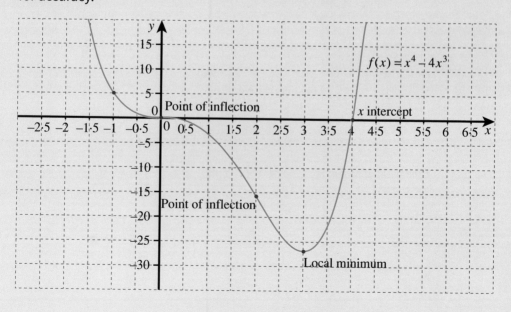

Matching derivatives

A common question is to match a graph to the graph of its derivative (first or second). There are a few things to check for.

- All stationary points of the original curve become roots (points on x-axis) on the graph of the derivative.

- If the original curve is increasing, the derivative is positive (the graph of the derivative will be above the x-axis).

- If the original curve is decreasing, the derivative is negative (the graph of the derivative will be below the x-axis).

A linear function has a constant as its derivative.

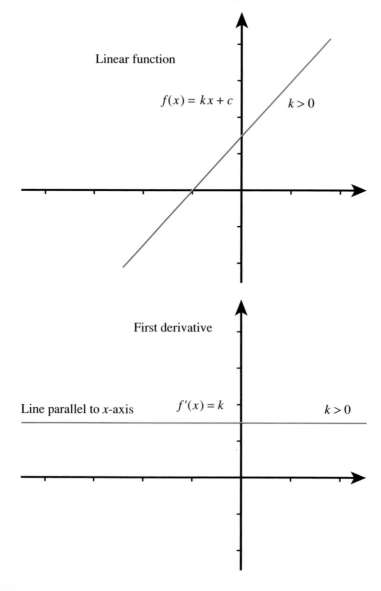

Linear function

$f(x) = kx + c$

$k > 0$

First derivative

Line parallel to x-axis

$f'(x) = k$

$k > 0$

A quadratic function has a linear derivative.

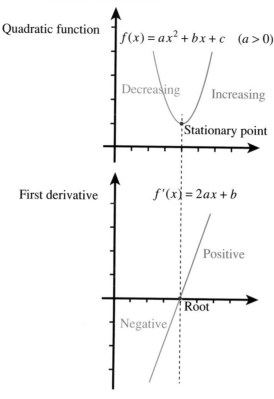

Quadratic function

$f(x) = ax^2 + bx + c \quad (a > 0)$

Decreasing   Increasing

Stationary point

First derivative

$f'(x) = 2ax + b$

Positive

Root

Negative

A cubic function has a quadratic derivative.

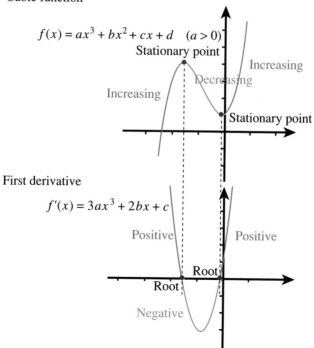

Cubic function

$f(x) = ax^3 + bx^2 + cx + d \quad (a > 0)$

Stationary point

Increasing

Decreasing

Increasing

Stationary point

First derivative

$f'(x) = 3ax^3 + 2bx + c$

Positive   Positive

Root

Root

Negative

A quartic function has a cubic derivative.

Quartic function

$$f(x) = ax^4 + bx^3 + cx^2 + dx + c \quad (a < 0)$$

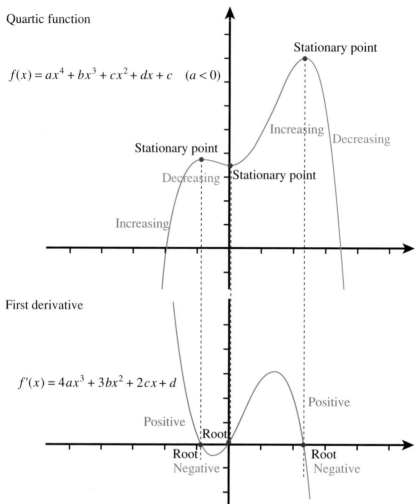

First derivative

$$f'(x) = 4ax^3 + 3bx^2 + 2cx + d$$

Examples

Each diagram below shows part of the graph of a function. Each is one of these: quadratic, cubic, trigonometric or exponential (not necessarily in that order).

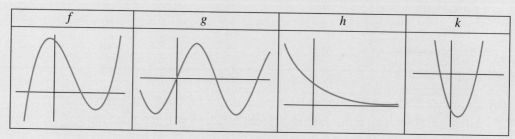

Each diagram below shows part of the graph of the first derivative of one of the above functions (not necessarily in the same order).

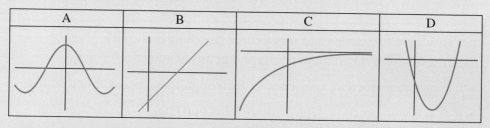

Each diagram below shows part of the graph of the second derivative of one of the original functions (not necessarily in the same order).

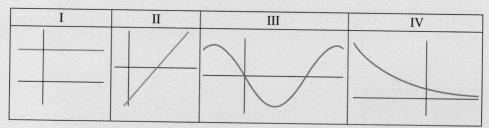

(a) Complete the table below by matching the function to its first derivative and its second derivative.

Type of function	Function	First derivative	Second derivative
Quadratic			
Cubic			
Trigonometric			
Exponential			

(b) For one row in the table, explain your choice of first derivative and second derivative.

(SEC 2013)

Solutions

(a)

Type of function	Function	First derivative	Second derivative
Quadratic	k	B	I
Cubic	f	D	II
Trigonometric	g	A	III
Exponential	h	C	IV

(b) Quadratic: When you differentiate a quadratic function you get a linear function. When you differentiate a linear function you get a constant.

Checklist

✓ Use GeoGebra to practise and check curve sketching and check local maximum and minimum points and points of inflection.

- If $f(x)$ is your function, type in input 'Extremum[f]' to check turning points.

- If $f(x)$ is your function, type in input 'Inflection Point[f]' to check points of inflection.

✓ Practise finding first and second derivatives of functions.

✓ Practise evaluating first and second derivatives.

✓ Know the method for the first and second derivative tests.

Differentiation 3

13

Learning objectives

In this chapter you will learn how to:

- Apply differentiation of functions to solve maximum and minimum problems
- Apply differentiation to real-life problems
- Use differentiation to find the slope of a tangent to a circle
- Apply differentiation to rates of change and related rates of change.

Differentiating with respect to other variables

Most of the differentiation examples we have seen so far have used x as the independent variable. Other variables are sometimes used for particular applications of differentiation. The important thing to remember is that you differentiate the function in exactly the same way, no matter what the independent variable is.

Some examples of variables that are often used are shown in the table below.

Independent variable	Dependent variable	Derivative	Rate of change
t (time)	s (displacement)	$\dfrac{ds}{dt}$	Displacement with respect to time = velocity
x (dimension)	A (area)	$\dfrac{dA}{dx}$	Area with respect to dimension of shape
t (time)	V (volume)	$\dfrac{dV}{dt}$	Volume with respect to time
r (radius)	P (perimeter)	$\dfrac{dP}{dr}$	Perimeter with respect to radius
t (time)	h (height)	$\dfrac{dh}{dt}$	Height with respect to time
t (time)	θ (measure of angle in radians)	$\dfrac{d\theta}{dt}$	Measure of angle with respect to time

Independent variable	Dependent variable	Derivative	Rate of change
t (time)	v (velocity)	$\dfrac{dv}{dt}$	Velocity with respect to time = acceleration
t (time)	S (surface area)	$\dfrac{dS}{dt}$	Surface area with respect to time

These are just a few of the common examples. It is important to label variables and use the correct notation when answering questions.

Maximum and minimum problems

A common exam scenario is to find the maximum or minimum of something, for example the volume of a box, or the area of a patio. You will often be given some constraints, such as the size of the cardboard available, or the number of paving slabs. Use the following steps to answer such questions.

1 Draw and label a diagram with appropriate variables. Sometimes a diagram is given in the question.

2 Decide what you are trying to maximise or minimise. Read the question carefully for key words such as 'at most', 'at least', 'greatest', 'least'.

3 Check if the quantity to be maximised or minimised is in terms of one or two variables. Find an equation linking the variables and write a function in terms of one variable only.

4 Differentiate the function with respect to the independent variable. Let derivative = 0 and solve the equation.

5 If there is more than one solution, use the second derivative test (see Chapter 12) to check if each solution is a maximum or a minimum.

Examples

A sheet of tin measuring 15 cm by 7 cm is shown in the diagram. A square with sides of length x is cut from each corner and a box is formed by folding up the sides.

(a) Find the dimensions of the box in terms of x.

(b) The volume of the box, $V(x)$, can be expressed as
$V(x) = ax^3 + bx^2 + cx + d,$
where $a, b, c, d \in \mathbb{R}$. Find the values of a, b, c and d.

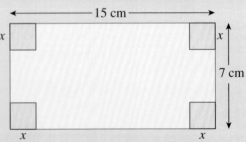

(c) Find the derivative of $V(x)$.

(d) What will be the dimensions of the box with the largest volume?

(e) Hence, find the largest volume of the box.

Solutions

(a) Height = x, width = $7 - 2x$, length = $15 - 2x$

(b) $V(x)$ = height × width × length = $(x)(7 - 2x)(15 - 2x)$

$\qquad = x(105 - 14x - 30x + 4x^2) = 105x - 44x^2 + 4x^3$

So $a = 4$, $b = -44$, $c = 105$, $d = 0$

(c) $\dfrac{dV}{dx} = 105 - 88x + 12x^2$

(d) For maximum volume set $\dfrac{dV}{dx} = 0$ and solve for x.

$12x^2 - 88x + 105 = 0 \Rightarrow (6x - 35)(2x - 3) = 0 \Rightarrow x = \dfrac{35}{6}$ or $x = \dfrac{3}{2}$

Test x values in the second derivative. $\dfrac{d^2x}{dy^2} > 0$ for a minimum point and $\dfrac{d^2x}{dy^2} < 0$ for a maximum point.

$\dfrac{d^2V}{dx^2} = 24x - 88$

$x = \dfrac{35}{6}$ cm $\Rightarrow \dfrac{d^2V}{dx^2} = 24\left(\dfrac{35}{6}\right) - 88 = 140 - 88 > 0$

This length is not possible anyway, as we cannot remove more than half the width of the sheet.

$x = \dfrac{3}{2}$ cm $\Rightarrow \dfrac{d^2V}{dx^2} = 24\left(\dfrac{3}{2}\right) - 88 = 36 - 88 = -52 < 0$

Therefore, a height of $\dfrac{3}{2}$ cm gives the maximum volume of the box. This means that the width is $7 - 2\left(\dfrac{3}{2}\right) = 4$ cm and the height is $15 - 2\left(\dfrac{3}{2}\right) = 12$ cm.

(e) Largest volume = $\dfrac{3}{2}$ × 4 × 12 = 72 cm^3

Examples

A window in the shape of a rectangle surmounted by a semicircle is designed to let in the maximum amount of light.

Clear glass is used for the semicircular part and the rectangular part.

The rectangle measures $2x$ metres in length and y metres in height, as shown in the diagram on page 204.

(a) If the perimeter of the whole window is 12 metres, express y in terms of x.

(b) Hence show that the area of the window, A, is given by $A = 12x - 2x^2 - \dfrac{\pi}{2}x^2$.

(c) Find the length and height that will give the maximum area and allow the maximum amount of light. Give your answer correct to 2 decimal places.

y

$2x$

Solutions

(a) Perimeter = perimeter of rectangle + perimeter of semicircle
$$= 2x + 2y + \pi x = 12$$
$$\Rightarrow 2y = 12 - 2x - \pi x \Rightarrow y = 6 - x - \frac{\pi x}{2}$$

(b) Area of whole window = area of semicircle + area of rectangle $= \dfrac{1}{2}\pi x^2 + 2xy$

$$A = \frac{1}{2}\pi x^2 + 2x\left(6 - x - \frac{\pi x}{2}\right) = \frac{1}{2}\pi x^2 + 12x - 2x^2 - \pi x^2 = 12x - 2x^2 - \frac{\pi}{2}x^2$$

(c) $\dfrac{dA}{dx} = 12 - 4x - \pi x = 0 \Rightarrow 12 = 4x + \pi x$

$$\Rightarrow x(4 + \pi) = 12 \Rightarrow x = \frac{12}{4 + \pi} = 1.68 \text{ m and } y = 6 - (1.68) - \frac{\pi}{2}(1.68) = 1.68 \text{ m}$$

Length $= 2x = 2(1.68) = 3.36$ m and height $= 1.68$ m.

Examples

The graph of the function $f(x) = x^2 - 6x + 12$ is shown in the diagram.

$A = (2, 4)$, $B = (-1, 0)$, $O = (0, 0)$. A triangle ABO is formed by joining these three points.

(a) Find the area of triangle ABO.

(b) A' is another point on the curve. If the area of triangle $A'BO$ = area of triangle ABO, find the co-ordinates of A'.

(c) $A' = (x, y)$ is any point on the curve, $B = (-x, 0)$ is a point on the negative side of the x-axis and $O = (0, 0)$. Show that the area, Q, of this triangle is given by $Q = \dfrac{1}{2}(x^3 - 6x^2 + 12x)$.

(d) Find $\dfrac{dQ}{dx}$ and hence find the maximum area of the triangle.

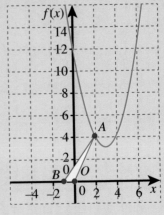

Solutions

(a) Area of triangle $= \frac{1}{2}$ (base × perpendicular height) $= \frac{1}{2}(1)(4) = 2$ square units

> **Point to note**
>
> You could also use the co-ordinate geometry formula for the area of a triangle from the *Formula and Tables* booklet page 18.

(b) $A' = (x, y)$, $B = (-1, 0)$, $O = (0, 0)$

Area of $A'BO = \frac{1}{2}\left| x_1 y_2 - x_2 y_1 \right| = \frac{1}{2}\left| 0 - (-y) \right| = 2$

$\Rightarrow \frac{1}{2}\left| y \right| = 2 \Rightarrow \left| y \right| = 4 \Rightarrow y = 4$ or $y = -4$

−4 isn't on the curve, so $y = 4$.

Find the value of x: $y = x^2 - 6x + 12 \Rightarrow 4 = x^2 - 6x + 12 \Rightarrow x^2 - 6x + 8 = 0$

$\Rightarrow (x - 4)(x - 2) = 0 \Rightarrow x = 4$ or $x = 2$

$(2, 4)$ is point A as given on the diagram, so $A' = (4, 4)$.

(c) Area $= Q = \frac{1}{2}$ (base × perpendicular height)

Base $= x$ units and perpendicular height $= y = f(x)$

So $Q = \frac{1}{2}(x)(x^2 - 6x + 12) = \frac{1}{2}(x^3 - 6x^2 + 12x)$

(d) $\frac{dQ}{dx} = \frac{1}{2}(3x^2 - 12x + 12)$

To find a local maximum or minimum, let $\frac{dQ}{dx} = 0$ and solve for x.

$3x^2 - 12x + 12 = 0 \Rightarrow x^2 - 4x + 4 = 0 \Rightarrow (x - 2)(x - 2) = 0$

$\Rightarrow x = 2$

Maximum area $= \frac{1}{2}(2)(2^2 - 12 + 12) = \frac{1}{2}(2)(4) = 4$ square units

Examples

$ADEC$ is a rectangle with $\left| AC \right| = 7$ m and $\left| AD \right| = 2$ m, as shown.

B is a point on $[AC]$ such that $\left| AB \right| = 5$ m.

P is a point on $[DE]$ such that $\left| DP \right| = x$ m.

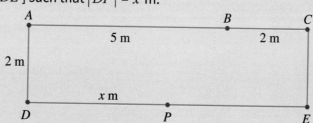

(a) Let $f(x) = |PA|^2 + |PB|^2 + |PC|^2$.

Show that $f(x) = 3x^2 - 24x + 86$, for $0 \leq x \leq 7$, $x \in \mathbb{R}$.

(b) The function $f(x)$ has a minimum value at $x = k$.

Find the value of k and the minimum value of $f(x)$. (SEC 2014)

Solutions

(a) The line segments used in $f(x)$ are the hypotenuses of the right-angled triangles APD, PBM and PCE, where M is the point on the bottom edge of the rectangle, directly below B.

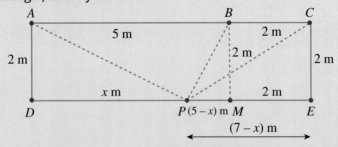

We can use Pythagoras to rewrite $f(x)$ in terms of x.

First find the distance $|PM|$.

$|PM| = |PE| - |ME| = (7 - x) - 2 = 5 - x$

$f(x) = |PA|^2 + |PB|^2 + |PC|^2$

$\quad = \left[|PD|^2 + |DA|^2\right] + \left[|PM|^2 + |MB|^2\right] + \left[|PE|^2 + |EC|^2\right]$

> Use Pythagoras to rewrite $f(x)$ in terms of known distances.

$\quad = x^2 + 2^2 + \left((5 - x^2) + 2^2\right) + \left((7 - x)^2 + 2^2\right)$

> Substitute in the known distances.

$\quad = x^2 + 4 + 25 - 10x + x^2 + 4 + 49 - 14x + x^2 + 4$

> Multiply out the brackets.

$\quad = 3x^2 - 24x + 86$

> Collect like terms to get the equation in the required form.

(b) Method one

$f(x) = 3x^2 - 24x + 86$

$f'(x) = 6x - 24$

$f''(x) = 6 > 0$

> The second derivative is greater than 0, so the function has a minimum point.

$$f'(x) = 0 \Rightarrow 6x - 24 = 0 \Rightarrow x = 4 = k$$

Set the first derivative to 0 and solve to find $x = k$.

$$f(4) = 3(4)^2 - 24(4) + 86 = 38$$

Evaluate $f(x)$ at $x = k = 4$.

The minimum value of $f(x)$ is 38.

Method two

This method involves rearranging $f(x)$ into a form where it is easy to see the minimum value.

$$f(x) = 3x^2 - 24x + 86$$
$$= 3\left(x^2 - 8x + \frac{86}{3}\right)$$
$$= 3\left[(x^2 - 8x + 16) + \frac{38}{3}\right]$$

Add and subtract 16 to complete the square.

$$= 3\left[(x - 4)^2 + \frac{38}{3}\right]$$

$(x - 4)^2$ must be positive, so the minimum value of the function occurs when $(x - 4)^2 = 0$, i.e. when $x = 4$. So $k = 4$.

$$f(4) = 3(4)^2 - 24(4) + 86 = 38$$

Evaluate $f(x)$ at $x = k = 4$.

The minimum value of $f(x)$ is 38.

Examples

A company uses waterproof paper to make disposable conical drinking cups. To make each cup, a sector AOB is cut from a circular piece of paper radius 9 cm. The edges AO and OB are then joined to form the cup, as shown.

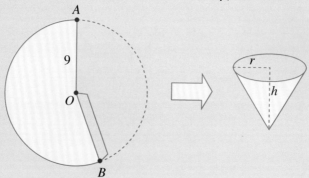

The radius of the rim of the cup is r, and the height of the cup is h.

(a) By expressing r^2 in terms of h, show that the capacity of the cup, in cm³, is given by the formula $V = \frac{\pi}{3}h(81 - h^2)$.

(b) There are two positive values of h for which the capacity of the cup is $\frac{154\pi}{3}$.

One of these values is an integer.

Find the two values.

Give the non-integer value correct to 2 decimal places.

(c) Find the maximum possible volume of the cup, correct to the nearest cm³.

(d) Complete the table below to show the radius, height and capacity of each of the cups involved in parts (b) and (c) above.

In each case, give the radius and height correct to 2 decimal places.

	Cups in part (b)		Cup in part (c)
Radius (r)			
Height (h)			
Capacity (V)	$\frac{154\pi}{3} \approx 161$ cm³	$\frac{154\pi}{3} \approx 161$ cm³	

(e) In practice, which one of the three cups above is the most reasonable shape for a conical cup? Give a reason for your answer.

(f) For the cup you have chosen in part (e), find the measure of the angle AOB that must be cut from the circular disc in order to make the cup.

Give your answer in degrees, correct to the nearest degree.

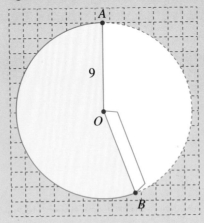

(SEC 2012)

Solutions

(a) The radius, height and slant height of the cone form a right angled triangle, so we can use Pythagoras.

$$r^2 + h^2 = 9^2$$
$$\Rightarrow r^2 = 81 - h^2$$

Now use the formula for the volume of a cone, and substitute in the formula for r^2 from above.

$$V = \frac{1}{3}\pi r^2 h = \frac{\pi h}{3}(81 - h^2)$$

(b) Equate the formula for V with the given capacity, and rearrange to form a cubic equal to zero.

$$\frac{\pi h}{3}(81 - h^2) = \frac{154\pi}{3}$$

$$\Rightarrow h(81 - h^2) = 154$$

$$\Rightarrow h^3 - 81h + 154 = 0$$

The integer root must be a factor of 154, so must be in $\{1, 2, 7, 11, 14, 22, 77, 154\}$. Try each in turn.

$(1)^3 - 81(1) + 154 = 74$, so 1 is not a solution.

$(2)^3 - 81(2) + 154 = 0$, so 2 is a solution and $(h - 2)$ is a factor of the cubic.

Use long division to find the other factors.

$$
\begin{array}{r}
h^2 + 2h - 77 \\
h - 2 \overline{)\, h^3 + 0h^2 - 81h + 154} \\
\underline{h^3 - 2h^2} \\
2h^2 - 81h \\
\underline{2h^2 - 4h} \\
-77h + 154 \\
\underline{-77h + 154} \\
0
\end{array}
$$

$$h^2 + 2h - 77 = 0$$

$$\Rightarrow (h + 1)^2 - 78 = 0$$

$$\Rightarrow h = -1 \pm \sqrt{78}$$

The positive solutions are $h = 2$ and $h \approx 7.83$.

(c) $V = \frac{\pi h}{3}(81 - h^2)$, $h \in [0, 9]$

$$= \frac{\pi}{3}(81h - h^3)$$

$$\frac{dV}{dh} = \frac{\pi}{3}(81 - 3h^2) = \pi(27 - h^2)$$

Setting $\frac{dV}{dh} = 0$ gives $\pi(27 - h^2) = 0 \Rightarrow h = \sqrt{27}$. This is clearly a maximum point, as $V(0) = V(9) = 0$.

Maximum volume $= \frac{\pi}{3}\left(81(\sqrt{27}) - (\sqrt{27})^3\right) = \frac{\pi}{3}\left(81\sqrt{27} - 27\sqrt{27}\right)$

$$= 18\sqrt{27}\pi \approx 29.4 \text{ cm}^3$$

(d)

	Cups in part (b)		Cup in part (c)
Radius (r)	8·77 cm	4·43 cm	7·35 cm
Height (h)	2 cm	7·83 cm	5·20 cm
Capacity (V)	$\dfrac{154\pi}{3} \approx 161$ cm^3	$\dfrac{154\pi}{3} \approx 161$ cm^3	274 cm^3

(e) The middle cup (radius 4·43 cm and height 7·83 cm) is the most reasonable shape. The other cups are much too wide and shallow to hold.

(f) Let θ be the required angle.

Circumference of rim $= 2\pi r \approx 8\cdot86\pi \approx 27\cdot86$ cm

$\theta = \dfrac{l}{r} = \dfrac{27\cdot86}{9} = 3\cdot096$ rad $\approx 177°$ 　　　Multiply the answer in radians by $\dfrac{180}{\pi}$ to get the answer in degrees.

Rates of change

In the table at the start of the chapter we saw examples of rates of change of one quantity with respect to another quantity.

The **rate of change of displacement with respect to time gives velocity** $v = \dfrac{ds}{dt}$.

Velocity can be positive or negative. This indicates the direction of travel. An object with negative velocity is moving in the opposite direction to an object with positive velocity.

If velocity = zero then the object is instantaneously at rest.

The **rate of change of velocity with respect to time is called acceleration** $a = \dfrac{d^2s}{dt^2} = \dfrac{dv}{dt}$.

Examples

A body moves in a straight line so that the distance, s metres, travelled after t seconds is given by the equation of motion

$$s = \frac{2}{3}t^3 - \frac{3}{2}t^2 + t.$$

(a) Find the velocity of the body after 2 seconds.

(b) Find the acceleration of the body after 1 second.

(c) After how many seconds is the body instantaneously at rest? Give your answer correct to 4 decimal places.

(d) Find the initial velocity of the object.

(e) Find the displacement when the acceleration is 12 m/s².

(f) Find the minimum velocity of the object.

Solutions

(a) Velocity $= v = \dfrac{ds}{dt} = \dfrac{2}{3}3t^2 - \dfrac{3}{2}2t + 1 = 2t^2 - 3t + 1$

$t = 2$ seconds $\Rightarrow v = 2(2)^2 - 3(2) + 1 = 20 - 6 + 1 = 3$ m/s

(b) Acceleration $= a = \dfrac{d^2s}{dt^2} = 4t - 3$

$t = 1$ second $\Rightarrow a = 4(1) - 3 = 1$ m/s²

(c) A body at rest has a velocity of $0 \Rightarrow \dfrac{ds}{dt} = 0$.

$2t^2 - 3t + 1 = 0 \Rightarrow (2t - 1)(t - 1) = 0 \Rightarrow t = \dfrac{1}{2}$ or $t = 1$

The object is at rest at 0·5 seconds and 1 second.

(d) The initial velocity is the velocity at $t = 0$. Substitute $t = 0$ into $\dfrac{ds}{dt}$ from part (a).

Initial velocity $= 2(0)^2 - 3(0) + 1 = 1$ m/s

(e) First find the time when acceleration is 12 m/s², by letting $a = 12$ from part (b) and solving for t.

$a = 12 \Rightarrow 4t - 3 = 12 \Rightarrow 4t = 15 \Rightarrow t = 3{·}75$ seconds

Substitute $t = 3{·}75$ into the original formula for displacement.

Displacement $= \dfrac{2}{3}(3{·}75)^3 - \dfrac{3}{2}(3{·}75)^2 + t = 17{·}8125 \approx 17{·}81$ m

(f) The minimum velocity occurs when the derivative of velocity, acceleration, is equal to zero.

$a = 4t - 3 = 0 \Rightarrow t = \dfrac{3}{4} = 0{·}75$ seconds

Substitute $t = 0{·}75$ into the formula for velocity.

Velocity $= 2(0{·}75)^2 - 3(0{·}75) + 1 = -0{·}125$ m/s

Point to note

Notice that the velocity in part (f) is negative. This means that the object was travelling at a speed of 0·125 m/s in the negative direction.

Top Tip

Remember to include units for displacement (m), velocity (m/s or m s^{-1}) and acceleration (m/s² or m s^{-2}). You'll lose marks if you leave them out.

Implicit differentiation

How do we differentiate functions of the type $x^2 + y^2 = 20$
or $x^2 + y^2 - 2x + y - 3 = 0$?

These are **implicit functions**.

> ## Point to note
>
> An implicit function is a function that does not directly relate one variable to another.
>
> Some implicit functions can easily be rewritten as explicit functions.
>
> For example, $x^2 + y^2 = 20$ can be rewritten as $y = \sqrt{20 - x^2}$.
>
> Other implicit functions are much harder to rewrite, for example,
>
> $\sin(xy)^2 + \cos\left(\dfrac{x}{y}\right) = \dfrac{2x}{y^3}$.

To differentiate an implicit function with respect to x, we can refer to the **chain rule** on page 25 of the *Formulae and Tables* booklet.

$$f'(x) = \frac{du}{dv} \cdot \frac{dv}{dx}$$

This can be written in more general terms as:

$$\frac{d(y)}{dx} = \frac{d(y)}{dy} \cdot \frac{dy}{dx} = 1\left(\frac{dy}{dx}\right) = \frac{dy}{dx}$$

$$\frac{d(y^2)}{dx} = \frac{d(y^2)}{dy} \cdot \frac{dy}{dx} = 2y\frac{dy}{dx}$$

In practical terms, to differentiate an implicit function we differentiate each term on both sides with respect to x. Whenever we come across a term containing y, we differentiate that term using the chain rule.

Example

The equation of a circle is $x^2 + y^2 = 20$. Find $\dfrac{dy}{dx}$ and hence find the slope of the tangent to the circle at the point $(2, 4)$.

Solution

$$\frac{d(x^2)}{dx} + \frac{d(y^2)}{dx} = \frac{d(20)}{dx}$$

Differentiate each term in turn with respect to x.

$f(x) = x^2 \Rightarrow f'(x) = 2x$ Differentiate x^2 as normal.

$g(x) = y^2 \Rightarrow g'(x) = 2y\left(\dfrac{dy}{dx}\right)$ Differentiate y^2 using the chain rule.

$h(x) = 20 \Rightarrow h'(x) = 0$ 20 is a constant, so it goes to 0 when it is differentiated.

Now put the differentiated terms together, and rearrange so that $\dfrac{dy}{dx}$ is on the left.

$$2x + 2y\left(\frac{dy}{dx}\right) = 0$$

$$2y\left(\frac{dy}{dx}\right) = -2x$$

$$\frac{dy}{dx} = \frac{-2x}{2y} = -\frac{x}{y}$$

At (2, 4), the slope of the tangent $= \dfrac{dy}{dx} = -\dfrac{x}{y} = -\dfrac{(2)}{(4)} = -\dfrac{1}{2}$.

Example

The equation of a circle, c, is $x^2 + y^2 - 2x - y + 1 = 0$.

Find the equation of the tangent to the circle at (1, 1).

Solution

$$\frac{d(x^2)}{dx} + \frac{d(y^2)}{dx} - \frac{d(2x)}{dx} - \frac{d(y)}{dx} + \frac{d(1)}{dx} = 0$$

$$2x + 2y\left(\frac{dy}{dx}\right) - 2 - \left(\frac{dy}{dx}\right) + 0 = 0$$

$\dfrac{dy}{dx}(2y - 1) = -2x + 2$ Rearrange, keeping $\dfrac{dy}{dx}$ terms on the left-hand side.

$$\frac{dy}{dx} = \frac{-2x + 2}{2y - 1}$$

Substitute (1, 1) into $\dfrac{dy}{dx}$ to find the slope of the tangent.

$$\frac{dy}{dx} = \frac{-2(1) + 2}{2(1) - 1} = 0$$

The equation of the tangent is $y - 1 = 0(x - 1) \Rightarrow y = 1$.

Related rates of change

We have seen some examples of rates of change. Now we can relate rates of change when we have one rate of change and we need to find another. We can do this using the chain rule.

For example, $\dfrac{dA}{dt} = \dfrac{dA}{dr}\dfrac{dr}{dt}$, $\dfrac{dh}{dt} = \dfrac{dh}{d\theta}\dfrac{d\theta}{dt}$, $\dfrac{dV}{dt} = \dfrac{dV}{dh}\dfrac{dh}{dt}$.

Method for solving related rates of change:

1. Draw a diagram (sometimes a diagram is given) and label it using appropriate variables (h = height, A = area, S = surface area, V = volume, P = perimeter, t = time, θ = angle, etc.).

2. Write down the relevant formulae for area, perpendicular height, volume, surface area of the shape or object.

3. Write an equation that relates the variables. You may have to combine two or more equations to get a single equation in terms of one variable. Write down what rate of change you are given.

4. Use the chain rule to connect all the rates of change: what is given, what you need to find, and the missing link.

5. Evaluate. Use the known value to find the unknown rate.

Example

The radius of a circle is increasing at the rate of 4 cm/s. Find the rate at which the area of the circle is increasing when the radius is 2 cm.

Solution

Draw a diagram of the circle and label the radius (r) and the area (A).

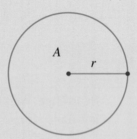

The relevant formula is $A = \pi r^2$. There is only one equation in this example.

We are given the rate of change of radius with respect to time: $\dfrac{dr}{dt} = 4$ cm/s.

We require the rate of change of area with respect to time: $\dfrac{dA}{dt}$.

Chain rule: $\dfrac{dA}{dt} = \dfrac{dA}{dr}\dfrac{dr}{dt}$.

The missing link is $\dfrac{dA}{dr} = 2\pi r$.

$\dfrac{dA}{dt} = \dfrac{dA}{dr}\dfrac{dr}{dt} \Rightarrow \dfrac{dA}{dt} = (2\pi r)(4) = 8\pi r$

Evaluate using $r = 2$ cm. $\dfrac{dA}{dt} = 8\pi(2) = 16\pi = 50{\cdot}3$ cm²/s

Example

A balloon leaves the ground 400 metres away from a base and rises vertically from a level field. At a specific instant the angle of elevation from the base is $\frac{\pi}{6}$ radians and the angle is increasing at the rate of 0·1 radians per minute. How fast is the balloon rising at that instant?

Solution

Point to note

Angle of elevation increasing with respect to time $= \dfrac{d\theta}{dt}$.

How fast balloon is rising $= \dfrac{dh}{dt}$.

Draw and label a diagram. Let θ be the angle of elevation and h be the height of the balloon.

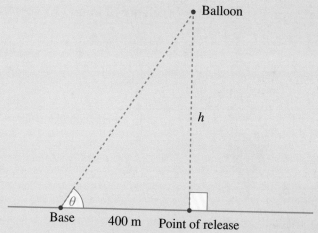

We have a right-angled triangle so we can use $\tan \theta = \dfrac{\text{opp}}{\text{adj}} = \dfrac{h}{400} \Rightarrow h = 400 \tan \theta$.

There is only one equation in this example.

We are given the rate of change of angle with respect to time: $\dfrac{d\theta}{dt} = 0\cdot1$ rad/minute.

We require the rate of change of height with respect to time: $\dfrac{dh}{dt}$.

Chain rule: $\dfrac{dh}{dt} = \dfrac{dh}{d\theta} \dfrac{d\theta}{dt}$

Remember

The derivative of $\tan \theta = \sec^2 \theta$.

The missing link is $\dfrac{dh}{d\theta} = 400 \sec^2 \theta$.

$\dfrac{dh}{dt} = (400 \sec^2 \theta)(0\cdot1)$

$$\sec\theta = \frac{1}{\cos\theta} = \frac{1}{\cos\frac{\pi}{6}} = \frac{1}{\frac{\sqrt{3}}{2}} = \frac{2}{\sqrt{3}}$$

Evaluate $\sec\theta$ at $\theta = \frac{\pi}{6}$.

$$\frac{dh}{dt} = 400\left(\frac{2}{\sqrt{3}}\right)^2(0\cdot1) = 400\left(\frac{4}{3}\right)(0\cdot1) = 53\cdot3 \text{ metres/minute}$$

Substitute into equation for $\frac{dh}{dt}$.

The balloon is rising at 53·3 metres/minute at that instant.

Example

Water is poured into a container in the shape of a cone at a rate of 9 m³/minute. The container has a perpendicular height of 4 metres and a base radius of 1·5 metres. Find how quickly the water level is rising when the water is 2 metres deep.

Solution

Draw a diagram of a cone. Label radius (r), depth of water (h), volume (V).

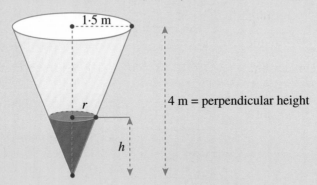

4 m = perpendicular height

We are given $\frac{dV}{dt}$, the rate of change of the volume of water with respect to time.

We require $\frac{dh}{dt}$, the rate of change of the water level with respect to time.

Chain rule: $\dfrac{dV}{dt} = \dfrac{dV}{dh}\dfrac{dh}{dt}$

The missing link is $\frac{dV}{dh}$. This means that we need a formula for V in terms of h.

$$V = \frac{1}{3}\pi r^2 h$$

From the diagram, we can connect the radius and depth using similar triangles.

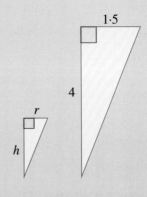

$$\frac{r}{h} = \frac{1\cdot5}{4} = \frac{3}{8} \Rightarrow 3h = 8r \Rightarrow r = \frac{3}{8}h$$

Combine the equations for V and h to get a formula for V in terms of h.

$$V = \frac{1}{3}\pi r^2 h = \frac{1}{3}\pi\left(\frac{3}{8}h\right)^2 h = \frac{3}{64}\pi h^3 \implies \frac{dV}{dh} = \frac{9}{64}\pi h^2$$

Now use the chain rule.

$$\frac{dV}{dt} = \frac{dV}{dh}\frac{dh}{dt} \implies (9) = \left(\frac{9}{64}\pi h^2\right)\left(\frac{dh}{dt}\right)$$

$$\implies \frac{dh}{dt}\pi h^2 = 64 \implies \frac{dh}{dt} = \frac{64}{\pi h^2}$$

Evaluate for $h = 2$: $\quad \dfrac{dh}{dt} = \dfrac{64}{\pi(2)^2} = \dfrac{16}{\pi} = 5{\cdot}09$

The water is rising at a rate of 5·09 metres/minute.

Checklist

✓ Know how to differentiate with respect to different variables.

✓ Practise the steps required for maximum and minimum problems.

✓ Always use a diagram and label it carefully.

✓ Read the question carefully and decide what quantity is required to be maximised or minimised.

✓ Practise the steps required for problems involving related rates of change.

14 Integration

Learning objectives

In this chapter you will learn how to:

- Recognise integration as the reverse process of differentiation
- Recognise the indefinite anti-derivative and distinct anti-derivative of a function
- Integrate sums, differences and constant multiples of the form
  - x^n where $n \in \mathbb{Q}$
  - a^x where $a \in \mathbb{R}, a > 0$
  - $\sin(ax)$ where $a \in \mathbb{R}$
  - $\cos(ax)$ where $a \in \mathbb{R}$
- Use the trapezoidal rule to approximate area
- Determine the areas of plane regions bounded by functions
- Use integration to find the average value of a function over an interval.

Introduction

We know the reverse process of moving clockwise is moving anti-clockwise. We need anti-virus software on our computer to stop or reverse any viruses. With calculus, **anti-differentiation** is the reverse process of differentiation.

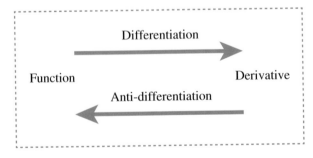

Examples

Match each function to its correct derivative from the list below. You may use each answer more than once.

$\cos(x)$	6	x	$2x$

Function $f(x)$	Derivative $f'(x)$
$\frac{1}{2}x^2$	
$\frac{1}{2}x^2 + 2$	
$6x$	
$6x + 3$	
$6x - 5$	
$\sin(x) - 4$	
$\sin(x)$	
$\sin(x) + 4$	
x^2	
$\frac{x^2}{2} - 1$	

Solutions

Function $f(x)$	Derivative $f'(x)$
$\frac{1}{2}x^2$	x
$\frac{1}{2}x^2 + 2$	x
$6x$	6
$6x + 3$	6
$6x - 5$	6
$\sin(x) - 4$	$\cos(x)$
$\sin(x)$	$\cos(x)$
$\sin(x) + 4$	$\cos(x)$
x^2	$2x$
$\frac{x^2}{2} - 1$	x

Notice that the derivatives of similar types of functions which include a constant are the same. This means that we have to include an arbitrary constant, $+c$, when we find the anti-derivative of any function. This is called the **constant of integration**.

The anti-derivative with the arbitrary constant is called the **indefinite form** of the anti-derivative, or the **indefinite integral** of the function. It is defined as the set of all anti-derivatives of the function.

We write it as $\int f(x) = F(x) + c$, where $\int$ is the integration symbol.

Function	Anti-derivative
6	$6x + c$
x	$\dfrac{x^2}{2} + c$
$\cos(x)$	$\sin(x) + c$
x^2	$\dfrac{x^3}{3} + c$

If we want a **distinct anti-derivative**, we simply replace c with any constant. Exam questions often give initial conditions that specify the constant to be used, or allow it to be worked out.

Working out the indefinite integral

The following sections show how to work out the indefinite integral for different types of function. The general form is shown in each case, followed by some examples.

Constants

Function $= k \Rightarrow$ Indefinite integral $= F(x) = kx + c$

Examples:

$f(x)$	$f'(x)$	Function	Indefinite integral
x	1	1	$x + c$
$2x$	2	2	$2x + c$

Functions of the form x^n

Function $= x^n \Rightarrow$ Indefinite integral $= F(x) = \dfrac{x^{n+1}}{n+1} + c$

Examples:

$f(x)$	$f'(x)$	Function	Indefinite integral
$\dfrac{x^2}{2}$	x	x	$\dfrac{x^2}{2} + c$
$\dfrac{x^3}{2}$	x^2	x^2	$\dfrac{x^3}{2} + c$
x^2	$2x$	$2x$	$x^2 + c$
x^3	$3x^2$	$3x^2$	$x^3 + c$

Point to note

$\int \dfrac{1}{x} = \ln|x| + c, x \neq 0$

$\int (f(x) \pm g(x))\, dx = \int f(x) \pm \int g(x)$

The integral of a sum or difference = sum or difference of the integrals.

$\int k\, f(x)\, dx = k \int f(x)\, dx$

The constant k can be moved outside the integral.

Examples

(a) Write down three distinct anti-derivatives of the function
$g: x \rightarrow x^3 - 3x^2 + 3, x \in \mathbb{R}$.

(b) Explain what is meant by the indefinite integral of a function f.

(c) Write down the indefinite integral of g, the function in part (a).

Solutions

(a) $\dfrac{x^4}{4} - x^3 + 3x + 1$

$\dfrac{x^4}{4} - x^3 + 3x - 5$

$\dfrac{x^4}{4} - x^3 + 3x + 20$

Point to note

Unless otherwise specified, any constant can be used for a distinct anti-derivative.

(b) The indefinite integral of a function f is the set of all anti-derivatives of f.

(c) $\int x^3 - 3x^2 + 3 = \dfrac{x^4}{4} - x^3 + 3x + c$

Example

A curve $f(x)$ contains the point $(-1, 0)$. If $f'(x) = 2x^2 - 6$, find $f(x)$.

Solution

$f(x)$ is the anti-derivative (indefinite integral) of $2x^2 - 6$.

$$\int 2x^2 - 6 = \frac{2x^3}{3} - 6x + c$$

$$f(x) = y = \frac{2x^3}{3} - 6x + c$$

$(-1, 0)$ is on the curve, so substituting $x = -1$ into the function gives a y value of 0.

$$0 = 2\frac{(-1)^3}{3} - 6(-1) + c$$

$$0 = \frac{-2}{3} + 6 + c \Rightarrow c = \frac{2}{3} - 6 = \frac{-16}{3}$$

$$f(x) = \frac{2x^3}{3} - 6x - \frac{16}{3}$$

> **Point to note**
>
> In this question we were given an initial condition (the point on the curve) so we could find the constant of integration.

Trigonometric functions

$$\int \cos(x)\, dx = \sin(x) + c$$

$$\int \cos(ax)\, dx = \frac{\sin(ax)}{a} + c, \text{ where } a \text{ is a constant}$$

$$\int \sin(x)\, dx = -\cos(x) + c$$

$$\int \sin(ax)\, dx = -\frac{\cos(ax)}{a} + c, \text{ where } a \text{ is a constant}$$

Point to note

Notice the change of sign for $\sin(x)$!

$f(x)$	$f'(x)$	Function	Indefinite integral
$\sin 2x$	$2\cos 2x$	$2\cos 2x$	$\sin 2x + c$
		$\cos 2x$	$\dfrac{\sin 2x}{2} + c$
$\cos 3x$	$-3\sin 3x$	$-3\sin 3x$	$\cos 3x + c$
		$\sin 3x$	$\dfrac{-\cos 3x}{3} + c$

Exponential functions

These formulae are on page 26 of the *Formulae and Tables* booklet.

$$\int e^x dx = e^x + c$$

$$\int e^{ax} dx = \frac{e^{ax}}{a} + c$$

$$\int a^x dx = \frac{a^x}{\ln a} + c$$

$f(x)$	$f'(x)$	Function	Indefinite integral
e^{3x}	$3e^{3x}$	$3e^{3x}$	$e^{3x} + c$
		e^{3x}	$\dfrac{e^{3x}}{3} + c$
4^x	$4^x \ln 4$	$4^x \ln 4$	$a^x + c$
		4^x	$\dfrac{4^x}{\ln 4} + c$

Numerical methods for finding area under a curve

Consider the graph of $f(x) = x^2$ as shown in the diagram. We want to find the area between the curve and the x-axis from $x = 0$ to $x = 4$.

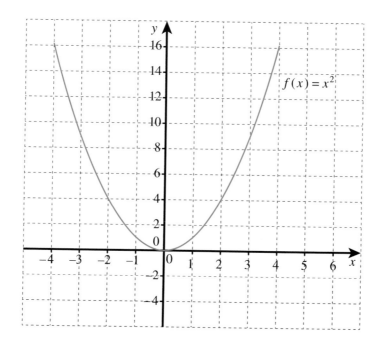

We require suitable shapes to approximate this area. A triangle would be okay, but rectangles or trapeziums would give a better approximation of the area.

Point to note

The formula for the area of a trapezium is on page 8 of the *Formulae and Tables* booklet.

$$A = \left(\frac{a + b}{2}\right)h$$

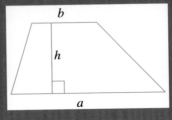

In the given diagram we are going to use one triangle (starting at $x = 0$) and three trapeziums to approximate the area under the curve. We can add each area or we can use the trapezoidal rule to get the answer.

Point to note

The trapezoidal rule is on page 12 of the *Formulae and Tables* booklet.

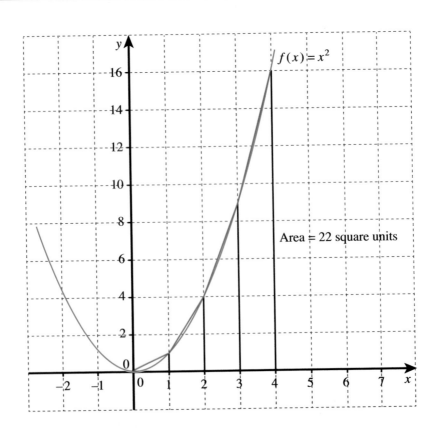

Top-Tip

An easy way to remember the trapezoidal rule is

Area $\approx \frac{h}{2}$[first height + last height + 2(sum of remaining heights)], where

h is the width of each interval and the heights correspond to the y values.

In the example, $h = 1$, first height = 0, last height = 16, remaining heights = 1, 4, 9.

Area $\approx \frac{1}{2}(0 + 16 + 2(1 + 4 + 9)) = \frac{1}{2}(16 + 28) = 22$ square units

In the above example, we could get a better approximation by increasing the number of trapezoids, so the width of each interval would get smaller.

The area beneath a function may be calculated using the limit of an infinite sum of thinner and thinner rectangles, as can be seen in this diagram.

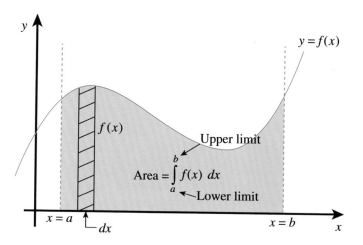

Area $= \int_{a}^{b} f(x)\,dx = F(b) - F(a) = $ area beneath function $f(x)$ from $x = a$ to $x = b$,

where:

$f(x)$ = height of rectangle

dx = width of a very thin rectangle

$\int$ is a summation symbol which represents the sum of the rectangles

a and b are the lower and upper limits

$F(a)$ and $F(b)$ are the indefinite integrals of the lower and upper limits (the constants cancel out).

Leibnitz used the integration symbol $\int$, which we still use today, as the sum of the areas under a curve.

> **Point to note**
>
> Use a definite integral to find the exact (true) area under a curve. This is called **definite integration**.

Examples

Evaluate the following:

(a) $\displaystyle\int_1^2 x^2\,dx$

(b) $\displaystyle\int_1^4 2 - \sqrt{t}\,dt$

(c) $\displaystyle\int_0^\pi 2\sin x\,dx$

(d) $\displaystyle\int_0^{\frac{\pi}{2}} (\sin 2x - \cos 3x)\,dx$

(e) $\displaystyle\int_1^2 \left(\frac{2}{x} - 4x\right) dx$

(f) $\displaystyle\int_0^1 e^{4x}\,dx$

(g) $\displaystyle\int_0^3 \frac{x^2 - 4}{x+2}\,dx$

Solutions

(a) $\displaystyle\int_1^2 x^2\,dx = \frac{x^3}{3}\bigg|_1^2 = \frac{(2)^3}{3} - \frac{(1)^3}{3} = \frac{7}{3}$

> **Point to note**
>
> The notation $F(x)\big|_a^b$ means $F(b) - F(a)$.
> It can also be written as $\left[F(x)\right]_a^b$.

(b) $\displaystyle\int_1^4 \left(2 - t^{\frac{1}{2}}\right) dt = \left|2t - \frac{t^{\frac{3}{2}}}{\frac{3}{2}}\right|_1^4 = \left(2t - \frac{2}{3}t^{\frac{3}{2}}\right)\bigg|_1^4 = \left(2(4) - \frac{2}{3}(4)^{\frac{3}{2}}\right) - \left(2(1) - \frac{2}{3}(1)^{\frac{3}{2}}\right)$

$= \left(8 - \frac{2}{3}(8)\right) - \left(2 - \frac{2}{3}(1)\right) = \left(\frac{8}{3}\right) - \left(\frac{4}{3}\right) = \frac{4}{3}$

(c) $\displaystyle\int_0^\pi 2\sin x \, dx = 2\int_0^\pi 2\sin x \, dx = -2\cos x \Big|_0^\pi = (-2\cos(\pi)) - (-2\cos(0))$

$$= (-2(-1)) - (-2(1)) = 2 + 2 = 4$$

(d) $\displaystyle\int_0^{\frac{\pi}{2}} \sin 2x - \cos 3x \, dx = \left(\frac{-\cos 2x}{2} - \frac{\sin 3x}{3}\right)\Big|_0^{\frac{\pi}{2}}$

$$= \left(\frac{-\cos 2\left(\frac{\pi}{2}\right)}{2} - \frac{\sin 3\left(\frac{\pi}{2}\right)}{3}\right) - \left(\frac{-\cos(0)}{2} - \frac{\sin(0)}{3}\right)$$

$$= \left(\frac{1}{2} + \frac{1}{3}\right) - \left(\frac{-1}{2}\right) = \frac{5}{6} + \frac{1}{2} = \frac{4}{3}$$

(e) $\displaystyle\int_1^2 \left(\frac{2}{x} - 4x\right) dx = 2\int \frac{1}{x}dx - 4\int x\,dx = \left(2\ln x - 4\frac{x^2}{2}\right)\Big|_1^2$

$$= \left[2\ln(2) - 4\left(\frac{(2)^2}{2}\right)\right] - \left[2\ln(1) - 4\left(\frac{(1)^2}{2}\right)\right]$$

$$= (2\ln 2 - 8) - (0 - 2) = 2\ln 2 - 6$$

(f) $\displaystyle\int_0^1 e^{4x} dx = \frac{e^{4x}}{4}\Big|_0^1 = \left(\frac{e^{4(1)}}{4}\right) - \left(\frac{e^{4(0)}}{4}\right) = \frac{e^4}{4} - \frac{1}{4} = \frac{e^4 - 1}{4}$

(g) $\displaystyle\frac{x^2 - 4}{x + 2} = \frac{(x-2)(x+2)}{(x+2)} = x - 2$ Simplify the function first.

$$\int_0^3 (x - 2)dx = \left(\frac{x^2}{2} - 2x\right)\Big|_0^3 = \left(\frac{(3)^2}{2} - 2(3)\right) - \left(\frac{(0)^2}{2} - 2(0)\right) = -\frac{3}{2}$$

When using definite integration:

- Area above the x-axis is positive
- Area under the x-axis is negative so use the absolute value to get a positive value for area
- If there are areas above and below the x-axis, find each area separately and add them
- Area about the y-axis to the right is positive
- Area about the y-axis to the left is negative so use the absolute value to have a positive value for area.

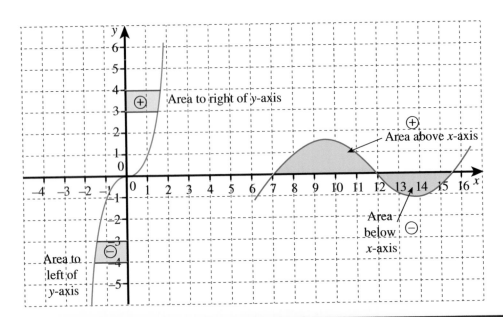

Examples

(a) Use the trapezoidal rule to approximate the area between the curve
$g(x) = x^2 - 4$ and the x-axis as shown in the diagram.

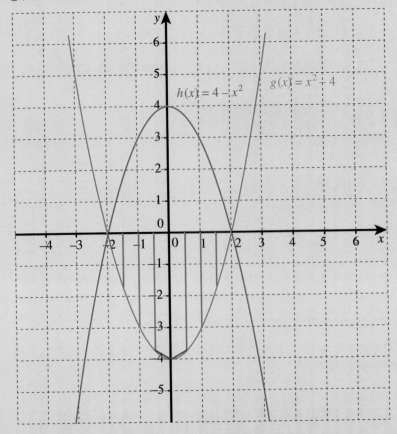

$h(x) = 4 - x^2$ $g(x) = x^2 - 4$

(b) Hence or otherwise find an approximate area between the curve $h(x)$ and the x-axis. Comment on your answers for both areas.

(c) Suggest a way to improve the approximation for each area.

(d) Find the exact value of the area between the curve $g(x) = x^2 - 4$ and the x-axis using integration. Hence, find the percentage error in your answer to part (a).

Solutions

(a) $g(x) = x^2 - 4$. Using a calculator we can evaluate the y values (heights).

First height $= g(-2) = 0$, last height $= g(2) = 0$

Remaining heights: $g(-1\cdot5) = -1\cdot75$, $g(-1) = -3$, $g(-0\cdot5) = -3\cdot75$, $g(0) = -4$, $g(0\cdot5) = -3\cdot75$, $g(1) = -3$, $g(1\cdot5) = -1\cdot75$

Notice the symmetry of the y values. This is obvious from the shape of the graph.

h = width of interval $= \dfrac{1}{2}$

Using the trapezoidal rule:

Area $\approx \dfrac{h}{2}$[first height + last height + 2(sum of remaining heights)]

$= 2[0 + 0 + 2(-1\cdot75 - 3 - 3\cdot75 - 4 - 3\cdot75 - 3 - 1\cdot75)]$

$= |-10\cdot5| = 10\cdot5$ square units

(b) Approximate area $= 10\cdot5$ square units

The area enclosed is the same, because $h(x)$ is the reflection of $g(x)$ in the x-axis.

(c) A better approximation for each area can be found by increasing the number of trapezoids used in calculating the area.

(d) Area $= \displaystyle\int_{-2}^{2} (x^2 - 4)\, dx = \dfrac{x^3}{3} - 4x \Big|_{-2}^{2} = \left(\dfrac{(2)^3}{3} - 4(2)\right) - \left(\dfrac{(-2)^3}{3} - 4(-2)\right)$

$= \left(\dfrac{-16}{3}\right) - \left(\dfrac{16}{3}\right) = -\dfrac{32}{3}$

Area $= \left|-\dfrac{32}{3}\right| = \dfrac{32}{3} = 10\dfrac{2}{3}$ square units

Percentage error $= \dfrac{10\dfrac{2}{3} - 10\cdot5}{10\dfrac{2}{3}} \times 100 = 1\cdot5625\%$

Examples

The diagram shows the graph of the function $y = \sin x$ in the domain $0 \le x \le \pi$, $x \in \mathbb{R}$.

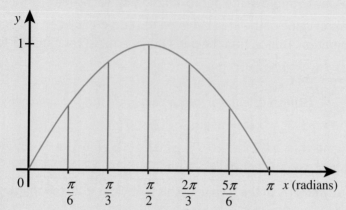

(a) Complete the table below, correct to 3 decimal places.

x	0	$\dfrac{\pi}{6}$	$\dfrac{\pi}{3}$	$\dfrac{\pi}{2}$	$\dfrac{2\pi}{3}$	$\dfrac{5\pi}{6}$	π
y							

(b) Use the trapezoidal rule to find the approximate area of the region enclosed between the curve and the x-axis in the given domain.

(c) Use integration to find the actual area of the region shown above.

(d) Find the percentage error in your answer to (b) above.

Solutions

(a)

x	0	$\dfrac{\pi}{6}$	$\dfrac{\pi}{3}$	$\dfrac{\pi}{2}$	$\dfrac{2\pi}{3}$	$\dfrac{5\pi}{6}$	π
y	0	0·5	0·866	1	0·866	0·5	0

(b) Use the y values from part (a).

$$A = \frac{h}{2}\left[y_1 + y_n + 2(y_2 + y_3 + y_4 + \ldots + y_{n-1})\right]$$

$$= \frac{\pi}{12}\left[0 + 0 + 2(0·5 + 0·866 + 1 + 0·866 + 0·5)\right]$$

$$= 1·95407$$

(c) $\displaystyle\int_0^\pi \sin x\,dx = -\cos x \Big|_0^\pi = -\cos(\pi) - (-\cos(0)) = -1 - 1 = -2$

Area $= |-2| = 2$.

(d) Percentage error $= \dfrac{2 - 1·95407}{2} \times 100 = 2·2965 = 2·3\%$.

To find the area bounded by a curve and the y-axis:

1 Write x as a function of y.

2 Integrate with respect to y and evaluate using limits.

Example

Find the area bounded by the curve $y = x^3$, the y-axis and the lines $y = 8$ and $y = 1$.

Solution

Write x as a function of y: $x^3 = y \Rightarrow x = y^{\frac{1}{3}}$.

Integrate with respect to y and evaluate using limits:

$$\text{Area} = \int_{1}^{8} y^{\frac{1}{3}} \, dy = \frac{3}{4} y^{\frac{4}{3}} \Big|_{1}^{8} = \left(\frac{3}{4}(8)^{\frac{4}{3}}\right) - \left(\frac{3}{4}(1)^{\frac{4}{3}}\right) = 12 - \frac{3}{4} = 11\frac{1}{4} \text{ square units}$$

To find the area bounded by a line and a curve or by a curve and a curve:

1 Find the co-ordinates where the line and curve or curve and curve intersect.

2 Subtract the two areas, or simply subtract the functions and integrate top function − bottom function.

3 Evaluate the bounded area using the limits.

Example

Find the points of intersection of the line and curve. Hence find the area of the bounded region.

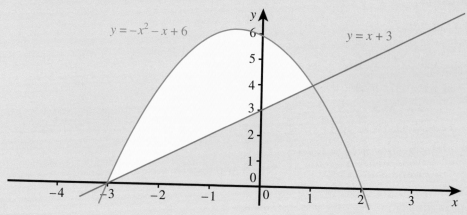

Solution

To find the points of intersection, equate the two functions and solve for x.

$-x^2 - x + 6 = x + 3 \Rightarrow x^2 + 2x - 3 = 0 \Rightarrow (x + 3)(x - 1) = 0 \Rightarrow x = -3 \text{ and } x = 1$

Substitute the solutions to find y.

$x = -3 \implies y = (-3) + 3 = 0$

$x = 1 \implies y = (1) + 3 = 4$

The graphs intersect at $(-3, 0)$ and $(1, 4)$.

To find the area, work out top function – bottom function and integrate.

Top function – bottom function = curve – line = $-x^2 - x + 6 - (x + 3) = -x^2 - 2x + 3$

$$\text{Area} = \int_{-3}^{1} -x^2 - 2x + 3 \, dx = -\frac{1}{3}x^3 - x^2 + 3x \Big|_{-3}^{1}$$

$$= \left[-\frac{1}{3}(1)^3 - (1)^2 + 3(1) \right] - \left[-\frac{1}{3}(-3)^3 - (-3)^2 + 3(-3) \right]$$

$$= \left[-\frac{1}{3} - 1 + 3 \right] - [9 - 9 - 9] = 10\frac{2}{3}$$

Examples

The functions f and g are defined for $x \in \mathbb{R}$ as

$f : x \mapsto 2x^2 - 3x + 2$ and $g : x \mapsto x^2 + x + 7$.

(a) Find the co-ordinates of the two points where the curves $y = f(x)$ and $y = g(x)$ intersect.

(b) Find the area of the region enclosed between the two curves.

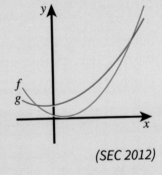

(SEC 2012)

Solutions

(a) $f(x) = g(x)$

$2x^2 - 3x + 2 = x^2 + x + 7$

$\implies x^2 - 4x - 5 = 0$

$\implies (x + 1)(x - 5) = 0$

$\implies x = -1$ and $x = 5$

$f(-1) = 2(-1)^2 - 3(-1) + 2 = 7$

$f(5) = 2(5)^2 - 3(5) + 2 = 37$

The points of intersection are $(-1, 7)$ and $(5, 37)$.

(b) $A = \int_{-1}^{5} (g(x) - f(x)) \, dx = \int_{-1}^{5} -x^2 + 4x + 5 \, dx$

$$= \frac{-x^3}{3} + 2x^2 + 5x \Big|_{-1}^{5} = \left[\frac{-(5)^3}{3} + 2(5)^2 + 5(5) \right] - \left[\frac{-(-1)^3}{3} + 2(-1)^2 + 5(-1) \right]$$

$$= \left[\frac{-125}{3} + 50 + 25 \right] - \left[\frac{1}{3} + 2 - 5 \right] = 36$$

The diagram shows the graph of $y = \sin x$ and $y = \cos x$ for $0 \leq x \leq \dfrac{\pi}{2}$. The two graphs intersect at the point P.

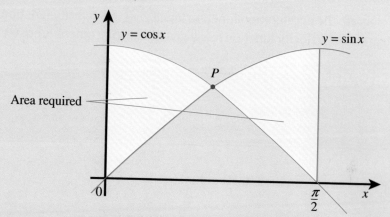

(a) Find the co-ordinates of the point P.

(b) Find the area of the shaded region.

Solutions

(a) $\sin x = \cos x \Rightarrow \dfrac{\sin x}{\cos x} = \dfrac{\cos x}{\cos x}$ Divide both sides by $\cos x$.

$\Rightarrow \tan x = 1 \Rightarrow x = \tan^{-1}(1) = \dfrac{\pi}{4}$ where $0 \leq x \leq \dfrac{\pi}{2}$

$x = \dfrac{\pi}{4} \Rightarrow y = \sin x = \sin\left(\dfrac{\pi}{4}\right) = \dfrac{1}{\sqrt{2}} = \dfrac{\sqrt{2}}{2}$

$P = (x, y) = \left(\dfrac{\pi}{4}, \dfrac{1}{\sqrt{2}}\right)$

(b) The areas shown in the diagram are equal areas. Area 1 (left) = Area 2 (right). Find Area 1 and then multiply the answer by 2.

$$\text{Area 1} = \int_{0}^{\frac{\pi}{4}} \text{top function} - \text{bottom function} = \int_{0}^{\frac{\pi}{4}} (\cos x - \sin x)\, dx$$

$$= \sin x - (-\cos x)\Big|_{0}^{\frac{\pi}{4}} = \sin x + \cos x\Big|_{0}^{\frac{\pi}{4}} = \left(\sin\left(\dfrac{\pi}{4}\right) + \cos\left(\dfrac{\pi}{4}\right)\right) - (\sin(0) + \cos(0))$$

$$= \left(\dfrac{\sqrt{2}}{2} + \dfrac{\sqrt{2}}{2}\right) - (1) = \sqrt{2} - 1$$

Total area = Area 1 $\times$ 2 = $2\left(\sqrt{2} - 1\right)$ = 0·8284 square units

Applications of integration

In the table below we can see the relationship between acceleration, velocity and displacement.

If we integrate the acceleration function it will give the velocity function, and if we integrate the velocity function it will give the displacement function.

Point to note

To find the constant of integration values we need more information. This is usually given as initial conditions in the question.

This process can be applied to other functions.

Function INTEGRATE →	Function INTEGRATE →	Function
Acceleration: $a(t)$	Velocity: $v(t)$	Displacement: $s(t)$
Example: $a(t) = 4t$ Linear	$v(t) = \dfrac{4t^2}{2} + c = 2t^2 + c$ Quadratic	$s(t) = \dfrac{2t^3}{3} + ct + k$ Cubic
Rate of change of height	Height	
Example: $\dfrac{dh}{dt} = 3t - 4$ Linear	$h(t) = \dfrac{3t^2}{2} - 4t + c$ Quadratic	——————
Rate of increase in number of bacteria	Number of bacteria	
Example: $\dfrac{dN}{dt} = 5e^t + 2$ Natural exponential	$N(t) = 5e^t + 2t + c$ Natural exponential	——————
Rate of change of volume	Volume	
Example: $\dfrac{dV}{dt} = -0{\cdot}5t^2 + 6t$ Quadratic	$V(t) = -\dfrac{0{\cdot}5t^3}{3} + \dfrac{6t^2}{2} + c$ $= -0{\cdot}1\dot{6}t^3 + 3t^2 + c$ Cubic	——————

Examples

The acceleration of an object is given by $a(t) = 4t$ m/s², as shown in the diagram below.

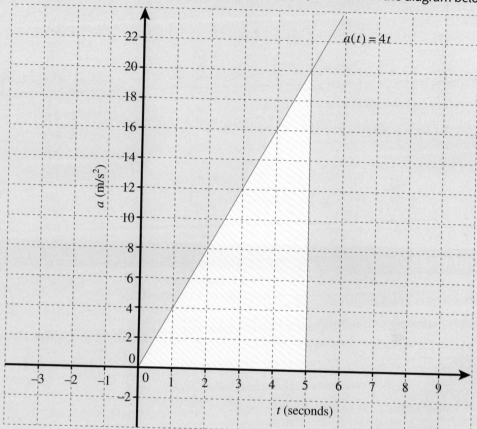

(a) Find the acceleration when $t = 5$ seconds.

(b) Find the velocity v in terms of t, given that $v = 0$ when $t = 0$.

(c) Hence find $v(5)$, the velocity of the object after 5 seconds.

(d) From the diagram of $a(t)$ verify your answer to part (c).

(e) Find the displacement s in terms of t, given that $s = 0$ when $t = 0$.

(f) Find the displacement when $t = 2$ seconds.

Solutions

(a) $t = 5 \implies a(t) = 4(5) = 20$ m/s²

(b) $v(t) = \int (4t)\, dt = 2t^2 + c$

We are given the initial conditions $v = 0$ when $t = 0$, so $v(0) = 2(0)^2 + c = 0$
$\implies c = 0$.

Therefore, $v(t) = 2t^2$.

(c) $t = 5 \implies v(t) = 2(5)^2 = 50$ m/s

(d) The area under an acceleration–time graph over an interval on the x-axis is the velocity over that interval. We can find the area under the graph of $a(t)$ for the interval $[0, 5]$ using the area of a triangle.

Area of triangle $= \frac{1}{2} bh = \frac{1}{2}(5)(20) = 50$, which matches the answer to part (c).

(e) $s(t) = \int 2t^2 \, dt = \dfrac{2t^3}{3} + k$

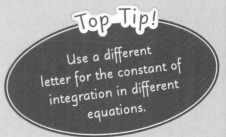

Top Tip!

Use a different letter for the constant of integration in different equations.

We are given the initial conditions $s = 0$

when $t = 0$, so $s(0) = \dfrac{2(0)^3}{3} + k = 0 \Rightarrow k = 0$.

Therefore $s(t) = \dfrac{2t^3}{3}$.

(f) $t = 2 \Rightarrow s(t) = \dfrac{2(2)^3}{3} = \dfrac{16}{3}\,\text{m} = 5\frac{1}{3}\,\text{m}$

Examples

The rate of change of the number of bacteria in a colony is given by $\dfrac{dN}{dt} = 5e^t + 2$. N is the number of bacteria in the colony and t is time measured in hours.

(a) Give a reason why the rate of change is increasing for all values of t where $t \geq 0$.

(b) Express N in terms of t using integration.

(c) If there were 20 bacteria in the colony at $t = 0$, find the number in the colony after 7 hours, correct to the nearest whole number.

Solutions

(a) The natural exponential function is an increasing function.

$e^0 = 1$, $e^t > 0 \Rightarrow 5e^t > 0$, and $2 > 0$.

This means that $5e^t + 2t > 0$ so the rate of change is increasing for all values of $t \geq 0$.

(b) $N = \int (5e^t + 2)\, dt = 5e^t + 2t + c$

(c) $N(t) = 5e^t + 2t + c$

We are given that $N = 20$ when $t = 0$, so $20 = 5e^{(0)} + 2(0) + c \Rightarrow 20 = 5 + c$ $\Rightarrow c = 15$. Therefore $N(t) = 5e^t + 2t + 15$.

$t = 7 \Rightarrow N(t) = 5e^{(7)} + 2(7) + 15 = 5512$

There are 5512 bacteria in the colony after 7 hours.

Examples

A sprinter's velocity over the course of a particular 100 metre race is approximated by the following model, where v is the velocity in metres per second and t is the time in seconds from the starting signal:

$$v(t) = \begin{cases} 0, & \text{for } 0 \leq t < 0 \cdot 2 \\ -0 \cdot 5t^2 + 5t - 0 \cdot 98, & \text{for } 0 \cdot 2 \leq t < 5 \\ 11 \cdot 52, & \text{for } t \geq 5 \end{cases}$$

(a) Sketch the graph of v as a function of t for the first 7 seconds of the race.

(b) Find the distance travelled by the sprinter in the first 5 seconds of the race.

(c) Find the sprinter's finishing time for the race. Give your answer correct to 2 decimal places.

(SEC Sample 2014)

Solutions

(a) This is a piecewise function made up of different pieces.

Notice that in the first 0·2 seconds the sprinter doesn't move, because velocity = 0. His is still in the blocks at this time.

From $0 \cdot 2 \leq t < 5$ the graph changes to a section of a quadratic curve. Velocity is increasing in this interval. We can sketch this by evaluating points from $t = 1$ to $t = 5$ inclusive.

Let $v(t) = -0 \cdot 5t^2 + 5t - 0 \cdot 98$

$v(1) = -0 \cdot 5(1)^2 + 5(1) - 0 \cdot 98 = 3 \cdot 52$

$v(2) = -0 \cdot 5(2)^2 + 5(2) - 0 \cdot 98 = 7 \cdot 02$

$v(3) = -0 \cdot 5(3)^2 + 5(3) - 0 \cdot 98 = 9 \cdot 52$

$v(4) = -0 \cdot 5(4)^2 + 5(4) - 0 \cdot 98 = 11 \cdot 02$

$v(5) = -0 \cdot 5(5)^2 + 5(5) - 0 \cdot 98 = 11 \cdot 52$

Then, from $t \geq 5$, the function changes to a straight line $v(t) = 11 \cdot 52$. Velocity is constant from this point.

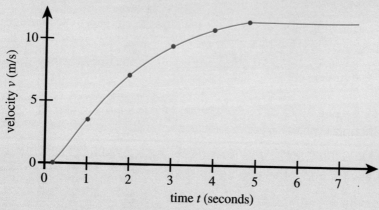

(b) We know that the sprinter doesn't move in the first 0·2 seconds. To find the distance (s) travelled in the first 5 seconds of the race we must find the integral of $v(t)$ for the time period $t = 0.2$ to $t = 5$.

$$s = \int_{0.2}^{5} v(t)\,dt$$

$$= \int_{0.2}^{5} (-0.5t^2 + 5t - 0.98)\,dt$$

$$= \frac{-0.5t^3}{3} + \frac{5t^2}{2} - 0.98t$$

The integration part is done. Now we substitute in the limits $t = 5$ and $t = 0.2$ and then subtract the answers.

$$s = \left[\frac{-0.5(5)^3}{3} + \frac{5(5)^2}{2} - 0.98(5)\right] - \left[\frac{-0.5(0.2)^3}{3} + \frac{5(0.2)^2}{2} - 0.98(2)\right] = 36.864 \text{ metres}$$

(c) The sprinter runs 36·9 m over the first 5 seconds. Now there is $100 - 36.684 = 63.316$ m to run at a constant speed of 11·52 m/s.

$$\text{speed} = \frac{\text{distance}}{\text{time}}$$

$$11.52 = \frac{63.316}{t} \Rightarrow t = \frac{63.316}{11.52} = 5.50 \text{ seconds}$$

Total time for race $= 5 + 5.50 = 10.50$ seconds.

Average velocity and average value of a function

Examples

The velocity of an object in m/s during the first 4 seconds is modelled by $v(t) = 3t - 1$, $0 \le t \le 4$.

(a) Complete the following table and use these values to calculate the average velocity of the object in the interval $1 \le t \le 4$.

t	1	2	3	4
$v = 3t - 1$				

(b) Graph the function $v(t)$.

(c) Find the area under the graph for the interval $1 \le t \le 4$ using integration.

(d) What does this area under the graph represent?

(e) Hence, find the average velocity of the object.

(f) Derive a formula for finding the average velocity of any object using integration.

Solutions

(a)

t	1	2	3	4
$v = 3t - 1$	2	5	8	11

Average velocity $= \dfrac{2 + 5 + 8 + 11}{4} = \dfrac{26}{4} = 6{\cdot}5$ m/s

(b)

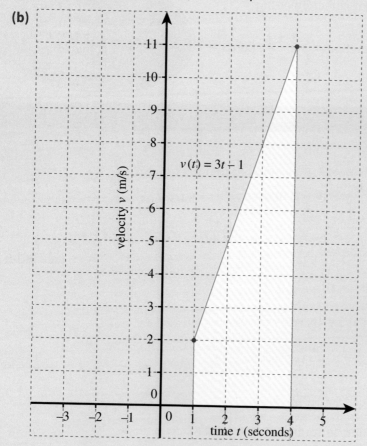

(c) Area under graph $= \displaystyle\int_{1}^{4}(3t - 1)\,dt = \dfrac{3t^2}{2} - t\Big|_{1}^{4} = \left(\dfrac{3(4)^2}{2} - (4)\right) - \left(\dfrac{3(1)^2}{2} - (1)\right)$

$$= (24 - 4) - \left(\dfrac{3}{2} - 1\right)$$

$$= (20) - \left(\dfrac{1}{2}\right) = 19{\cdot}5 \text{ square units}$$

(d) This value represents the displacement of the object over the interval $1 \le t \le 4$.

(e) Average velocity of object $= \dfrac{\text{displacement}}{\text{time taken}} = \dfrac{19{\cdot}5}{4-1} = \dfrac{19{\cdot}5}{3} = 6{\cdot}5 \text{ m/s}$

Note that this is the same answer as in part (a).

(f) Average velocity $= \dfrac{\text{displacement}}{\text{time taken}} = \dfrac{\int_1^4 3t-1}{4-1} = \dfrac{\int_a^b v(t)}{b-a} = \dfrac{1}{b-a}\int_a^b v(t)\,dt.$

We can extend the formula in the above example to any velocity function or any continuous function.

Average value of a function $= \dfrac{1}{b-a}\displaystyle\int_a^b f(x)\,dx$

Top Tip!

Learn this formula. It is not in the Formulae and Tables booklet.

Examples

(a) Find $\displaystyle\int 5\cos 3x\,dx$.

(b) The slope of the tangent of $y = f(x)$ at each point (x, y) is $2x - 2$.
The curve cuts the x-axis at $(-2, 0)$.

   (i) Find the equation of $f(x)$.

   (ii) Find the average value of $f(x)$ over the interval $0 \le x \le 3,\ x \in \mathbb{R}$.

(SEC 2014)

Solutions

(a) $\displaystyle\int 5\cos 3x\,dx = 5\int \cos 3x\,dx = 5\dfrac{\sin 3x}{3} + c = \dfrac{5}{3}\sin 3x + c$

(b) **(i)** $f(x) = \displaystyle\int (2x - 2)\,dx = x^2 - 2x + c$

At $x = -2,\ y = 0 \Rightarrow 0 = (2)^2 + 2(2) + c \Rightarrow 0 = 4 + 4 + c \Rightarrow c = -8$

Hence, $f(x) = x^2 - 2x - 8$.

(ii) The average value formula is $\dfrac{1}{b-a}\displaystyle\int_a^b f(x)\,dx.$

$$\frac{1}{3-0}\int_0^3 (x^2 - 2x - 8)\,dx = \frac{1}{3}\left[\frac{x^3}{3} - x^2 - 8x\right]_0^3$$

$$= \frac{1}{3}\left[\left(\frac{(3)^3}{3} - (3)^2 - 8(3)\right) - \left(\frac{(0)^3}{3} - (0)^2 - 8(0)\right)\right] = \frac{1}{3}(-24) = -8$$

✓ Practise finding anti-derivatives of different functions.

✓ Practise finding the constant of integration given initial conditions.

✓ Integrate sums, differences and constant multiples of functions of the form

- x^a where $x \in \mathbb{Q}$

- a^x where $a \in \mathbb{R}, a > 0$

- $\sin ax$ where $a \in \mathbb{R}$

- $\cos ax$ where $a \in \mathbb{R}$.

✓ Know how to find the area between a line and a curve or between a curve and a curve with respect to the x-axis or y-axis.

15 Complex Numbers

Learning objectives

In this chapter you will learn how to:

- Understand the origin of and the need for complex numbers
- Express complex numbers in rectangular form $a + bi$ and illustrate them on an Argand diagram
- Interpret the modulus as distance from the origin on an Argand diagram
- Investigate the operations of addition, multiplication, subtraction and division with complex numbers in rectangular form $a + bi$ and the geometrical interpretation of these operations
- Calculate the conjugates of sums and products of complex numbers
- Solve quadratic equations having complex roots and interpret the solutions
- Use the conjugate root theorem to find the roots of polynomials
- Express complex numbers in polar form
- Work with complex numbers in rectangular and polar form to solve quadratic and other equations, including those in the form $z^n = a$, where $n \in \mathbb{Z}$ and $z = r\left(\cos \theta + i \sin \theta\right)$
- Use De Moivre's theorem
- Use applications such as the nth roots of unity, $n \in \mathbb{N}$, and identities such as $\cos 3\theta = 4\cos^3\theta - 3\cos\theta$.

Introduction

When Italian mathematicians Cardano (1501–1576) and Tartaglia (1499–1557) were working on solutions to cubic equations, they found that expressions involving the square roots of negative numbers arose. This led to the study of complex numbers, which are used today in science, computer game design, engineering and many other areas.

Roots of negative numbers

You have already learnt that the square of any number is positive, e.g. $(2)^2 = 4$, $(-2)^2 = 4$, $(n)^2 = (-n)^2$. So how do you solve the equation $x = \sqrt{-1}$?

The solution to this equation is a little number called i (also known as an **imaginary number**, or iota).

$$\sqrt{-1} = i \implies i^2 = -1$$

The following table shows some examples.

Negative root	Imaginary number
$\sqrt{-4}$	$\sqrt{4(-1)} = 2i$
$\sqrt{-49}$	$\sqrt{49(-1)} = 7i$
$\sqrt{-100}$	$\sqrt{100(-1)} = 10i$
$\sqrt{-125}$	$\sqrt{125(-1)} = 5\sqrt{5}\,i$
$\sqrt{-\dfrac{1}{4}}$	$\sqrt{\dfrac{1}{4}(-1)} = \dfrac{1}{2}i = \dfrac{i}{2}$
$\sqrt{-0 \cdot 125}$	$\sqrt{0 \cdot 125(-1)} = \dfrac{\sqrt{2}}{4}i = \dfrac{\sqrt{2}i}{4}$

A **complex number** consists of a **real part** and an **imaginary part**. Complex numbers are often denoted by z, z_1, z_2, etc. or by Greek letters such as ω (omega). The set of all complex numbers is denoted by $\mathbb{C}$.

Point to note

A complex number, z, is any number of the form $z = a + bi$, $a, b \in \mathbb{R}$, $i^2 = -1$.

a is called the real part of z, denoted Re (z), and b is called the imaginary part of z, denoted Im (z).

For example, if $z = 2 - 3i$ then Re $(z) = 2$ and Im $(z) = -3$.

Point to note

Every real number is also a complex number with an imaginary part of 0. For example, $4 = 4 + 0i$.

The set of real numbers is a subset of the set of complex numbers. $\mathbb{R} \subset \mathbb{C}$.

The set of complex numbers is $\mathbb{C} = \{a + bi \mid a \in \mathbb{R},\ b \in \mathbb{R},\ i^2 = -1\}$. This is on page 23 of the *Formulae and Tables* booklet.

Examples

(a) Solve the equation $z^2 + 25 = 0$. Express your answer in the form $a + bi$, where $a, b \in \mathbb{R}$.

(b) Simplify i^3 and i^4.

Solutions

(a) $z^2 + 25 = 0 \implies z^2 = -25 \implies z = \pm\sqrt{-25} = 0 \pm 5i$

(b) $i^3 = i^2(i) = (-1)(i) = -i$

$i^4 = i^2 i^2 = (-1)(-1) = 1$

Powers of i

The powers of i repeat in a cyclic pattern.

Powers of i	i^1	i^2	i^3	i^4	i^5	i^6	i^7	i^8
Simplified form	i	-1	$-i$	1	i	-1	$-i$	1

Top Tip

When simplifying powers of i, divide the exponent by 4.

- If the remainder is 0, the answer is $i^0 = 1$
- If the remainder is 1, the answer is $i^1 = i$
- If the remainder is 2, the answer is $i^2 = -1$
- If the remainder is 3, the answer is $i^3 = -i$.

Examples

(a) Simplify i^{12} and i^{59}.

(b) Simplify $(2i)^7$.

Solutions

(a) $\dfrac{12}{4} = 3$ with no remainder, so $i^{12} = 1$.

$\dfrac{59}{4} = 4$ with a remainder of 3, so $i^{59} = -i$.

(b) $(2i)^7 = 128\,i^7$

$\dfrac{7}{4} = 1$ with a remainder of 3, so $128\,i^7 = 128(-i) = -128i$.

Argand diagrams

The **Argand diagram**, invented by Jean-Robert Argand (1768–1822), is used to represent numbers on the **complex plane**. It is similar to a Cartesian diagram, with two perpendicular axes. The horizontal axis is called the **real axis (Re)** and is used to plot the real part of a complex number. The vertical axis is called the **imaginary axis (Im)** and is used to plot the imaginary part.

Plotting different powers of i on an Argand diagram makes it easy to see the cyclic pattern.

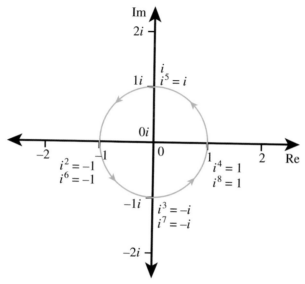

Modulus of a complex number

The modulus of a complex number z is denoted as $|z|$. The modulus is the distance from the origin to the complex number on the Argand diagram.

For any complex number $z = a + bi$, $|z| = \sqrt{a^2 + b^2}$.

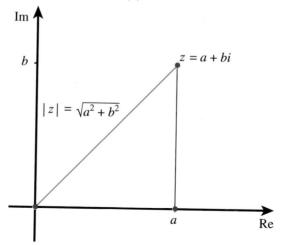

Examples

(a) Plot the following on an Argand diagram: $z_1 = 4 + 3i$, $z_2 = -2 + i$, $z_3 = 2 - i$.

(b) Find $|z_1|$, $|z_2|$, $|z_3|$.

(c) Hence, find which complex number is furthest away from the origin.

(d) Show that $|z_2| = |z_3|$. Find two other complex numbers which have the same modulus and plot these on an Argand diagram. What geometrical shape is formed by these complex numbers? Give a reason for your answer.

(e) If $|t + ti| = |z_1|$, find two possible values of t, where $t \in \mathbb{R}$.

Solutions

(a)

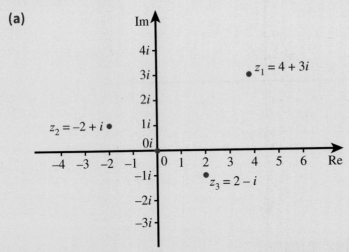

(b) $|z| = \sqrt{a^2 + b^2}$

$|z_1| = \sqrt{4^2 + 3^2} = \sqrt{16 + 9} = \sqrt{25} = 5$

$|z_2| = \sqrt{(-2)^2 + 1^2} = \sqrt{5}$

$|z_3| = \sqrt{2^2 + (-1)^2} = \sqrt{5}$

(c) z_1 is the complex number furthest away from the origin. $|z_1| > |z_2|$ and $|z_1| > |z_3|$.

(d) From part (b), $|z_2| = |z_3| = \sqrt{5}$. Both complex numbers are a distance of $\sqrt{5}$ units from the origin.

Two other complex numbers with the same modulus are $z_4 = 2 + i$ and $z_5 = -2 - i$.

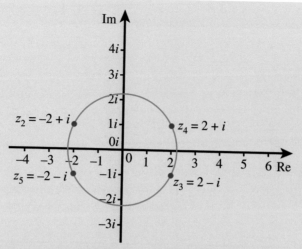

These complex numbers lie on a circle of radius $\sqrt{5}$. It includes all complex numbers which are a distance of $\sqrt{5}$ units from the origin.

(e) $|t + ti| = |z|$

$\Rightarrow \sqrt{t^2 + t^2} = \sqrt{25}$

$\Rightarrow 2t^2 = 25$ Square both sides.

$\Rightarrow t^2 = \dfrac{25}{2}$

$\Rightarrow t = \pm\dfrac{5}{\sqrt{2}}$

Operations with complex numbers
Addition and subtraction

To add complex numbers:

- Add real parts to real parts.
- Add imaginary parts to imaginary parts.

To subtract complex numbers:

- Subtract real parts from real parts.
- Subtract imaginary parts from imaginary parts.

$z_1 = a + bi,\ z_2 = c + di$

$z_1 + z_2 = (a + c) + (b + d)i$

$z_1 - z_2 = (a - c) + (b - d)i$

Examples

$z_1 = \sqrt{3} - i$, $z_2 = 2\sqrt{3} + 5i$

Express in the form $a + bi$:

(a) $z_1 + z_2$

(b) $z_2 - z_1$.

Solutions

(a) $z_1 + z_2 = \left(\sqrt{3} + 2\sqrt{3}\right) + \left(-1 + 5\right)i = 3\sqrt{3} + 4i$

(b) $z_2 - z_1 = \left(2\sqrt{3} - \sqrt{3}\right) + \left(5 - (-1)\right)i = \sqrt{3} + 6i$

> **Top Tip**
>
> Always use brackets when subtracting complex numbers, to avoid making sign errors in the exam.

Multiplication

To multiply a complex number by a real number, multiply both the real and imaginary parts of the complex number by the real number.

$z = x + yi$, $k \in \mathbb{R}$

$kz = k(x + yi) = kx + kyi$

To multiply two complex numbers, multiply out the terms in the same way as multiplying pairs of brackets.

$z_1 = a + bi$, $z_2 = c + di$

$z_1 z_2 = (a + bi)(c + di)$

$\qquad = a(c + di) + bi(c + di)$

$\qquad = ac + adi + bci + i^2 bd \quad i^2 = -1$, so $i^2 bd$ becomes $-bd$.

$\qquad = ac - bd + (ad + bc)i$

> **Point to note**
>
> $z^2 = (a + bi)^2 = a^2 - b^2 + 2abi$

$z_1 = 2 - i$, $z_2 = 3 - 2i$, $z_3 = 0 + i$

Express in the form $a + bi$:

(a) $2z_1 + 3z_3$

(b) $z_1 z_2$.

Solutions

(a) $2z_1 + 3z_3 = 2(2 - i) + 3(0 + i) = 4 - 2i + 3i = 4 + i$

(b) $z_1 z_2 = (2 - i)(3 - 2i)$

$= 2(3 - 2i) - i(3 - 2i)$

$= 6 - 4i - 3i + 2i^2$

$= 6 - 2 - 7i$

$= 4 - 7i$

Conjugate of a complex number

The **conjugate** of a complex number is its reflection in the real axis. If $z = a + bi$, the conjugate of z is $\bar{z} = a - bi$.

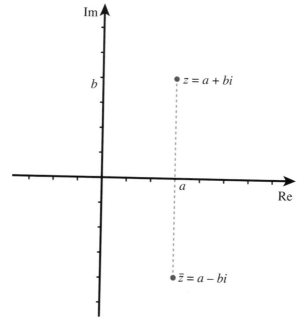

Adding conjugates: $z + \bar{z} = a + bi + a - bi = 2a$.

Multiplication of conjugates: $(a + bi)(a - bi) = a^2 + b^2$. This result will be useful when dividing complex numbers.

Point to note

Adding a complex number to its conjugate, and multiplying a complex number by its conjugate, both result in a real number.

The following table shows some examples of complex numbers and their conjugates.

$z = a + bi$	$\bar{z} = a - bi$	$z\bar{z} = a^2 + b^2$
$1 + 2i$	$1 - 2i$	$1^2 + 2^2 = 5$
$2 - 3i$	$2 + 3i$	$2^2 + (-3)^2 = 4 + 9 = 13$
$-1 + i$	$-1 - i$	$(-1)^2 + 1^2 = 2$
$1 + \sqrt{3}i$	$1 - \sqrt{3}i$	$1^2 + \left(\sqrt{3}\right)^2 = 1 + 3 = 4$
$0 + 4i$	$0 - 4i$	$0^2 + 4^2 = 16$

Division

When dividing complex numbers we multiply above and below by the **conjugate of the denominator**.

Examples

$z_1 = 2 - 3i,\ z_2 = 1 + 2i$

Find the values of x and y, where $x, y \in \mathbb{R}$, in:

(a) $x + yi = \dfrac{z_1}{z_2}$

(b) $x + yi = \dfrac{1}{z_1}$.

Solutions

(a) $\dfrac{z_1}{z_2} = \dfrac{2 - 3i}{1 + 2i} = \dfrac{2 - 3i}{1 + 2i} \times \dfrac{1 - 2i}{1 - 2i} = \dfrac{2(1 - 2i) - 3i(1 - 2i)}{1 + 4}$

$= \dfrac{2 - 2i - 3i + 6i^2}{5} = \dfrac{2 - 5i - 6}{5} = \dfrac{-4 - 5i}{5} = -\dfrac{4}{5} - i$

$\Rightarrow x = -\dfrac{4}{5},\ y = -1$

(b) $\dfrac{1}{z_1} = \dfrac{1}{2 + 3i} = \dfrac{1}{2 + 3i} \times \dfrac{2 - 3i}{2 - 3i} = \dfrac{2 - 3i}{4 + 9} = \dfrac{2 - 3i}{13} = \dfrac{2}{13} - \dfrac{3}{13}i$

$\Rightarrow x = \dfrac{2}{13},\ y = -\dfrac{3}{13}$

Geometrical transformations of complex numbers

Addition

Geometrically, addition of complex numbers is similar to vector addition.

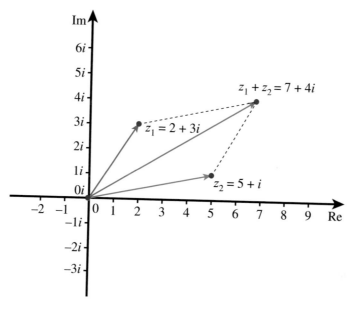

As shown in the diagram, the addition of two complex numbers z_1 and z_2 constructs a parallelogram, with $z_1 + z_2$ being the diagonal of the parallelogram starting from the origin.

This can also be described as a translation. If $z_1 = 2 + 3i$ is a translation of 2 units to the right and 3 units up, and $z_2 = 5 + i$ is a translation of 5 units to the right and 1 unit up, then $z_1 + z_2$ is a translation of $2 + 5 = 7$ units to the right, and $3 + 1 = 4$ units up $= 7 + 4i$.

Subtraction

Subtracting a complex number is the same as adding the negative of the complex number.

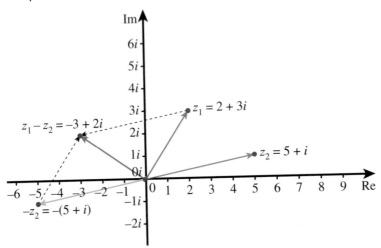

As with addition, subtraction of complex numbers constructs a parallelogram, and can be described as a translation. If $z_1 = 2 + 3i$ is a translation of 2 units to the right and 3 units up, and $z_2 = 5 + i$ is a translation of 5 units to the right and 1 unit up, then $-z_2$ is a translation of 5 units to the left and 1 unit down.

To work out $z_1 - z_2$, translate by 2 units to the right followed by 5 to the left, which gives a total of 3 to the left. Then translate by 3 units up followed by 1 unit down, which gives a total of 2 units up. So $z_1 - z_2 = -3 + 2i$.

Multiplication by a real number

Multiplying a complex number, z, by a real number, k, where $k > 1$, enlarges, or stretches, z by a scale factor of k. The modulus of z is also increased by a scale factor of k. If $0 < k < 1$, multiplication results in a reduction, or contraction, of z.

Multiplying a complex number by -1 gives a complex number of the same modulus but in the opposite direction.

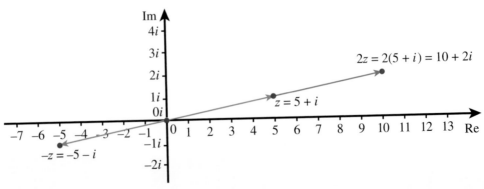

Multiplication by i and $-i$

Multiplying a complex number by i is the same as a rotation of 90° anti-clockwise about the origin.

Multiplying a complex number by $-i$ is the same as a rotation of 90° clockwise about the origin.

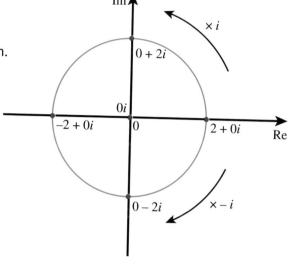

Multiplication by a complex number

There are several noteworthy features of multiplication by a complex number, illustrated in the diagram below.

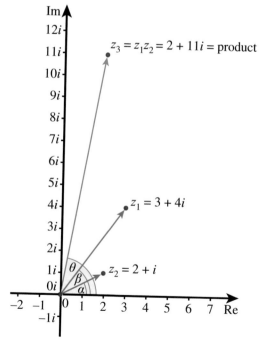

$$\left|z_1\right| = \sqrt{25},\ \left|z_2\right| = \sqrt{5},\ \left|z_3\right| = \sqrt{125} = \sqrt{5}\sqrt{25}$$

$$\alpha = \tan^{-1}\left(\frac{1}{2}\right) \approx 27°,\ \beta = \tan^{-1}\left(\frac{4}{3}\right) \approx 53°,\ \theta = \tan^{-1}\left(\frac{11}{2}\right) \approx 80° = \alpha + \beta$$

When you multiply two complex numbers:

- the **modulus** of the result is the **product** of the moduli of the two original numbers, $|z_1 z_2| = |z_1||z_2|$
- the **argument** of the result is the **sum** of the arguments of the two original numbers, $\arg(z_1 z_2) = \arg(z_1) + \arg(z_2)$.

Point to note

The **argument** of a complex number is the clockwise angle of the number from the positive real axis.

Division

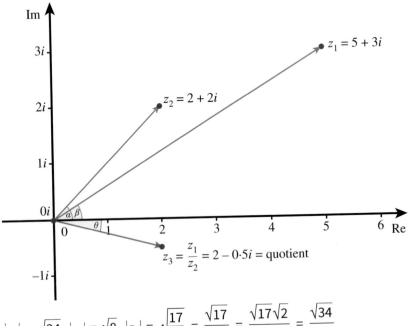

$|z_1| = \sqrt{34}, \; |z_2| = \sqrt{8}, \; |z_3| = \sqrt{\frac{17}{4}} = \frac{\sqrt{17}}{2} = \frac{\sqrt{17}\sqrt{2}}{2\sqrt{2}} = \frac{\sqrt{34}}{\sqrt{8}}$

$\alpha = \tan^{-1}\left(\frac{5}{3}\right) \approx 59°, \; \beta = \tan^{-1}\left(\frac{2}{2}\right) = 45°, \; \theta = \tan^{-1}\left(\frac{0\cdot5}{2}\right) \approx 14° = \alpha - \beta$

When you divide two complex numbers:

- the **modulus** of the result is the **quotient** of the moduli of the two original numbers, $\left|\dfrac{z_1}{z_2}\right| = \dfrac{|z_1|}{|z_2|}$
- the **argument** of the result is the **difference** of the arguments of the two original numbers, $\arg\left(\dfrac{z_1}{z_2}\right) = \arg(z_1) - \arg(z_2)$.

Equality of complex numbers

If $a + bi = c + di$ then $a = c$ and $b = d$.

To solve equations involving complex numbers, equate real parts with real parts and imaginary parts with imaginary parts.

Example

If $(x + yi)^2 = 4i$, $x, y \in \mathbb{R}$, find the values of x and y.

Solution

$(x + yi)^2 = 4i \Rightarrow x^2 - y^2 + 2xyi = 0 + 4i$ Multiply out the brackets.

$x^2 - y^2 = 0$ Equate real parts.

$2xy = 4 \Rightarrow xy = 2 \Rightarrow y = \dfrac{2}{x}$ Equate imaginary parts.

Substitute $y = \dfrac{2}{x}$ into the equation $x^2 - y^2 = 0$.

$x^2 - \left(\dfrac{2}{x}\right)^2 = 0$

$x^2 - \dfrac{4}{x^2} = 0$

$x^4 - 4 = 0$ Multiply each term by x^2.

$(x^2 - 2)(x^2 + 2) = 0$ Factorise and solve for $x \in \mathbb{R}$.

$x^2 = 2 \Rightarrow x = \pm\sqrt{2}$

$x^2 + 2 = 0$ has no real solutions.

$y = \dfrac{2}{x} = \pm \dfrac{2}{\sqrt{2}} = \pm\sqrt{2}$

Complex equations

Example

Solve the equation $z^2 + z + 1 = 0$ for $z \in \mathbb{C}$.

Solution

We use the quadratic formula: $z = \dfrac{-b \pm \sqrt{b^2 - 4ac}}{2a}$

$a = 1, \quad b = 1, \quad c = 1$

$$z = \frac{-(1) \pm \sqrt{(1)^2 - 4(1)(1)}}{2(1)}$$

$$\Rightarrow z = \frac{-1 \pm \sqrt{1 - 4}}{2}$$

$$\Rightarrow z = \frac{-1 \pm \sqrt{-3}}{2}$$

$$\Rightarrow z = \frac{-1 \pm \sqrt{3}i}{2}$$

The answer gives roots which are conjugates.

Example

Given that $z = 2 - 3i$ and $\bar{z} = 2 + 3i$ are roots of the equation
$az^2 + bz + c = 0$ where $a, b, c \in \mathbb{R}$, find the values of a, b and c.

Remember

Remember the formula for forming a quadratic given the roots:

$z^2 - $ (sum of roots)$z +$ product of roots $= 0$.

Solution

Sum of roots $= 2 - 3i + 2 + 3i = 4$

Product of roots $= (2 - 3i)(2 + 3i) = 4 + 9 = 13$

$z^2 - 4z + 13 = 0$

$a = 1, \ b = -4, \ c = 13$

Conjugate root theorem

In the previous two examples we saw that the roots of the quadratic were a conjugate pair. This can be applied to other equations (e.g. cubic equations) as long as the coefficients are real.

Point to note

If $f(z) = 0$ is an equation with real coefficients and if z_1 is a root of the equation then the conjugate of z_1 is also a root of the equation.

Examples

Given that $f(z) = z^3 - 1$:

(a) find a real root of $f(z) = 0$

(b) hence, find two complex roots of $f(z) = 0$.

Solutions

(a) $z^3 - 1 = 0 \Rightarrow z^3 = 1 \Rightarrow z = \sqrt[3]{1}$

So $z = 1$ is a root of $f(z) = 0$.

(b) If $z = 1$ is a root then $z - 1$ must be a factor.

Use long division to find another factor.

$$
\begin{array}{r}
z^2 + z + 1 \\
z - 1 \overline{) z^3 + 0z^2 + 0z + 1} \\
\underline{-z^3 + z^2} \\
z^2 + 0z \\
\underline{-z^2 + z} \\
z - 1 \\
\underline{-z + 1} \\
0 \quad 0
\end{array}
$$

No remainder.

The other factor is $z^2 + z + 1 = 0$. This was solved in a previous example

to get $z = \dfrac{-1 \pm \sqrt{3}i}{2}$.

Examples

Let $z_1 = 1 - 2i$, where $i^2 = -1$.

(a) The complex number z_1 is a root of the equation $2z^3 - 7z^2 + 16z - 15 = 0$.
Find the other two roots of the equation.

(b) (i) Let $w = z_1 \bar{z}_1$, where $\bar{z}_1$ is the conjugate of z_1. Plot $z_1, \bar{z}_1$ and w on an Argand diagram and label each point.

(ii) Find the measure of the acute angle, $\bar{z}_1 w z_1$, formed by joining $\bar{z}_1$ to w to z_1 on the diagram drawn in part (i). Give your answer to the nearest degree.

(SEC 2014)

Solutions

(a) $z_1 = 1 - 2i$ is a root $\Rightarrow \bar{z}_1 = 1 + 2i$ is a root.

$(z - 1 + 2i)(z - z - 2i) = z^2 - 2z + 5$ is a factor.

Hence, $(z^2 - 2z + 5)(az + b) = 2z^3 - 7z^2 + 16z - 15$.

Equate coefficients: $a = 2$ and $b - 2a = -7 \Rightarrow b = -3$.

The other factor is $2z - 3$, so the third root is $z = \dfrac{3}{2}$.

(b) **(i)** $w = (1 - 2i)(1 + 2i) = 5$

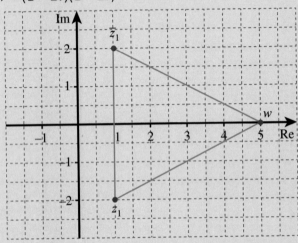

(ii)

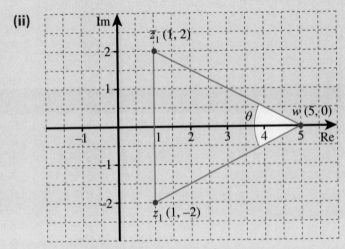

Let the required angle be θ as shown.

The line wz_1 forms a right angle with the real axis, so $\tan\left(\dfrac{1}{2}\theta\right) = \dfrac{2}{4}$

$\Rightarrow \dfrac{1}{2}\theta = 26 \cdot 57 \Rightarrow \theta = 53 \cdot 14 \approx 53°$.

$f(z) = z^3 + z^2(-5 - 2i) + z(6 + 10i) - 12i$

(a) Show that $2i$ is a root of $f(z)$.

(b) Find all the solutions of $f(z) = 0$.

Solutions

(a) Substitute $2i$ into the function.

$(2i)^3 + (2i)^2(-5 - 2i) + 2i(6 + 10i) - 12i = 8i^3 + (-4)(-5 - 2i) + 12i + 20i^2 - 12i$

$= -8i + 20 + 8i + 12i - 20 - 12i = 0$ as required.

(b) If $z = 2i$ is a root then $z - 2i$ is a factor.

$(z - 2i)(z^2 + az + b) = z^3 + z^2(-5 - 2i) + z(6 + 10i) - 12i$

Equating coefficients:

$z^3 + az^2 + bz - 2iz^2 - 2aiz - 2ib$ on the left-hand side

Equate coefficients of z^2 terms on left and right:

$a - 2i = -5 - 2i \implies a = -5$

Equate coefficients of z terms on left and right:

$b = 6$

So $z^2 + az + b = z^2 - 5z + 6$.

Factorise and solve to find the roots:

$(z - 3)(z - 2) = 0 \implies z = 3$ or $z = 2$

The three roots are $2i$, 3 and 2.

> ### Point to note
>
> We can't use the conjugate root theorem here because the coefficients of $f(z)$ are **not real**.

Polar form of a complex number

On the Argand diagram the complex number $z = x + yi$ can be defined using rectangular/Cartesian co-ordinates (x, y) or polar co-ordinates (r, θ).

The polar form of a complex number $z = x + yi$ is $z = r(\cos\theta + i\sin\theta)$, where $r = |z| = \sqrt{x^2 + y^2}$ and θ = argument of z (the angle between z and the positive side of the real axis). This is illustrated in the diagram on page 260.

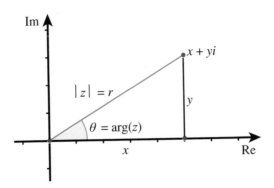

$$\sin\theta = \frac{\text{opp}}{\text{hyp}} = \frac{y}{r} \Rightarrow y = r\sin\theta$$

$$\cos\theta = \frac{\text{adj}}{\text{hyp}} = \frac{x}{r} \Rightarrow x = r\cos\theta$$

Therefore, $x + iy = r\cos\theta + ir\sin\theta = r(\cos\theta + i\sin\theta)$, which is the polar form of z.

The following table shows how arg (z) is calculated for complex numbers in different quadrants. We can define arg (z) in degrees or radians.

$z = x + iy$	$1 + i$ (first quadrant)
Diagram	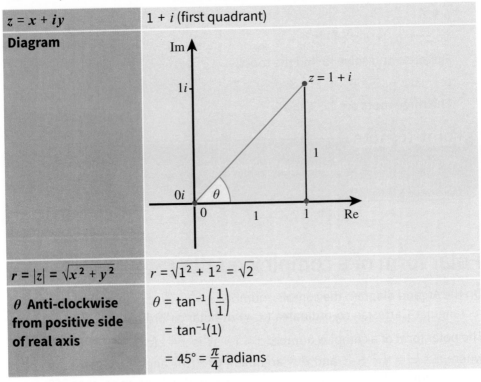
$r = \|z\| = \sqrt{x^2 + y^2}$	$r = \sqrt{1^2 + 1^2} = \sqrt{2}$
θ **Anti-clockwise from positive side of real axis**	$\theta = \tan^{-1}\left(\dfrac{1}{1}\right)$ $= \tan^{-1}(1)$ $= 45° = \dfrac{\pi}{4}$ radians

$z = x + iy$	$-1 + \sqrt{3}i$ (second quadrant)
Diagram	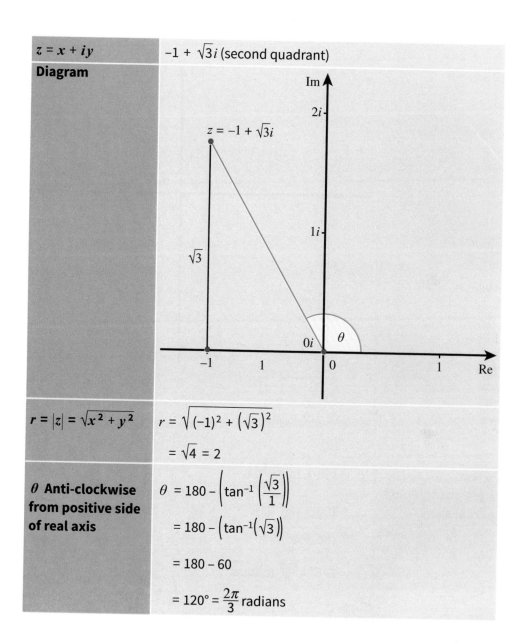
$r = \|z\| = \sqrt{x^2 + y^2}$	$r = \sqrt{(-1)^2 + \left(\sqrt{3}\right)^2}$ $= \sqrt{4} = 2$
θ **Anti-clockwise from positive side of real axis**	$\theta = 180 - \left(\tan^{-1}\left(\dfrac{\sqrt{3}}{1}\right)\right)$ $= 180 - \left(\tan^{-1}\left(\sqrt{3}\right)\right)$ $= 180 - 60$ $= 120° = \dfrac{2\pi}{3}$ radians

$z = x + iy$	$-3 - 3i$ (third quadrant)
Diagram	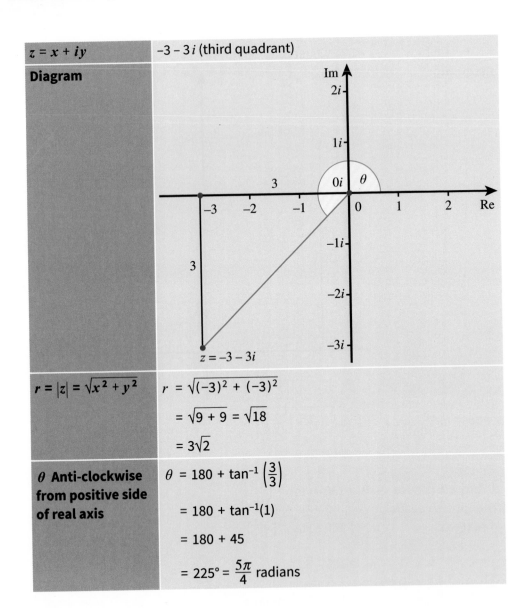
$r = \|z\| = \sqrt{x^2 + y^2}$	$r = \sqrt{(-3)^2 + (-3)^2}$ $= \sqrt{9 + 9} = \sqrt{18}$ $= 3\sqrt{2}$
θ **Anti-clockwise from positive side of real axis**	$\theta = 180 + \tan^{-1}\left(\dfrac{3}{3}\right)$ $= 180 + \tan^{-1}(1)$ $= 180 + 45$ $= 225° = \dfrac{5\pi}{4}$ radians

$z = x + iy$	$4 - \sqrt{2}\, i$ (fourth quadrant)
Diagram	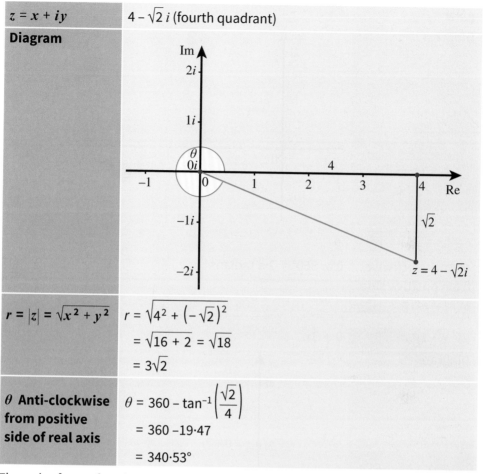
$r = \|z\| = \sqrt{x^2 + y^2}$	$r = \sqrt{4^2 + \left(-\sqrt{2}\right)^2}$ $= \sqrt{16 + 2} = \sqrt{18}$ $= 3\sqrt{2}$
θ Anti-clockwise from positive side of real axis	$\theta = 360 - \tan^{-1}\left(\dfrac{\sqrt{2}}{4}\right)$ $= 360 - 19\cdot47$ $= 340\cdot53°$

The polar form of each complex number in the table can be deduced from the r and θ values.

$$1 + i = \sqrt{2}\left(\cos\frac{\pi}{4} + i\sin\frac{\pi}{4}\right)$$

$$-1 + \sqrt{3}i = 2\left(\cos\frac{2\pi}{3} + i\sin\frac{2\pi}{3}\right)$$

$$-3 - 3i = 3\sqrt{2}\left(\cos\frac{5\pi}{4} + i\sin\frac{5\pi}{4}\right)$$

$$4 - \sqrt{2}i = 3\sqrt{2}\left(\cos(340\cdot53°) + i\sin(340\cdot53°)\right)$$

Complex numbers on the axes

It is very easy to find r and θ for complex numbers that lie on the axes.

- Plot the complex number z.
- r = distance from the origin to z (obvious from the diagram).
- θ = angle between positive side of real axis and z (also obvious from the diagram).

$z = x + iy$	$4 + 0i$
Diagram	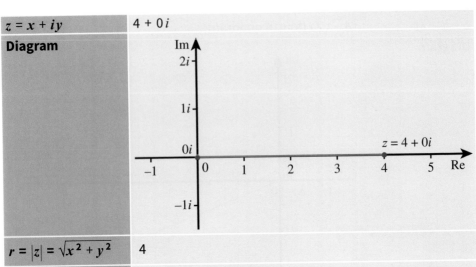
$r = \|z\| = \sqrt{x^2 + y^2}$	4
θ Anti-clockwise from positive side of real axis	0 or 360° = 2π radians

$z = x + iy$	$0 + 3i$
Diagram	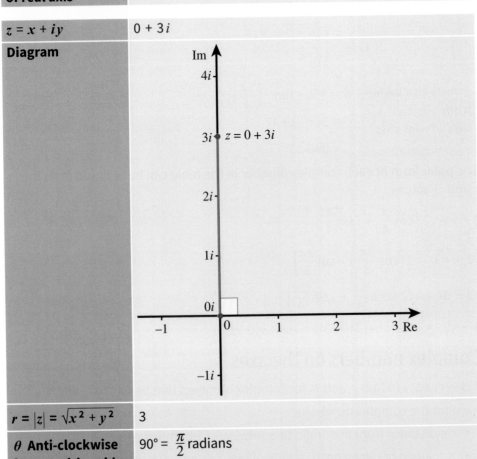
$r = \|z\| = \sqrt{x^2 + y^2}$	3
θ Anti-clockwise from positive side of real axis	90° = $\dfrac{\pi}{2}$ radians

$z = x + iy$	$-8 + 0i$
Diagram	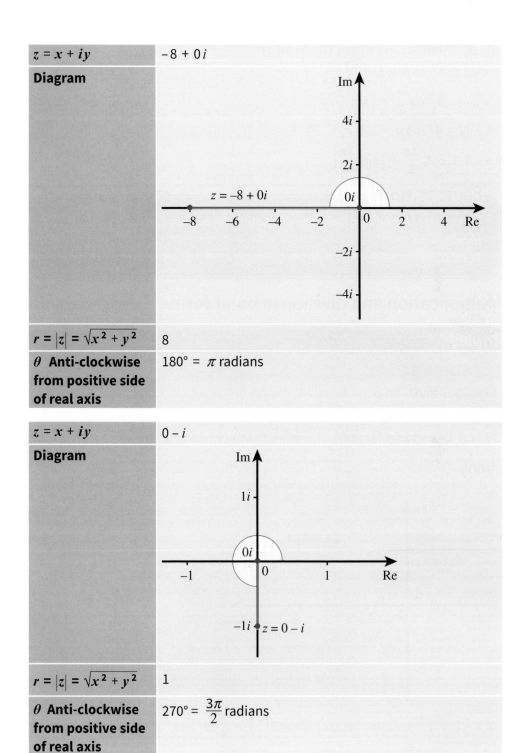
$r = |z| = \sqrt{x^2 + y^2}$	8
θ **Anti-clockwise from positive side of real axis**	$180° = \pi$ radians

$z = x + iy$	$0 - i$
Diagram	
$r = |z| = \sqrt{x^2 + y^2}$	1
θ **Anti-clockwise from positive side of real axis**	$270° = \dfrac{3\pi}{2}$ radians

The polar forms can be deduced as follows.

$4 + 0i = 4(\cos 0 + i \sin 0)$

$0 + 3i = 3\left(\cos \dfrac{\pi}{2} + i \sin \dfrac{\pi}{2}\right)$

$-8 + 0i = 8(\cos \pi + i \sin \pi)$

$0 - i = 1\left(\cos \dfrac{3\pi}{2} + i \sin \dfrac{3\pi}{2}\right)$

> **Point to note**
>
> To convert from polar form to rectangular form, just evaluate with a calculator.
> For example, $8(\cos \pi + i \sin \pi) = 8(-1 + 0i) = -8 + 0i$

Multiplication and division in polar form

Examples

$z = 1 + i$ and $\omega = 1 - i$

(a) Express z and ω in polar form.

(b) Find $z\omega$ in rectangular and polar form. Comment on your answer.

(c) Find $\dfrac{z}{\omega}$ in rectangular and polar form. Comment on your answer.

Solutions

(a)

$|z| = \sqrt{1^2 + 1^2} = \sqrt{2}$ and $\arg(z) = \tan^{-1}\left(\dfrac{1}{1}\right) = \dfrac{\pi}{4}$ so $z = \sqrt{2}\left(\cos \dfrac{\pi}{4} + i \sin \dfrac{\pi}{4}\right)$ in polar form.

$|\omega| = \sqrt{1^2 + 1^2} = \sqrt{2}$ and $\arg(\omega) = 2\pi - \tan^{-1}\left(\dfrac{1}{1}\right) = 2\pi - \dfrac{\pi}{4} = \dfrac{7\pi}{4}$ so

$\omega = \sqrt{2}\left(\cos \dfrac{7\pi}{4} + i \sin \dfrac{7\pi}{4}\right)$ in polar form.

(b) Rectangular form: $z\omega = (1 + i)(1 - i) = 1 + i - i - i^2 = 1 - (-1) = 2 + 0i$

Notice that this is the product of a conjugate pair, so we get a real number on the real axis. Therefore the polar form is $z\omega = 2(\cos 0 + i \sin 0)$.

We could also have found the polar form by multiplying the moduli and adding the arguments of z and ω.

$|z||\omega| = \sqrt{2} \times \sqrt{2} = 2$ and $\arg(z) + \arg(\omega) = \dfrac{\pi}{4} + \dfrac{7\pi}{4} = 2\pi$, so

$z\omega = 2(\cos 2\pi + i \sin 2\pi) = 2(\cos 0 + i \sin 0)$.

> ### Remember
> An angle of 2π is in the same position on the x-axis as an angle of 0.

(c) Rectangular form: $\dfrac{z}{\omega} = \dfrac{1 + i}{1 - i} = \dfrac{1 + i}{1 - i} \times \dfrac{1 + i}{1 + i} = \dfrac{(1 + i)^2}{1 + 1} = \dfrac{1 + 2i + i^2}{2} = \dfrac{2i}{2}$

$$= i = 0 + i$$

Notice that this is on the imaginary axis. Therefore the polar form

is $\dfrac{z}{\omega} = \cos\dfrac{\pi}{2} + i \sin\dfrac{\pi}{2}$.

We could also have found the polar form by dividing the moduli and subtracting the arguments.

$\dfrac{|z|}{|\omega|} = \dfrac{\sqrt{2}}{\sqrt{2}} = 1$ and $\arg(z) - \arg(\omega) = \dfrac{\pi}{4} - \dfrac{7\pi}{4} = \dfrac{-3\pi}{2}$.

Remember that the negative angle $\dfrac{-3\pi}{2}$ is the same as the positive angle $\dfrac{\pi}{2}$,

so $\dfrac{z}{\omega} = \cos\dfrac{\pi}{2} + i \sin\dfrac{\pi}{2}$.

De Moivre's theorem

De Moivre's theorem states:

if $z = r(\cos\theta + i \sin\theta)$ then $z^n = [r(\cos\theta + i \sin\theta)]^n = r^n(\cos n\theta + i \sin n\theta)$, where $n \in \mathbb{Q}$. This is on page 20 of the *Formulae and Tables* booklet.

See Chapter 16 for the proof of this theorem.

Applications

De Moivre's theorem can be used:

- to raise complex numbers to a power
- to find roots of complex numbers
- to prove trigonometric identities.

(a) Use De Moivre's theorem to evaluate $\left(\cos\dfrac{2\pi}{3} + i\sin\dfrac{2\pi}{3}\right)^2$.

(b) Write $3 - \sqrt{3}i$ in polar form and hence express $\left(3 - \sqrt{3}i\right)^3$ in the form $x + yi$.

Solutions

(a) By De Moivre's theorem, $z = r(\cos\theta + i\sin\theta) \Rightarrow z^n = r^n(\cos n\theta + i\sin n\theta)$.

$$\left(\cos\dfrac{2\pi}{3} + i\sin\dfrac{2\pi}{3}\right)^2 = \cos 2\left(\dfrac{2\pi}{3}\right) + i\sin 2\left(\dfrac{2\pi}{3}\right) = \cos\dfrac{4\pi}{3} + i\sin\dfrac{4\pi}{3}$$

Evaluate to get $-\dfrac{1}{2} - \dfrac{\sqrt{3}}{2}i$.

(b) Plot $3 - \sqrt{3}i$, then find r and θ and use them to find the polar form.

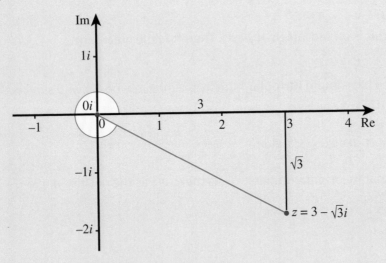

$$r = |z| = \sqrt{3^2 + \left(-\sqrt{3}\right)^2} = \sqrt{9 + 3} = \sqrt{12} = 2\sqrt{3}$$

$$\theta = 360 - \tan^{-1}\dfrac{3}{\sqrt{3}} = 330° = \dfrac{11\pi}{6}\text{ radians}$$

$3 - \sqrt{3}i = r(\cos\theta + i\sin\theta) = 2\sqrt{3}\left(\cos\dfrac{11\pi}{6} + i\sin\dfrac{11\pi}{6}\right)$ in polar form.

Apply De Moivre's theorem, with $n = 3$.

$$\left(3 - \sqrt{3}i\right)^3 = \left(2\sqrt{3}\right)^3\left(\cos 3\left(\dfrac{11\pi}{6}\right) + i\sin 3\left(\dfrac{11\pi}{6}\right)\right)$$

$$= 24\sqrt{3}\left(\cos\dfrac{11\pi}{2} + i\cos\dfrac{11\pi}{2}\right)$$

$$= 24\sqrt{3}\,(0 - i) = 0 - 24\sqrt{3}i$$

Examples

$z = \dfrac{4}{1 + \sqrt{3}i}$ is a complex number, where $i^2 = -1$.

(a) Verify that z can be written as $1 - \sqrt{3}i$.

(b) Plot z on an Argand diagram and write z in polar form.

(c) Use De Moivre's theorem to show that $z^{10} = -2^9(1 - \sqrt{3}i)$.   *(SEC 2013)*

Solutions

(a) Method one

$$z = \frac{4}{1 + \sqrt{3}i} = \frac{4}{1 + \sqrt{3}i} \times \frac{1 - \sqrt{3}i}{1 - \sqrt{3}i}$$ Multiply top and bottom by the conjugate of $1 + \sqrt{3}i$.

$$= \frac{4 - 4\sqrt{3}i}{1 + 3} = 1 - \sqrt{3}i$$

Method two

If $z = \dfrac{4}{1 + \sqrt{3}i} = 1 - \sqrt{3}i$ then $4 = (1 + \sqrt{3}i)(1 - \sqrt{3}i) = (1)^2 + (\sqrt{3})^2 = 4 \checkmark$

So z can be written as $1 - \sqrt{3}i$.

(b)

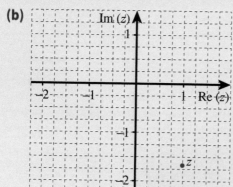

$r = |z| = \sqrt{1^2 + 3^2} = \sqrt{4} = 2$

$\theta = 2\pi - \tan^{-1}\dfrac{\sqrt{3}}{1} = 2\pi - \dfrac{\pi}{3} = \dfrac{5\pi}{3}$

$z = r(\cos\theta + i\sin\theta) = 2\left(\cos\dfrac{5\pi}{3} + i\sin\dfrac{5\pi}{3}\right)$

(c) $z^{10} = \left[2\left(\cos\dfrac{5\pi}{3} + i\sin\dfrac{5\pi}{3}\right)\right]^{10}$

$= 2^{10}\left(\cos\dfrac{5\pi}{3} + i\sin\dfrac{5\pi}{3}\right)^{10} = 2^{10}\left(\cos\dfrac{50\pi}{3} + i\sin\dfrac{50\pi}{3}\right)$ By De Moivre's theorem.

$= 2^{10}\left(\cos\dfrac{2\pi}{3} + i\sin\dfrac{2\pi}{3}\right) = 2^{10}\left(-\dfrac{1}{2} + i\dfrac{\sqrt{3}}{2}\right) = -2^9(1 - \sqrt{3}i)$ as required.

To find the roots of complex numbers such as $\sqrt{1 - i}$, $\sqrt[3]{1 + 0i}$, $\sqrt[4]{8i}$ we require more than one solution. For example, $\sqrt{1 - i}$ will have two solutions, $\sqrt[3]{1 + 0i}$ has three solutions and $\sqrt[4]{8i}$ has four solutions.

How do we generate these solutions?

Remember from trigonometry that to generate more solutions we add $360n$ or $2n\pi$ radians to an angle, where $n \in \mathbb{Z}$. We can apply this to the polar form and call it the **general polar form** of the complex number.

> **Point to note**
>
> General polar form: $z = x + yi$,
> $z = r\left[\cos(\theta + 2n\pi) + i\sin(\theta + 2n\pi)\right]$, where $n \in \mathbb{Z}$.

We can then apply De Moivre's theorem to the general polar form to find the solutions.

Example

Solve the equation $z^2 = 4i$.

Solution

We need to write z as a complex number to a power.

$$z = \sqrt{4i} = (4i)^{\frac{1}{2}}$$

Plot z^2, and hence find its modulus, r and argument, θ.

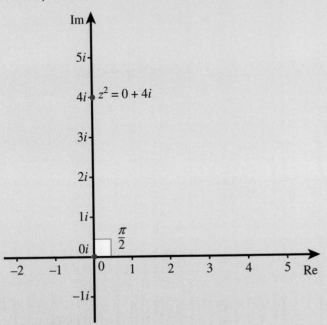

We can see from the diagram that $r = 4$, $\theta = \dfrac{\pi}{2}$.

In general polar form, $z^2 = 4\left[\cos\left(\dfrac{\pi}{2} + 2n\pi\right) + i\sin\left(\dfrac{\pi}{2} + 2n\pi\right)\right]$.

Therefore, by De Moivre's theorem,

$$z = (z^2)^{\frac{1}{2}} = 4^{\frac{1}{2}}\left[\cos\frac{1}{2}\left(\frac{\pi}{2} + 2n\pi\right) + i\sin\frac{1}{2}\left(\frac{\pi}{2} + 2n\pi\right)\right]$$

$$= 2\left[\cos\left(\frac{\pi}{4} + n\pi\right) + i\sin\left(\frac{\pi}{4} + n\pi\right)\right]$$

There are two solutions required to a quadratic, so substitute in $n = 0$ and $n = 1$.

$$n = 0 \Rightarrow z = 2\left[\cos\left(\frac{\pi}{4} + (0)\pi\right) + i\sin\left(\frac{\pi}{4} + (0)\pi\right)\right] = 2\left[\cos\left(\frac{\pi}{4}\right) + i\sin\left(\frac{\pi}{4}\right)\right]$$

$$= 2\left(\frac{\sqrt{2}}{2} + i\frac{\sqrt{2}}{2}\right) = \sqrt{2} + \sqrt{2}i$$

$$n = 1 \Rightarrow z = 2\left[\cos\left(\frac{\pi}{4} + (1)\pi\right) + i\sin\left(\frac{\pi}{4} + (1)\pi\right)\right] = 2\left[\cos\left(\frac{5\pi}{4}\right) + i\sin\left(\frac{5\pi}{4}\right)\right]$$

$$= 2\left(-\frac{\sqrt{2}}{2} - i\frac{\sqrt{2}}{2}\right) = -\sqrt{2} - \sqrt{2}i$$

The two solutions are $z = \sqrt{2} + \sqrt{2}i$ and $z = -\sqrt{2} - \sqrt{2}i$

Examples

The complex number z has modulus $5\dfrac{1}{16}$ and argument $\dfrac{4\pi}{9}$.

(a) Find, in polar form, the four complex fourth roots of z. (That is, find the four values of w for which $w^4 = z$.)

(b) z is marked on the Argand diagram. On the same diagram, show the four answers to part (a).

(SEC 2012)

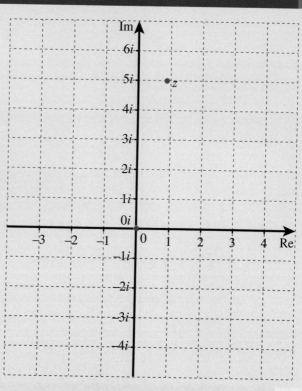

Solutions

(a) $z = 5\dfrac{1}{16}\left(\cos\dfrac{4\pi}{9} + i\sin\dfrac{4\pi}{9}\right)$

$$= \dfrac{81}{16}\left(\cos\left(\dfrac{4\pi}{9} + 2n\pi\right) + i\sin\left(\dfrac{4\pi}{9} + 2n\pi\right)\right)$$

Write z in general polar form.

$w^4 = z \Rightarrow w = z^{\frac{1}{4}}$

$$\Rightarrow w = \sqrt[4]{\dfrac{81}{16}}\left(\cos\left(\dfrac{\dfrac{4\pi}{9} + 2n\pi}{4}\right) + i\sin\left(\dfrac{\dfrac{4\pi}{9} - 2n\pi}{4}\right)\right),$$

$n = 0, 1, 2, 3$ By De Moivre's theorem.

$$\Rightarrow w = \dfrac{3}{2}\left(\cos\left(\dfrac{\pi}{9} + \dfrac{n\pi}{2}\right) + i\sin\left(\dfrac{\pi}{9} + \dfrac{n\pi}{2}\right)\right), n = 0, 1, 2, 3$$

$$\Rightarrow w_1 = \dfrac{3}{2}\left(\cos\left(\dfrac{\pi}{9}\right) + i\sin\left(\dfrac{\pi}{9}\right)\right), \qquad w_2 = \dfrac{3}{2}\left(\cos\left(\dfrac{11\pi}{18}\right) + i\sin\left(\dfrac{11\pi}{18}\right)\right),$$

$$w_3 = \dfrac{3}{2}\left(\cos\left(\dfrac{10\pi}{9}\right) + i\sin\left(\dfrac{10\pi}{9}\right)\right), \quad w_4 = \dfrac{3}{2}\left(\cos\left(\dfrac{29\pi}{18}\right) + i\sin\left(\dfrac{29\pi}{18}\right)\right)$$

(b)

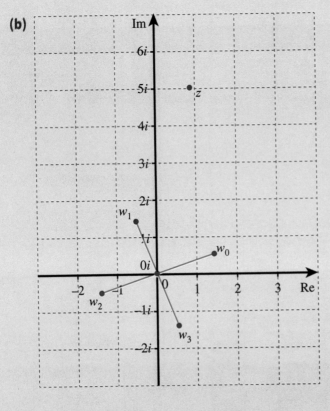

Notice that the roots are on a circle centre $(0, 0)$ and radius 1·5 units and positioned 90° from each other.

Examples

(a) **(i)** Write the complex number $1 - i$ in polar form.

  (ii) Use De Moivre's theorem to evaluate $(1 - i)^9$, giving your answer in rectangular form.

(b) A complex number z has modulus greater than 1.

  The three numbers z, z^2 and z^3 are shown on the Argand diagram.

  One of them lies on the imaginary axis as shown.

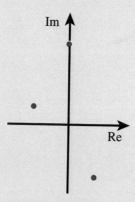

  (i) Label the points on the diagram to show which point corresponds to which number.

  (ii) Find θ, the argument of z.

  (SEC 2011)

Solutions

(a) **(i)**

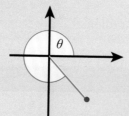

$$r = \sqrt{1^2 + 1^2} = \sqrt{2}, \ \theta = 2\pi - \tan^{-1}\left(\frac{1}{1}\right) = \frac{7\pi}{4} \text{ radians}$$

$$1 - i = \sqrt{2}\left(\cos\left(\frac{7\pi}{4}\right) + i\sin\left(\frac{7\pi}{4}\right)\right)$$

> **Point to note**
>
> It would also be correct to write θ as $-\frac{\pi}{4}$ radians, $-45°$ or $315°$.

(ii) $(1 - i)^9 = \left(\sqrt{2}\left(\cos\left(\frac{-\pi}{4}\right) + i\sin\left(\frac{-\pi}{4}\right)\right)\right)^9$ Use $\theta = -\frac{\pi}{4}$, as this is easiest

to work with.

$$= (\sqrt{2})^9 \left(\cos\left(-\frac{9\pi}{4}\right) + i\sin\left(-\frac{9\pi}{4}\right)\right)$$

$$= 16\sqrt{2}\left(\frac{1}{\sqrt{2}} - \frac{1}{\sqrt{2}}i\right)$$

$$= 16 - 16i$$

(b) (i)

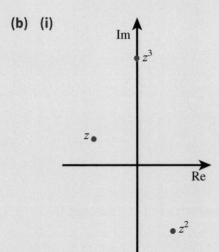

(ii) By De Moivre's theorem, z^3 has argument $3\theta = (90 + 360n)°$, so z has argument $\theta = (30 + 120n)°$.

z is in the second quadrant, so $\theta = 150°$ or $\frac{5\pi}{6}$ radians.

Example

Solve $z^4 - 1 = 0$.

Plot the solutions on an Argand diagram and comment on the pattern of the roots.

Solution

We could solve the equation by finding the general polar form, applying De Moivre's theorem and substituting in values for n as in previous examples.

We can also solve the equation using factors.

$$z^4 - 1 = (z^2 - 1)(z^2 + 1) = 0$$

$$z^2 = 1 \implies z = \pm\sqrt{1} = \pm1$$

$$z^2 = -1 \implies z = \pm\sqrt{-1} = \pm i$$

The fourth roots are 1, -1, i and $-i$.

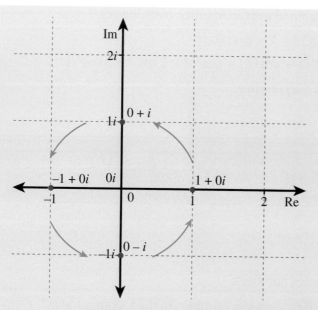

We can see from the diagram that the roots form a pattern. Each root can be found by rotating the preceding root 90° anti-clockwise about the origin.

Point to note

Similar patterns can be found for other types of root, but the angle of rotation will change.

De Moivre's theorem can be used to prove the identity
$\cos 3\theta = 4\cos^3 \theta - 3\cos \theta$.

Expand $(\cos \theta + i \sin \theta)^3$ using De Moivre's theorem to get $\cos 3\theta + i \sin 3\theta$.

Expand $(\cos \theta + i \sin \theta)^3$ using the binomial expansion of $(x + y)^3$ to get
$\cos^3\theta + 3\cos^2\theta\,(i \sin \theta) + 3\cos \theta\,(i^2 \sin^2\theta) + i^3 \sin^3\theta$

$= \cos^3\theta + 3i\cos^2\theta \sin \theta - 3\cos \theta \sin^2\theta - i \sin^3\theta.$

Remember

$i^2 = -1, \; i^3 = -i$

Equating the two results:
$\cos 3\theta + i \sin 3\theta = \cos^3 \theta + 3i\cos^2\theta \sin \theta - 3\cos \theta \sin^2\theta - i \sin^3\theta$

Equate real parts:
$\cos 3\theta = \cos^3\theta - 3\cos \theta \sin^2\theta$

Now simplify by replacing $\sin^2 \theta$ with an identity involving $\cos \theta$.

$\cos^2 \theta + \sin^2 \theta = 1 \Rightarrow \sin^2 \theta = 1 - \cos^2 \theta$

$\cos 3\theta = \cos^3 \theta - 3 \cos \theta (1 - \cos^2 \theta) = \cos^3 \theta - 3 \cos \theta + 3 \cos^3 \theta$

$\cos 3\theta = 4 \cos^3 \theta - 3 \cos \theta$ as required.

> **Point to note**
>
> We can also prove the identity $\sin 3\theta = 3 \sin \theta - 4 \sin^3 \theta$ by equating the imaginary parts and then simplifying.

Checklist

- ✓ Know how to plot complex numbers.

- ✓ Practise finding r and θ for complex numbers in the four quadrants and on the axes.

- ✓ Practise finding the polar form of a complex number and using De Moivre's theorem for complex numbers.

- ✓ Practise finding the general polar form and roots of complex numbers.

- ✓ Know the geometrical interpretation associated with the operations of complex numbers.

- ✓ Know how to prove trigonometric identities.

Proof by Induction

16

Learning objectives

In this chapter you will learn how to prove by induction:

- Simple identities such as the sum of the first n natural numbers and the sum of a finite geometric series
- Simple identities such as $n! > 2^n$, $2^n \geq n^2$ $(n \geq 4)$, $(1 + x)^n \geq 1 + nx$ $(x > -1)$
- Factorisation results such as 2 is a factor of $3^n - 1$
- De Moivre's theorem for $n \in \mathbb{N}$.

Introduction

Mathematical induction is a method of proof used to establish that a given statement or proposition is true for all natural numbers. It is a 'rolling proof', similar to a domino effect.

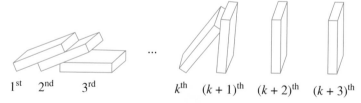

1st 2nd 3rd ... k^{th} $(k + 1)^{th}$ $(k + 2)^{th}$ $(k + 3)^{th}$

Steps involved in proof by induction:

1. Prove that the proposition or statement $P(n)$ is true for the smallest value in question, usually $n = 1$.
2. Assume the proposition is true for $n = k$.
3. Prove that the proposition is true for $n = k + 1$ (the next domino).
4. The proposition is true for $n = 1$. If the proposition is true for $n = k$, then it will be true for $n = k + 1$. Therefore by induction it is true for all n where n is a natural number.

Series

Example

Prove, by induction, that the sum of the first n natural numbers,

$1 + 2 + 3 + \ldots + n$, is $\dfrac{n(n + 1)}{2}$.

(SEC 2014)

Solution

1 Show that $P(n)$ is true for $n = 1$.

$$P(1): 1 = \frac{(1)((1) + 1)}{2} = 1 \quad \checkmark$$

2 Assume that $P(n)$ is true for $n = k$.

$$1 + 2 + 3 + \ldots + k = \frac{k(k + 1)}{2}$$

3 Prove that $P(n)$ is true for $n = k + 1$.

$$P(k + 1): 1 + 2 + 3 + \ldots + k + (k + 1) = \frac{(k + 1)((k + 1) + 1)}{2} = \frac{(k + 1)(k + 2)}{2}$$

Because $P(k)$ is true, we can rewrite the left-hand side as

$$\frac{k(k + 1)}{2} + (k + 1) = \frac{k(k + 1)}{2} + \frac{2(k + 1)}{2} \qquad \text{Multiply the second term by } \frac{2}{2}.$$

$$= \frac{(k + 1)(k + 2)}{2} \quad \text{as required.}$$

Hence, $P(k + 1)$ is true.

4 $P(1)$ is true, so $P(2)$ is true, and so on. Hence, by induction, $P(n)$ is true for all $n \in \mathbb{N}$.

Example

Prove by induction that $S_n = \dfrac{a(1 - r^n)}{1 - r}$ for all $n \in \mathbb{N}$.

Point to note

This is the formula for the sum of a finite geometric series.

Solution

1 Show that $P(n)$ is true for $n = 1$.

$$S_1 = \frac{a(1 - r^{(1)})}{1} = a \text{ (first term of geometric series} = a) \quad \checkmark$$

2 Assume that $P(n)$ is true for $n = k$.

$$S_k = \frac{a(1 - r^k)}{1 - r}$$

3 Prove that $P(n)$ is true for $n = k + 1$.

> **Remember**
>
> Recall that in a geometric series, $T_n = ar^{n-1} \Rightarrow T_{n+1} = ar^n$
> and $S_{n+1} = S_n + T_{n+1}$.

$$S_{k+1} = S_k + T_{k+1} = \frac{a(1 - r^k)}{1 - r} + ar^k$$

$$= \frac{a(1 - r^k)}{1 - r} + \frac{ar^k(1 - r)}{1 - r} = \frac{a(1 - r^k + r^k - r^{k+1})}{1 - r}$$

$$= \frac{a(1 - r^{k+1})}{1 - r} \quad \text{as required.}$$

Hence, $P(k + 1)$ is true.

4 $P(1)$ is true, so $P(2)$ is true, and so on. Hence, by induction, $P(n)$ is true for all $n \in \mathbb{N}$.

Divisibility

The key phrases used here are 'is divisible by' and 'is a factor of'.

Example

Prove that $3^n - 1$ is divisible by 2, for all natural numbers.

Solution

Point to note

The symbol | means 'is divisible by'.

1 Show that $P(n)$ is true for $n = 1$.

$P(1)$: $3^1 - 1 = 2 | 2$ ✓

2 Assume that $P(n)$ is true for $n = k$.

$P(k)$: $3^k - 1 | 2$

3 Prove that $P(n)$ is true for $n = k + 1$.

$P(k + 1)$: $3^{k+1} - 1 | 2$

$3^{k+1} - 1 = 3^k(3) - 1 = 3^k(2 + 1) - 1 = 2(3^k) + 3^k - 1$

$2(3^k)$ and $3^k - 1$ are both divisible by 2.

$\therefore\ 2(3^k) + 3^k - 1 | 2$

4 $P(1)$ is true, so $P(2)$ is true, and so on. Hence, by induction, $P(n)$ is true for all $n \in \mathbb{N}$.

Example

Prove by induction that $7^n - 2^n$ is divisible by 5 for all values of $n \in \mathbb{N}$.

Solution

1 Show that $P(n)$ is true for $n = 1$

$P(1)$: $7^1 - 2^1 = 7 - 2 = 5|5$ ✓

2 Assume that $P(n)$ is true for $n = k$.

$P(k)$: $7^k - 2^k|5$

3 Prove that $P(n)$ is true for $n = k + 1$.

$P(k + 1)$: $7^{k+1} - 2^{k+1}|5$

$7^{k+1} - 2^{k+1} = 7^k(7) - 2^k(2) = 7^k(5 + 2) - 2^k(2) = 5(7^k) + 2(7^k - 2^k)$

Both $5(7^k)$ and $2(7^k - 2^k)$ are divisible by 5.

$\therefore 5(7^k) + 2(7^k - 2^k)|5$

4 $P(1)$ is true, so $P(2)$ is true, and so on. Hence, by induction, $P(n)$ is true for all $n \in \mathbb{N}$.

Inequalities

> **Point to note**
>
> If $a \geq b$ and $b \geq c$ then $a \geq c$. If $a \leq b$ and $b \leq c$ then $a \leq c$.
> $a^2 \geq 0$ for $a \in \mathbb{R}$.

Example

Prove by induction that $2^n \geq n^2$ for $n \geq 4$, $n \in \mathbb{N}$.

Solution

1 Show that $P(n)$ is true for $n = 4$.

$P(4)$: $2^4 \geq 4^2 \Rightarrow 16 \geq 16$ ✓

2 Assume that $P(n)$ is true for $n = k$.

$P(k)$: $2^k \geq k^2$

3 Prove that $P(n)$ is true for $n = k + 1$.

$P(k + 1)$: $2^{k+1} \geq (k + 1)^2 \, [a \geq c]$

From $P(k)$ we know that $2^k \geq k^2 \Rightarrow 2(2^k) \geq 2k^2 \Rightarrow 2^{k+1} \geq 2k^2 \, [a \geq b]$

We need to show that $2k^2 \geq (k+1)^2 \, [b \geq c]$.

$2k^2 \geq (k+1)^2 \Rightarrow 2k^2 \geq k^2 + 2k + 1 \Rightarrow k^2 - 2k \geq 1$. This is true for $k \geq 4$.

$\therefore P(k+1)$ is true.

4 $P(4)$ is true, so $P(5)$ is true, and so on. Hence, by induction, $P(n)$ is true for all $n \geq 4$, $n \in \mathbb{N}$.

Example

Prove by induction that $n! > 2^n$ for $n \geq 4$, $n \in \mathbb{N}$.

Solution

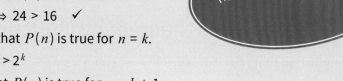

Point to note

$(n+1)! = (n+1)n!$

1 Show that $P(n)$ is true for $n = 4$

$4! > 2^4 \Rightarrow 24 > 16$ ✓

2 Assume that $P(n)$ is true for $n = k$.

$P(k)$: $k! > 2^k$

3 Prove that $P(n)$ is true for $n = k + 1$.

$P(k+1)$: $(k+1)! > 2^{k+1}$

From $P(k)$ we know that $k! > 2^k \Rightarrow (k+1)k! > 2^k(k+1)$

$$\Rightarrow (k+1)! > 2^k(k+1)$$

We proceed in a similar way to the previous example.

We need to show that $2^k(k+1) > 2^{k+1}$.

$2^k(k+1) > 2^{k+1} \Rightarrow k+1 > \dfrac{2^{k+1}}{2^k} = 2$

$k + 1 > 2$ is true for $k \geq 4$.

$\therefore P(k+1)$ is true.

4 $P(4)$ is true, so $P(5)$ is true, and so on. Hence, by induction, $P(n)$ is true for all $n \geq 4$, $n \in \mathbb{N}$.

Example

Prove by induction that $(1+x)^n \geq 1 + nx$, $x > -1$, $n \in \mathbb{N}$.

1 Show that $P(n)$ is true for $n = 1$.

$P(1)$: $(1+x)^1 \geq 1 + 1x \Rightarrow 1 + x \geq 1 + x$ ✓

2 Assume that $P(n)$ is true for $n = k$.

$P(k)$: $(1+x)^k \geq 1 + kx$

3 Prove that $P(n)$ is true for $n = k + 1$.

$P(k + 1)$: $(1 + x)^{k+1} \geq 1 + (k + 1)x$

From $P(k)$ we know that $(1 + x)^k \geq 1 + kx \Rightarrow (1 + x)^k (1 + x) \geq (1 + kx)(1 + x)$

$$\Rightarrow (1 + x)^{k+1} \geq (1 + kx)(1 + x)$$

We proceed in a similar way to the previous example.

We need to show that $(1 + kx)(1 + x) \geq 1 + (k + 1)x$.

$(1 + kx)(1 + x) \geq 1 + (k + 1)x \Rightarrow 1 + kx + x + kx^2 \geq 1 + (k + 1)x$

$$\Rightarrow 1 + (k + 1)x + kx^2 \geq 1 + (k + 1)x$$

$$\Rightarrow kx^2 \geq 0 \qquad \text{This is true for } x > -1, k \in \mathbb{N}.$$

$\therefore P(k + 1)$ is true.

4 $P(1)$ is true, so $P(2)$ is true, and so on. Hence, by induction, $P(n)$ is true for all $n \in \mathbb{N}$.

Proof of De Moivre's theorem by induction

Prove by induction that $(\cos \theta + i \sin \theta)^n = \cos n\theta + i \sin n\theta$ if n is a positive integer ($n \in \mathbb{N}$).

1 Show that $P(n)$ is true for $n = 1$.

$P(1)$: $(\cos \theta + i \sin \theta)^{(1)} = \cos(1)\theta + i \sin(1)\theta$ ✓

2 Assume that $P(n)$ is true for $n = k$.

$P(k)$: $(\cos \theta + i \sin \theta)^k = \cos k\theta + i \sin k\theta$

3 Prove that $P(n)$ is true for $n = k + 1$.

$P(k + 1)$: $(\cos \theta + i \sin \theta)^{k+1} = [\cos(k + 1)\theta + i \sin(k + 1)\theta]$

$(\cos\theta + i \sin\theta)^{k+1} = (\cos \theta + i \sin \theta)^k(\cos \theta + i \sin \theta)$

$$= (\cos k\theta + i \sin k\theta)(\cos \theta + i \sin \theta) \qquad \text{By } P(k).$$

$$= \cos k\theta \cos\theta - \sin k\theta \sin\theta + i(\cos k\theta \sin \theta + \sin k\theta \cos \theta)$$

$$= \cos(k + 1)\theta + i \sin(k + 1)\theta \qquad \text{Using trigonometric identities.}$$

$\therefore P(k + 1)$ is true.

4 $P(1)$ is true, so $P(2)$ is true, and so on. Hence, by induction, $P(n)$ is true for all $n \in \mathbb{N}$.

Checklist

✓ Learn the method of proof by induction for all the examples in this chapter.

Binomial Theorem 17

Learning objectives

In this chapter you will learn how to:

- Work with binomial coefficients and apply the binomial theorem
- Recognise the general term of a binomial expansion and apply it to a binomial distribution.

$\binom{n}{r}$ notation

The symbol $\binom{n}{r}$ is the **binomial coefficient**, and represents the number of ways of choosing r objects from a set of n objects. It is often said aloud as 'n choose r'.

> **Top-Tip**
>
> The symbols $n\,Cr$ and $C(n,\,r)$ mean the same as $\binom{n}{r}$.

The formula is on page 20 of the *Formulae and Tables* booklet.

$$\binom{n}{r} = n\,Cr = C(n, r) = \frac{n!}{(n-r)!\,r!}$$

$$\binom{5}{3} = \frac{5!}{(5-3)!\,3!} = \frac{5!}{2!\,3!} = \frac{5 \times 4 \times 3 \times 2 \times 1}{2 \times 1 \times 3 \times 2 \times 1} = 10$$

We can check this on a calculator using the $n\,Cr$ button.

Examples

Evaluate:

(a) $\binom{6}{3}$ (b) $\binom{7}{5}$ (c) $\binom{3}{0} + \binom{3}{1} + \binom{3}{2} + \binom{3}{3}$.

Solutions

(a) $\binom{6}{3} = \dfrac{6!}{(6-3)!\,3!} = 20$ (b) $\binom{7}{5} = \binom{7}{2} = \dfrac{7!}{(7-2)!\,2!} = 21$

(c) $\binom{3}{0} + \binom{3}{1} + \binom{3}{2} + \binom{3}{3} = 1 + 3 + 3 + 1 = 8$

Binomial coefficients and Pascal's triangle

To construct **Pascal's triangle**, start with a 1 at the top, and arrange rows of numbers below in a triangular pattern. Each number is the sum of the two numbers above it.

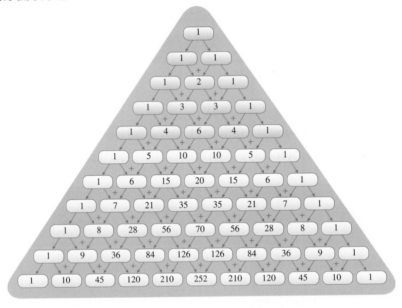

There are many interesting features of Pascal's triangle, not least that it can be written using binomial coefficients.

$$\binom{0}{0}$$

$$\binom{1}{0} \quad + \quad \binom{1}{1}$$

$$\binom{2}{0} \quad + \quad \binom{2}{1} \quad + \quad \binom{2}{2}$$

$$\binom{3}{0} \quad + \quad \binom{3}{1} \qquad \binom{3}{2} \qquad \binom{3}{3}$$

$$\binom{4}{0} \qquad \binom{4}{1} \qquad \binom{4}{2} \qquad \binom{4}{3} \qquad \binom{4}{4}$$

Pascal's triangle can be used to expand a binomial.

A binomial is an expression with two terms, such as $a + b$.

Expanding a binomial means taking a binomial raised to the power of n, such as $(a + b)^n$, and multiplying out the brackets.

$$(a + b)^0 = 1$$
$$(a + b)^1 = 1a + 1b$$
$$(a + b)^2 = 1a^2 + 2ab + 1b^2$$
$$(a + b)^3 = 1a^3 + 3a^2b + 3ab^2 + 1b^3$$
$$(a + b)^4 = 1a^4 + 4a^3b + 6a^2b^2 + 4ab^3 + 1b^4$$
$$(a + b)^5 = 1a^5 + 5a^4b + 10a^3b^2 + 10a^2b^3 + 5ab^4 + 1b^5$$

Note that:

- Each row has one more term than the previous row.
- In each row, the powers of a decrease and the powers of b increase.

Binomial theorem

The **binomial theorem** gives a formula for expanding a binomial. It is on page 20 of the *Formulae and Tables* booklet.

$$(x + y)^n = \sum_{r=0}^{n} \binom{n}{r} x^{n-r} y^r$$

$$= \binom{n}{0} x^n + \binom{n}{1} x^{n-1} y + \binom{n}{2} x^{n-2} y^2 + \dots + \binom{n}{r} x^{n-r} y^r + \dots + \binom{n}{n} y^n$$

- The expansion of $(x + y)^n$ has $n + 1$ terms, e.g. $(x + y)^3$ has 4 terms in its expansion.
- The x term will start with a power of n and then decrease to a power of 0.
- The y term will start with a power of 0 and then increase to a power of n.
- The sum of the powers of any term will equal n.
- The sum of the binomial coefficients of any expansion $= 2^n$.
- The general term of a binomial expansion is $\binom{n}{r} x^{n-r} y^r$.

Example

Write out the binomial expansion of **(a)** $(x + y)^3$ **(b)** $(x - y)^3$.

Solutions

(a) $(x + y)^3 = \binom{3}{0}x^3y^0 + \binom{3}{1}x^2y^1 + \binom{3}{2}x^1y^2 + \binom{3}{3}x^0y^3 = x^3 + 3x^2y + 3xy^2 + y^3$

Notice how the x term powers decrease and the y term powers increase.

(b) $(x - y)^3 = \binom{3}{0}x^3(-y)^0 + \binom{3}{1}x^2(-y)^1 + \binom{3}{2}x^1(-y)^2 + \binom{3}{3}x^0(-y)^3$

$\qquad = x^3 - 3x^2y + 3xy^2 - y^3$

Notice the pattern of signs. When the y term of the binomial is negative, the odd powers of y in the expansion have a negative coefficient.

Example

Write out the binomial expansion of $\left(3x^2 + \dfrac{2}{x}\right)^3$ and hence find the term independent of x.

Solution

$\left(3x^2 + \dfrac{2}{x}\right)^3 = \binom{3}{0}(3x^2)^3 + \binom{3}{1}(3x^2)^2\left(\dfrac{2}{x}\right) + \binom{3}{2}(3x^2)^1\left(\dfrac{2}{x}\right)^2 + \binom{3}{3}\left(\dfrac{2}{x}\right)^3$

$\qquad = 27x^6 + 54x^3 + 36 + \dfrac{8}{x^3}$

The third term in the expansion, 36, is the term independent of x. The power of x in this term is the same in the numerator and the denominator, so they cancel out.

Example

Show that $(1 + x)^4 - (1 - x)^4 = 8x(1 + x^2)$, and hence evaluate $\left(1 + \sqrt{3}\right)^4 - \left(1 - \sqrt{3}\right)^4$. Give your answer in the form $k\sqrt{3}$, where $k \in \mathbb{N}$.

Solution

$(1 + x)^4 = 1 + 4x + 6x^2 + 4x^3 + x^4$

$(1 - x)^4 = 1 - 4x + 6x^2 - 4x^3 + x^4$

Top Tip

You can use the binomial theorem or Pascal's triangle to work out expansions. Here it is easier to use Pascal's triangle, because 1 is a term in the expansion.

Subtracting these results gives

$$1 + 4x + 6x^2 + 4x^3 + x^4 - (1 - 4x + 6x^2 - 4x^3 + x^4)$$

$$= 1 + 4x + 6x^2 + 4x^3 + x^4 - 1 + 4x - 6x^2 + 4x^3 - x^4$$

$$= 4x + 4x + 4x^3 + 4x^3 = 8x + 8x^3 = 8x(1 + x^2)$$

Notice that the even terms cancel each other out.

So $x = \sqrt{3} \Rightarrow (1 + \sqrt{3})^4 - (1 - \sqrt{3})^4 = 8\sqrt{3}(1 + (\sqrt{3})^2) = 8\sqrt{3}(1 + 3) = 32\sqrt{3}$.

General term of binomial expansion

The general term of a binomial expansion is $t_{r+1} = \binom{n}{r} x^{n-r} y^r$. This is included in the binomial theorem on page 20 of the *Formulae and Tables* booklet.

Examples

(a) Find the coefficient of x^4 in the expansion of $(1 - 3x)^6$.

(b) Find the value of the middle term if $x = 0.25$.

Solutions

(a) $t_{r+1} = \binom{n}{r} x^{n-r} y^r$

In this question $n = 6$. We require a term with $x^4 \Rightarrow r = 4 \Rightarrow t_5 = \binom{6}{4} 1^{6-4} (-3x)^4$

$t_5 = 15(1)^2 (81x^4) = 1215 x^4$

So the coefficient of x^4 is 1215.

(b) The expansion will have seven terms, so the middle term is the fourth term. $n = 6$ and $r + 1 = 4$ so $r = 3$.

$t_4 = \binom{6}{3} 1^{6-3} (-3x)^3 = 20(1)^3 (-27x^3) = -540x^3 = -540(0.25)^3 = \dfrac{-135}{16}$

Examples

(a) Write out the first three terms of the binomial expansion of $\left(x^2 + \dfrac{1}{\sqrt{x}}\right)^{15}$.

(b) Find the term independent of x.

Solutions

(a) $\binom{15}{0}(x^2)^{15} + \binom{15}{1}(x^2)^{14}\left(\dfrac{1}{\sqrt{x}}\right)^1 + \binom{15}{2}(x^2)^{13}\left(\dfrac{1}{\sqrt{x}}\right)^2 = x^{30} + 15\dfrac{x^{28}}{\sqrt{x}} + 105x^{25}$

(b) $t_{r+1} = \binom{n}{r} x^{n-r} y^r$, $n = 15$

Extract powers of x from the general term. We know that the independent power of x has a power of zero.

$$(x^2)^{15-r}\left(\frac{1}{\sqrt{x}}\right)^r = \frac{x^{30-2r}}{x^{\frac{r}{2}}} = x^{30-\frac{5r}{2}}$$

$$\therefore x^{30-\frac{5r}{2}} = x^0 \Rightarrow 30 - \frac{5r}{2} = 0 \Rightarrow 30 = \frac{5r}{2} \Rightarrow r = 12$$

Using the general term, with $n = 15$ and $r = 12$

$$t_{13} = \binom{15}{12}(x^2)^{15-12}\left(\frac{1}{\sqrt{x}}\right)^{12} = 455\frac{x^6}{x^6} = 455$$

Binomial distribution

The **binomial distribution** gives a formula for the probability of r successes when n trials (called **Bernoulli trials**) are carried out. It is given on page 33 of the *Formulae and Tables* booklet.

$$P(X = r) = \binom{n}{r} p^r q^{n-r}, \ r = 0, ..., n$$

- Each trial has two possible outcomes: success or failure.
- The trials are independent of each other.
- The probability of success is the same for each trial.
- p = probability of success, q = probability of failure, n = number of trials, r = number of successes.

This section is just a brief introduction to the binomial distribution. It is covered in more detail in the probability chapters in Book 2.

Example

A fair coin is flipped eight times. Find the probability that a head appears exactly four times.

Solution

$n = 8$, $r = 4$, $p = \dfrac{1}{2}$, $q = \dfrac{1}{2}$

$$P(X = r) = \binom{n}{r} p^r q^{n-r}$$

$$P(X = 4) = \binom{8}{4}\left(\frac{1}{2}\right)^4\left(\frac{1}{2}\right)^4 = 70\left(\frac{1}{2}\right)^8 = \frac{70}{256} = 0 \cdot 2734$$

✓ Practise using Pascal's triangle and the binomial theorem.

✓ Be careful when expanding terms, especially with exponents and negative signs.

✓ Practise using your calculator to evaluate nCr when n and r are known.

✓ Show your work carefully, and make terms clear when using the binomial theorem.

Questions to Practise

If you have a difficulty with a question do the following.

- Write the page number and the question number in the boxes provided.

- Practise the question. Each time you practise, tick a box.

- Usually, five ticks will indicate that you have mastered the difficulty.

This is a very efficient study method.

Page Number	Question Number						Page Number	Question Number					
		☐	☐	☐	☐	☐			☐	☐	☐	☐	☐
		☐	☐	☐	☐	☐			☐	☐	☐	☐	☐
		☐	☐	☐	☐	☐			☐	☐	☐	☐	☐
		☐	☐	☐	☐	☐			☐	☐	☐	☐	☐
		☐	☐	☐	☐	☐			☐	☐	☐	☐	☐
		☐	☐	☐	☐	☐			☐	☐	☐	☐	☐
		☐	☐	☐	☐	☐			☐	☐	☐	☐	☐
		☐	☐	☐	☐	☐			☐	☐	☐	☐	☐
		☐	☐	☐	☐	☐			☐	☐	☐	☐	☐
		☐	☐	☐	☐	☐			☐	☐	☐	☐	☐
		☐	☐	☐	☐	☐			☐	☐	☐	☐	☐
		☐	☐	☐	☐	☐			☐	☐	☐	☐	☐
		☐	☐	☐	☐	☐			☐	☐	☐	☐	☐
		☐	☐	☐	☐	☐			☐	☐	☐	☐	☐
		☐	☐	☐	☐	☐			☐	☐	☐	☐	☐

Page Number	Question Number						Page Number	Question Number					
		☐	☐	☐	☐	☐			☐	☐	☐	☐	☐
		☐	☐	☐	☐	☐			☐	☐	☐	☐	☐
		☐	☐	☐	☐	☐			☐	☐	☐	☐	☐
		☐	☐	☐	☐	☐			☐	☐	☐	☐	☐
		☐	☐	☐	☐	☐			☐	☐	☐	☐	☐
		☐	☐	☐	☐	☐			☐	☐	☐	☐	☐
		☐	☐	☐	☐	☐			☐	☐	☐	☐	☐
		☐	☐	☐	☐	☐			☐	☐	☐	☐	☐
		☐	☐	☐	☐	☐			☐	☐	☐	☐	☐
		☐	☐	☐	☐	☐			☐	☐	☐	☐	☐
		☐	☐	☐	☐	☐			☐	☐	☐	☐	☐
		☐	☐	☐	☐	☐			☐	☐	☐	☐	☐
		☐	☐	☐	☐	☐			☐	☐	☐	☐	☐
		☐	☐	☐	☐	☐			☐	☐	☐	☐	☐
		☐	☐	☐	☐	☐			☐	☐	☐	☐	☐
		☐	☐	☐	☐	☐			☐	☐	☐	☐	☐
		☐	☐	☐	☐	☐			☐	☐	☐	☐	☐
		☐	☐	☐	☐	☐			☐	☐	☐	☐	☐
		☐	☐	☐	☐	☐			☐	☐	☐	☐	☐
		☐	☐	☐	☐	☐			☐	☐	☐	☐	☐
		☐	☐	☐	☐	☐			☐	☐	☐	☐	☐
		☐	☐	☐	☐	☐			☐	☐	☐	☐	☐
		☐	☐	☐	☐	☐			☐	☐	☐	☐	☐
		☐	☐	☐	☐	☐			☐	☐	☐	☐	☐
		☐	☐	☐	☐	☐			☐	☐	☐	☐	☐
		☐	☐	☐	☐	☐			☐	☐	☐	☐	☐
		☐	☐	☐	☐	☐			☐	☐	☐	☐	☐

Page Number	Question Number						Page Number	Question Number					
		☐	☐	☐	☐	☐			☐	☐	☐	☐	☐
		☐	☐	☐	☐	☐			☐	☐	☐	☐	☐
		☐	☐	☐	☐	☐			☐	☐	☐	☐	☐
		☐	☐	☐	☐	☐			☐	☐	☐	☐	☐
		☐	☐	☐	☐	☐			☐	☐	☐	☐	☐
		☐	☐	☐	☐	☐			☐	☐	☐	☐	☐
		☐	☐	☐	☐	☐			☐	☐	☐	☐	☐
		☐	☐	☐	☐	☐			☐	☐	☐	☐	☐
		☐	☐	☐	☐	☐			☐	☐	☐	☐	☐
		☐	☐	☐	☐	☐			☐	☐	☐	☐	☐
		☐	☐	☐	☐	☐			☐	☐	☐	☐	☐
		☐	☐	☐	☐	☐			☐	☐	☐	☐	☐
		☐	☐	☐	☐	☐			☐	☐	☐	☐	☐
		☐	☐	☐	☐	☐			☐	☐	☐	☐	☐
		☐	☐	☐	☐	☐			☐	☐	☐	☐	☐
		☐	☐	☐	☐	☐			☐	☐	☐	☐	☐
		☐	☐	☐	☐	☐			☐	☐	☐	☐	☐
		☐	☐	☐	☐	☐			☐	☐	☐	☐	☐
		☐	☐	☐	☐	☐			☐	☐	☐	☐	☐
		☐	☐	☐	☐	☐			☐	☐	☐	☐	☐
		☐	☐	☐	☐	☐			☐	☐	☐	☐	☐
		☐	☐	☐	☐	☐			☐	☐	☐	☐	☐
		☐	☐	☐	☐	☐			☐	☐	☐	☐	☐
		☐	☐	☐	☐	☐			☐	☐	☐	☐	☐
		☐	☐	☐	☐	☐			☐	☐	☐	☐	☐
		☐	☐	☐	☐	☐			☐	☐	☐	☐	☐
		☐	☐	☐	☐	☐			☐	☐	☐	☐	☐
		☐	☐	☐	☐	☐			☐	☐	☐	☐	☐

Page Number	Question Number						Page Number	Question Number					
		☐	☐	☐	☐	☐			☐	☐	☐	☐	☐
		☐	☐	☐	☐	☐			☐	☐	☐	☐	☐
		☐	☐	☐	☐	☐			☐	☐	☐	☐	☐
		☐	☐	☐	☐	☐			☐	☐	☐	☐	☐
		☐	☐	☐	☐	☐			☐	☐	☐	☐	☐
		☐	☐	☐	☐	☐			☐	☐	☐	☐	☐
		☐	☐	☐	☐	☐			☐	☐	☐	☐	☐
		☐	☐	☐	☐	☐			☐	☐	☐	☐	☐
		☐	☐	☐	☐	☐			☐	☐	☐	☐	☐
		☐	☐	☐	☐	☐			☐	☐	☐	☐	☐
		☐	☐	☐	☐	☐			☐	☐	☐	☐	☐
		☐	☐	☐	☐	☐			☐	☐	☐	☐	☐
		☐	☐	☐	☐	☐			☐	☐	☐	☐	☐
		☐	☐	☐	☐	☐			☐	☐	☐	☐	☐
		☐	☐	☐	☐	☐			☐	☐	☐	☐	☐
		☐	☐	☐	☐	☐			☐	☐	☐	☐	☐
		☐	☐	☐	☐	☐			☐	☐	☐	☐	☐
		☐	☐	☐	☐	☐			☐	☐	☐	☐	☐
		☐	☐	☐	☐	☐			☐	☐	☐	☐	☐
		☐	☐	☐	☐	☐			☐	☐	☐	☐	☐
		☐	☐	☐	☐	☐			☐	☐	☐	☐	☐
		☐	☐	☐	☐	☐			☐	☐	☐	☐	☐
		☐	☐	☐	☐	☐			☐	☐	☐	☐	☐
		☐	☐	☐	☐	☐			☐	☐	☐	☐	☐
		☐	☐	☐	☐	☐			☐	☐	☐	☐	☐
		☐	☐	☐	☐	☐			☐	☐	☐	☐	☐
		☐	☐	☐	☐	☐			☐	☐	☐	☐	☐
		☐	☐	☐	☐	☐			☐	☐	☐	☐	☐

Page Number	Question Number						Page Number	Question Number					
		☐	☐	☐	☐	☐			☐	☐	☐	☐	☐
		☐	☐	☐	☐	☐			☐	☐	☐	☐	☐
		☐	☐	☐	☐	☐			☐	☐	☐	☐	☐
		☐	☐	☐	☐	☐			☐	☐	☐	☐	☐
		☐	☐	☐	☐	☐			☐	☐	☐	☐	☐
		☐	☐	☐	☐	☐			☐	☐	☐	☐	☐
		☐	☐	☐	☐	☐			☐	☐	☐	☐	☐
		☐	☐	☐	☐	☐			☐	☐	☐	☐	☐
		☐	☐	☐	☐	☐			☐	☐	☐	☐	☐
		☐	☐	☐	☐	☐			☐	☐	☐	☐	☐
		☐	☐	☐	☐	☐			☐	☐	☐	☐	☐
		☐	☐	☐	☐	☐			☐	☐	☐	☐	☐
		☐	☐	☐	☐	☐			☐	☐	☐	☐	☐
		☐	☐	☐	☐	☐			☐	☐	☐	☐	☐
		☐	☐	☐	☐	☐			☐	☐	☐	☐	☐
		☐	☐	☐	☐	☐			☐	☐	☐	☐	☐
		☐	☐	☐	☐	☐			☐	☐	☐	☐	☐
		☐	☐	☐	☐	☐			☐	☐	☐	☐	☐
		☐	☐	☐	☐	☐			☐	☐	☐	☐	☐
		☐	☐	☐	☐	☐			☐	☐	☐	☐	☐
		☐	☐	☐	☐	☐			☐	☐	☐	☐	☐
		☐	☐	☐	☐	☐			☐	☐	☐	☐	☐
		☐	☐	☐	☐	☐			☐	☐	☐	☐	☐
		☐	☐	☐	☐	☐			☐	☐	☐	☐	☐
		☐	☐	☐	☐	☐			☐	☐	☐	☐	☐
		☐	☐	☐	☐	☐			☐	☐	☐	☐	☐
		☐	☐	☐	☐	☐			☐	☐	☐	☐	☐
		☐	☐	☐	☐	☐			☐	☐	☐	☐	☐